MW01069647

THE TRANSCENDENT FUNCTION

THE TRANSCENDENT FUNCTION

Jung's Model of Psychological Growth through Dialogue with the Unconscious

Jeffrey C. Miller

STATE UNIVERSITY OF NEW YORK PRESS

Published by
State University of New York Press, Albany

Printed in the United States of America

For information, contact State University of New York Press, Albany, NY
www.sunypress.edu

Production, Laurie Searl
Marketing, Jennifer Giovanni

Library of Congress Cataloging-in-Publication Data

Miller, Jeffrey C., 1951–
The transcendent function : Jung's model of psychological growth through dialogue with the unconscious / Jeffrey C. Miller.
p. cm.
Includes bibliographical references (p.) and index.
ISBN 0-7914-5977-2 (alk. paper)—ISBN 0-7914-5978-0 (pbk. : alk. paper)
1. Individuation (Psychology) 2. Subconsciousness. I. Jung, C. G. (Carl Gustav), 1875–1961. Transzendente Funktion. II. Title.

BF175.5.I53M55 2003
155.2'5—dc22 2003060636

10 9 8 7 6 5 4 3 2 1

CONTENTS

FOREWORD

Dr. Jeffrey Miller has produced a truly significant and creative work. I have been engaged with Jung's transcendent function for many years and love reading about it. Miller's text is at once inspired, scholarly, and well crafted. The quotes from Jung are great and the appendices will be a tremendous resource for generations of Jung scholars. The author's detailed comparison of the 1916 and 1958 versions of Jung's essay strikes me as a stroke of genius. By combining his skills as a lawyer with depth psychological scholarship, Jeffrey Miller did something that has never been done before, that is, he found a way to highlight each and every change Jung made in a clear, accessible way. On the one hand, Dr. Miller's method of textual comparison is simple and self-evident. On the other hand, the creative process that guided him to it is a living example of the transcendent function.

The author's interest and excitement in his topic are palpable. The reader is taken on a memorable journey, approaching the transcendent function from multiple perspectives. In chapter 1, Dr. Miller provides the reader with important material concerning Jung's ideas about the unconscious. He looks at the transcendent function as psyche's way to bring the realms of consciousness and the unconscious into a dialogue with each other toward psychological growth and individuation. Miller also introduces an idea that he explores in greater depth later in the work, that is, the transcendent function allows us to discover new perspectives in every situation that were previously hidden or unseen.

Chapter 2 provides the reader with a fascinating tour through Jung's essay, *The Transcendent Function.* Dr. Miller analyzes its central ideas and themes, and he also compares and contrasts the 1916 and 1958 versions of the essay to show how some of Jung's ideas shifted and developed over time. From his comparison, additional valuable themes emerge.

Chapters 3 and 4 may be the most interesting for scholars and serious readers of Jung. Miller examines each reference to the transcendent function in Jung's written works—including his letters and lectures—in a thematic way. What emerges from the author's painstaking methodology is an image of a web representing the interconnectedness of key Jungian concepts, with the transcendent function at or near the center. Another way to say this: The author makes a compelling case for the centrality of the transcendent function in analytical psychology.

Following his impressive scholarly analysis of Jung's essay in the early chapters, Dr. Miller provides interesting texture to and applications of the transcendent function in the chapters that follow. Chapter 5 explores links between the transcendent function and analogous material in other psychologies. Then chapter 6 takes the material into a deeper imaginal landscape. Guided by Jung, the author approaches the transcendent function as an archetypal process inherent in psychological life. This material is both interesting and thought provoking, as Miller seems to allow the transcendent function itself to work through his writing, providing new, lively connections in a playful and imaginative way.

Chapter 7 concludes with a discussion of the transcendent function in everyday life. This last step is an important one in Dr. Miller's work since he presents the transcendent function as more than a tool for the analyst in the consulting room; the transcendent function is at the same time an omnipresent reality in all psychological life.

Following Dr. Miller's text, a set of invaluable appendices provide the reader with critical reference material about the transcendent function: Appendix A is Miller's clear, thorough, original textual comparison of the 1916 and 1958 versions of Jung's essay *The Transcendent Function;* Appendix B is a listing of every single mention of the transcendent function in Jung's written works, published letters, and public seminars; Appendix C is a review of literature written by Jungian authors on the transcendent function.

In summary, Dr. Miller provides the reader with a comprehensive view of one of Jung's most important early works. In addition to tracing its vital and central role in Jung's analytical psychology, Miller links the transcendent function to other psychological theories, as well as to ancient and contemporary philosophical, scientific, social, artistic, and religious traditions. He gives examples of ways it appears in everyday life and in human relationships. Again, Dr. Miller mirrors the transcendent function itself as he goes deeply into a particular aspect while at the same time amplifying it with wide ranging scholarship.

In discussing the scope of his study, Jeffrey Miller notes that his "book does not venture into the related and important area of the clinical application of the transcendent function." Even so, I highly recommend it to students and professionals across the psychotherapies. The most effective method of psychotherapeutic treatment is one that aligns itself with the natural, integrative function of the psyche. In this sense, a method and its underlying healing function are two aspects of the same thing.

To conclude, this book is all about the creative, integrative, healing function in the psyche that unites the opposites. I turn now to Jeffrey Miller's outstanding contribution, which speaks for itself.

Joan Chodrow

PREFACE

The transcendent function is the core of Carl Jung's theory of psychological growth and the heart of what he called "individuation," the process by which one is guided in a teleological way toward the person he or she is meant to be. This book exhaustively reviews the transcendent function through the seminal essay that bears its name, Jung's other writings, commentary by others, and exploration by the author. It analyzes the 1958 version of the essay "The Transcendent Function" from Jung's *Collected Works,* the original version written in 1916, and every reference Jung made to the transcendent function in his written works, his letters, and his public seminars. In addition to describing the transcendent function within Jung's psychology, this book hypothesizes that it became his root metaphor for psychological growth or even psyche itself. It compares and contrasts the transcendent function with transitional and mediatory phenomena from other schools of psychology, identifies its deeper foundational even archetypal roots, and suggests ways that it can be vivified in everyday life.

Jung's theory of individuation, that a person is pulled forward in a purposive way by psyche, was a central departure from the theories of Sigmund Freud, whose drive theory posited that a person's life was largely determined by the push of early life events and traumas. Jung believed that psychological growth and individuation were only possible through an ongoing conversation between consciousness and the unconscious. He felt that every idea, attitude, or image in consciousness was opposed or compensated for by another in the unconscious and that the two struggled with each other in a kind of polarized dance. If these opposites were held in swaying tension, he posited, a new, third thing would emerge that was not a mixture of the two but qualitatively different. This mechanism he called the "transcendent function." It was key to his thinking because only through a process of engaging in the transcendent function can a person foster the psychological growth that leads to individuation.

Jung first explored this key process in 1916, soon after his break from Freud, in a paper called "The Transcendent Function." Though he went on to refer to the concept extensively in eight of his other written works, in four published letters, and in five public seminars, the paper was not published until 1957 when it was discovered by the students of the C. G. Jung Institute in Zurich. Jung revised the paper in 1958 for inclusion in the *Collected Works* in 1960. Appendix A presents a word-by-word comparison of the two versions to show how Jung's thinking changed on the subject. This book is the first to analyze and review the excerpts about the transcendent function in Jung's written works, published letters, and public seminars. Through this process, the book presents a scholarly overview of the transcendent function's role within the Jungian paradigm.

From this Jungian foundation, the book compares and contrasts the transcendent function with mediatory and transitional concepts from other schools of psychology. Object relations (Winnicott and Klein), ego psychology (Freud), self-psychology (Kohut), archetypal psychology (Hillman), gestalt therapy, client-centered therapy, and cognitive-behavioral therapy are all analyzed in this context. This study also explores the deeper roots and archetypal foundations of the transcendent function as a psychological construct. Finally, the book seeks to usher the transcendent function from the abstract realm of psychological theory into the world of modern life. It concludes with a discussion of how the transcendent function can be animated in human relationships, and cultural dialogue in our day-to-day lives in the form of a metaphoric field, a third area between ourselves and whatever or whomever we are interacting with, that invites the emergence of new attitudes, situations, or perspectives.

ACKNOWLEDGMENTS

Many have contributed to this book. I owe a great debt of gratitude to Robert Romanyshyn, Ph.D., whose powerful writings and teachings about the significance of metaphor in psychological life, alchemical thinking, the neither/nor urge of the psyche, and the detrimental aspects of science and technology, all more fully explored in the book, formed a foundation upon which important synthesizing concepts in the later parts of the book were built. I also thank Michael Geis, M.D., who introduced me to the transcendent function essay; and to Glen Slater, Ph.D., who helped fashion the early structure of the project. Much of my ultimate thinking and synthesis was made possible through discussion with my dear friend, Joe Belichick. I also acknowledge Maria Chiaia, Ph.D., Patricia Speier, M.D., Pilar Montero, Ph.D., Randy Charlton, M.D., John Beebe, M.D., Michael Horne, M.D., and Thomas Kirsch, M.D., for their time and feedback during the creation of this work. Most important, I could not have given this work the passion and commitment I did without the love and patience of my wife, Kathleen, with whom I try to live the transcendent function every day.

Grateful acknowledgment is also given to the Estate of C. G. Jung and to Derek George Hunter, Nigel J. Hunter, and Richard Michael Hunter, the surviving heirs to A. R. Pope, for the copyright permission to use Pope's English translation of the 1916 version of Jung's essay "The Transcendent Function" published in pamphlet format in 1957 in Appendix A. Finally, thanks to Princeton University Press and Taylor & Francis for the copyright permission to use R.F.C. Hull's translation of the 1958 version of "The Transcendent Function," published in 1960 in volume 8 of *The Collected Works of C. G. Jung*.

CHAPTER ONE

INTRODUCTION TO THE TRANSCENDENT FUNCTION

DEVELOPMENT OF THE EGO IN WESTERN CONSCIOUSNESS

The last three millennia have witnessed the development of the logical, thinking human being. Beginning with the ancient Greeks, Western civilization has marched inexorably toward the elusive goal of the autonomous, rational human. Through the emergence of Christianity, the awakening of the Middle Ages, the Renaissance and Reformation, the Scientific Revolution of Copernicus, Kepler, Galileo, and Newton, the Philosophical Revolution of Bacon and Descartes, and into the Industrial Revolution and the modern age, Western consciousness has moved seemingly single-mindedly toward what may best be expressed in the Cartesian *cogito*—"I think, therefore I am." Many have argued that this rational, empirical, scientific thrust was necessary for the evolution of the human intellect so that we may comprehend the physical laws of matter, the order of the cosmos, and the processes of nature. Whatever its cause, this procession has led to a focus on the importance of the thinker's self-awareness.

In psychological terms, the march represents the development, indeed many would say an inflation, of the individual ego[1] that could apprehend separateness from the gods, from other humans, and from the surrounding world. With ego development came the ideas of self-determination, personal freedom, individual uniqueness, self-awareness, indeed the *self* as it is used in many areas of psychology today. Many would say (see, e.g. Romanyshyn, 1989), however, that these benefits came at a cost: a disunion with the undifferentiated consciousness that previously connected people; an amnesia regarding "*participation mystique*"[2] with the natural world; a repudiation of the *anima mundi*, the soul of the world, that created the fabric of community; and a devaluation of unprovable and unscientific concepts like intuition, unknowing, fantasy, symbol, imagination, dreams, and emotions. Largely incompatible with the developing, rational ego, these disowned but necessary parts of human consciousness were relegated to the hidden terrain of the unconscious, where they must inevitably be reclaimed.

EMERGENCE OF DEPTH PSYCHOLOGY AND EMPHASIS ON THE UNCONSCIOUS

In hindsight it came as no surprise, then, that at the beginning of the twentieth century, when the scientific paradigm, the Industrial Revolution, and Cartesian dualism were moving ahead at full throttle, Sigmund Freud and Carl Jung gave birth to the field of depth psychology, that branch of psychology that gives primacy to the unconscious. Though the unconscious had a long history in areas outside of psychology, Freud and Jung were the first to give it close clinical scrutiny. Yet almost one hundred years later, we have merely begun to apprehend the significance, scope, and impact of the unconscious. It still sits beneath, before, and around us—or more accurately, we are immersed in it—as a profound mystery, the boundaries, effects, and implications of which we have only begun to fathom. With roots in the earliest efforts to understand consciousness itself, depth psychology seeks to go yet further and find what is beneath it.

> "Depth psychology," the modern field whose interest is in the unconscious levels of the psyche—that is, the deeper meanings of soul—is itself no modern term. "Depth" reverberates with a significance echoing one of the first philosophers of antiquity. All depth psychology has been summed up by this fragment of Heraclitus: "You could not discover the limits of soul *(psyche)*, even if you traveled every road to do so; such is the depth *(batun)* of its meaning *(logos)*." (Hillman, 1975, p. xvii)

Depth psychology yearns to apprehend, indeed to integrate, what is beyond our conscious grasp, the deeper meanings of soul as expressed in dreams, images, and metaphors of the unconscious.

Freud felt that the unconscious was limited to contents rejected or repressed from consciousness. In his view, the unconscious was a kind of backwater carrying the stagnant refuse repudiated as too painful or intolerable to the conscious mind. In contrast, Jung believed the unconscious to be not only the territory of repression but also a mysterious landscape of autonomous, teleological intelligence that compensates for, supplements, even opposes consciousness. First articulated in his 1913 paper "On Psychic Energy" (1928/1960), Jung's idea was that the unconscious guides us in a purposeful way

This theoretical leap required Jung to enunciate a psychic mechanism through which such guidance takes place. He called the core of that mechanism the transcendent function, a dialogue between the unconscious and consciousness through which a new direction emerges. The concept of the purposive unconscious operating through the transcendent function became the hub of Jung's psychology and represented an irreparable break from Freud. Jung eventually came to believe that one cannot individuate, that is, cannot become the person he or she is truly meant to be, without conversing with and coming to terms with the unconscious. The transcendent function is the primary means through which that reconciliation is accomplished. Conceived and explored quite early in the development of Jung's psychology, the transcendent function is implicated in many of his other key concepts (e.g., the role of symbol and fantasy, individuation, the archetypes, the Self[3]), indeed may be the wellspring from whence they flow.

PRIMER ON THE TRANSCENDENT FUNCTION

In the essay bearing its name written in 1916 but not published until 1957, the transcendent function is described by Jung as arising "from the union of conscious and unconscious contents" (1957/1960, p. 69). The paper describes a "synthetic" or "constructive" method (p. 73) through which unconscious components can be united with conscious perceptions to produce a wholly new perspective. Indeed, the word *transcendent* was used by Jung to signify the transition from one attitude to another (p. 73). Explaining how such unconscious contents could be elicited and brought into a dialogue with consciousness, Jung stated, "It is exactly as if a dialogue were taking place between two human beings with equal rights" (p. 89). He summarized the transcendent function that emerges as follows:

> The shuttling to and fro of arguments and affects represents the transcendent function of opposites. The confrontation of the two positions generates a tension charged with energy and creates a living, third thing—not a logical stillbirth in accordance with the principle *tertium non datur* but a movement out of the suspension between the opposites, a living birth that leads to a new level of being, a new situation. (p. 90)

Simply put, the transcendent function is crucial to the central mission of depth psychology, which is to access, explore, and integrate the unconscious, and thereby apprehend the deeper meanings of soul. As Jung wrote in his 1958 prefatory note to "The Transcendent Function" prepared for the *Collected Works*:

> As its [the essay's] basic argument is still valid today, it may stimulate the reader to a broader and deeper understanding of the problem. This problem is identical with the universal question: How does one come to terms in practice with the unconscious? (1957/1960, p. 67)

Jung believed that the conscious and unconscious contain opposite, compensatory, or complementary material and that psyche's natural tendency is to strive to bring the conscious and unconscious positions together for the purpose of integrating them. Fundamental to his theory is the idea that conscious and unconscious opposites can be bridged by the emergence of a symbol from the fantasy-producing activity of psyche. The symbol, in turn, produces something that is not merely an amalgam of or compromise between the two opposites but rather a "living, third thing . . . a living birth that leads to a new level of being, a new situation" (p. 90). Thus, the essence of the transcendent function is a confrontation of opposites, one from consciousness and one from the unconscious, from which emerges some new position or perspective:

> Standing in a compensatory relationship to both, the transcendent function enables thesis and antithesis to encounter one another on equal terms. That which is capable of uniting these two is a metaphorical statement (the symbol) which itself transcends time and conflict, neither adhering to nor partaking of one side or the other but somehow common to both and offering the possibility of a new synthesis. The word *transcendent* is expressive of the presence of a capacity to transcend the destructive tendency to pull (or be pulled) to one side or the other. (Samuels, Shorter, and Plaut, 1986, p. 151)

At the heart of the transcendent function is transformation, a shift in consciousness. "Expressing itself by way of the symbol, [the transcendent function] facilitates a transition from one psychological attitude or condition to another" (Samuels, Shorter, and Plaut, 1986, p. 150). Indeed, "Jung considered the transcendent function to be the most significant factor in psychological process" (p. 150). Though its full implications are beyond the scope of this introduction, suffice it to say that Jung posited the transcendent function to be of central importance, particularly in the self-regulating functions of the psyche and in the individuation process:

> The transcendent function, which plays the role of an autonomous regulator, emerges and gradually begins to work as the process of individuation begins to unfold. For Jung, it is in the activation of the transcendent function that true maturity lies. (Humbert, 1988, p. 125)

Moreover, Jung held that the transcendent function was crucial to the process of individuation and the drive toward wholeness by the Self. As Hall and Nordby (1973) state:

> The first step toward integration is, as we have just seen, individuation of *all* aspects of the personality. The second stage is controlled by what Jung calls the *transcendent function*. This function is endowed with the capability of uniting all of the opposing trends in the personality and of working toward the goal of wholeness. The aim of the transcendent function, Jung writes, is "the realization, in all of its aspects, of the personality originally hidden away in the embryonic germplasm; the production and unfolding of the original potential wholeness." *The transcendent function is the means by which the unity or self archetype is realized* [italics added]. Like the process of individuation, the transcendent function is inherent in the person. (p. 84)

The transcendent function has to do with opening a dialogue between the conscious and unconscious to allow a living, third thing to emerge that is neither a combination of nor a rejection of the two. It has a central role in the self-regulating nature of the psyche, individuation, and the Self's drive toward wholeness.

Beyond its importance to Jungian psychology, the transcendent function is a subject that has broader significance to depth psychology. The transcendent function is an archetypal process that implicates other archetypal processes that can be found in the theories and writings of other depth psychologists. The concepts of a psychic struggle between polarized segments of consciousness, mechanisms that mediate such antitheses, transformation through the liminal spaces between such opposing forces, and the "third" emerging from the struggle of the "two" are all ideas that recur in the field of depth psychology. Indeed, the transcendent function may be an expression of a larger human urge to reconcile ontological quandaries such as spirit and matter, subject and object, inner and outer, idea and thing, form and substance, thought and feeling. Viewed in this way, the transcendent function can be thought of as an archetypal phenomenon,[4] ubiquitous to and inherent in human experience, that implicates liminality, initiation, transformation, and transcendence.

Depth psychology is intimately involved in all these enterprises. The depth psychological perspective beholds all phenomena with the exhortations, "I don't know" and "Something is happening here that I cannot see." It seeks the unseen and liminal, that which is buried beneath or lies between the layers of what is perceptible. Jung and Freud initiated the "movement beneath and between" and that course is being followed by adherents in both schools.

One contemporary expression of these ideas can be found in archetypal psychology, an offshoot of Jungian psychology,[5] which identifies "soul" as that which seeks deeper meaning and provides the connective tissue between the seen and the hidden. As Hillman, a powerful contemporary advocate of depth psychology's message, states:

> By *soul* I mean, first of all, a perspective rather than a substance, a viewpoint toward things rather than a thing itself. This perspective is reflective; it mediates events and make differences between ourselves and everything that happens. Between us and events, between the doer and the deed, there is a reflective moment—and soul-making means differentiating the middle ground. (1975, p. xvi)

There is a confluence between the soul-making aspiration of depth psychology and the telos of the transcendent function: a mediation of conscious and unconscious, a seeking of the reflective vantage point between ourselves and the events we perceive, a striving to have revealed that which remains hidden. Having accepted as its destiny the recovery and integration of the unconscious from domination by logical, rational consciousness, depth psychology struggles with ways in which to accomplish its charge. The transcendent function is fundamental to both the substance of that vocation and methods of pursuing it.

SCOPE AND ORGANIZATION OF THE WORK

This book is a theoretical and analytical examination of the transcendent function and the concepts it implicates. The exploration begins in chapter 2 with a detailed review and analysis of "The Transcendent Function," one of three important essays that Jung wrote in 1916, soon after his break with Freud and during his struggles with the images of the unconscious. That chapter reviews and compares the 1916 version and the revised version prepared by Jung in 1958 for inclusion in the *Collected Works*. It investigates Jung's thinking on the key topics that emerge from the essay and refers to Appendix A, which contains a comparison of the two, showing every addition to and deletion from the 1916 version that Jung made in creating the 1958 version.

Chapter 3 traces Jung's thinking about the transcendent function by way of the dozens of references he made to it in eight other written works, five public seminars, and four published letters. It addresses such questions as: How exactly does the transcendent function work? Does the transcendent function operate on its own or can it be prompted in some way? How does the transcendent function interact with other key Jungian concepts such as individuation, the Self, and the archetypes? Reference is made to relevant excerpts from each of the written works, seminars, and letters. Appendix B gives a complete list of all those references together with the pages surrounding each reference that the author believes give the reader the material necessary for the reference to be fully understood. The research that led to this chapter yielded an important realization: that the references to the transcendent function implicate just about every core Jungian concept. The references are addressed thematically in the framework of key topics in Jung's paradigm.

Chapter 4 springs from the analysis in chapter 3 and posits that the transcendent function is centrally located in the complex web of Jungian concepts. Indeed, it makes the proposition that the transcendent function is Jung's root metaphor for psyche itself or for becoming psychological and is the wellspring from whence flowed much of the rest of Jung's imaginal, depth psychology. It then makes an attempt to set forth and analyze, both in words and images, the core components of the transcendent function. The chapter concludes by posing questions that flow from the idea of the transcendent function as a root metaphor: Does it find expression in the theories of others? Is the transcendent function reflective of deeper, even archetypal, expressions of psyche?

Chapter 5, working from the premise that the transcendent function may be seen as a metaphor for becoming psychological or for psychological transformation, compares and contrasts the transcendent function with the theories of others. Notwithstanding the uniqueness of Jung's thinking on the transcendent function (i.e., the dynamic opposition of the psyche, the role of fantasy and symbol in mediating such antitheses, the emergence of something larger than the ego that is purposeful, even numinous and holy, and the potentiating of a transformative result), many schools of psychology struggle with the relationships between self/other, me/not-me, known/unknown. Here the book engages in a lively dialogue about whether there is any relationship between the transcendent function and transitional/mediatory phenomena hypothesized by others.

Chapter 6 shifts to an exploration of the deeper roots or archetypal basis of the transcendent function. Viewed through this lens, the transcendent function is conceptualized as ubiquitous to psychological experience, a way that the psyche seeks connections between disparate elements in order to continually evolve and grow. It implicates deeper patterns in the psyche, including the binary oppositions inherent in consciousness, the chasm between subject and object, archetypal patterns of liminality and initiation, the archetypal energies of Hermes (the god of boundaries and connections between realms), the deeper foundations of three (the number embodied by the transcendent function, i.e. the emergence of the third from the polarity of two), and the search for a connection with the Divine. Through an examination of these patterns, chapter 6 posits that the transcendent function is an archetypal process that represents what the chapter calls the "neither/nor" and "autochthonous" urges of the psyche. Though somewhat abstract, this discussion of the deeper patterns of psyche is the natural analytic destination of any comprehensive discussion of the transcendent function.

The book concludes in chapter 7 by turning to more practical concerns: How can we better recognize and apply the transcendent function in our lives? Here the transcendent function is used as a tool for everyday living, to prompt a conversation between that which is known/conscious/acknowledged and that which is unknown/unconscious/hidden, a dialogue through which something new emerges. It uses analogies to alchemy to emphasize that the essence of the transcendent function is to allow something new to emerge from things that are in seemingly irreconcilable conflict. Through these concepts, the transcendent function is then applied to relationships, social and cultural issues (e.g., race relations, gun control, abortion, gender differences, democratic discourse), and day-to-day living. Chapter 7 proposes a model for deepening relationships and for revisioning the deep rifts we see in social and cultural issues. Finally, it shifts the focus to everyday living, showing how the transcendent function allows us to see all the world as a way of embodying, relating to, and integrating the unconscious.

It is important to note here that this book does not venture into the related and important area of the clinical application of the transcendent function. In the essay that bears its name, Jung introduced the method of active imagination as a way to prompt the occurrence of the transcendent function in analysis. That is the proper topic for a separate work and is reserved for a future volume. It is also a subject that has received treatment by others. Readers who wish to add a clinical dimension to the theories and analysis offered herein would be well served to consult the work of Chodorow (1997), Hannah (1953), von Franz (1980), Dallett (1982), and Johnson (1986). In addition, Appendix C provides a literature review of sources that discuss the transcendent function in ways that are less central to the focus of this book.

CHAPTER TWO

DETAILED ANALYSIS OF THE TRANSCENDENT FUNCTION ESSAY

"The Transcendent Function" essay was seminal in the development of key aspects of Jung's metapsychology. In it he explores foundational concepts such as the omnipresence of the unconscious, its compensatory relationship to consciousness, its synthetic (as opposed to purely reductive) nature, the role of the analyst in mediating the transcendent function, methods for accessing material from the unconscious, the importance of purpose and meaning in working with the unconscious, the interaction between ego and the unconscious, and the interaction of the opposites in consciousness and the unconscious that allows psychological transformation. These themes will be explored below through a review of the text of this groundbreaking essay.

1916: HISTORICAL CONTEXT FOR THE TRANSCENDENT FUNCTION

Given that the transcendent function is a bridge between the conscious and unconscious, it should come as no surprise that Jung wrote "The Transcendent Function" in 1916 when he was himself actively engaging in making such a connection. After his break with Freud in or around 1912,[1] Jung went through several years of what he himself called "a period of uncertainty" (1989c, p. 170). Jung stated flatly that "it would be no exaggeration to call it a state of disorientation" (p. 170) and that he "lived as if under constant inner pressure" (p. 173). In response to the disturbances, Jung meticulously reviewed, not once but twice, all the details of his life "with particular emphasis to childhood memories" (p. 173), but to no avail. This amounted to Jung's unsuccessful attempt to deal with the turmoil rationally with primary emphasis on the linear logic of consciousness. In a kind of surrender, Jung decided to submit to a conversation with the unconscious:

> But this retrospection led to nothing but a fresh acknowledgment of my ignorance. Thereupon I said to myself, "Since I know nothing at all, I shall simply do whatever occurs to me." Thus I consciously submitted myself to the impulses of the unconscious. (p. 173)

Jung's capitulation was a seminal moment in depth psychology because it acknowledged for the first time the purposive, teleological nature of the unconscious. Indeed, that decision may be said to be the birth of the transcendent function in Jung's thinking, an explicit recognition of the fact that psychological growth requires a partnership between conscious and unconscious.

During the next several years Jung was buffeted by the turbulent forces of the unconscious. He dreamt prodigiously, was invaded by symbolic visions, and dialogued with fantasy figures. In response, Jung experimented with several forms of self-healing: using stones from the lakeshore behind his house to build a miniature town, journaling about his experiences, and actively engaging in interactions with the visions that appeared to him. Jung describes the release of the unconscious images in overwhelming terms:

> An incessant stream of fantasies had been released, and I did my best not to lose my head but to find some way to understand these strange things. I stood helpless before an alien world; everything in it seemed difficult and incomprehensible. I was living in a constant state of tension; often I felt as if gigantic blocks of stone were tumbling down upon me. One thunderstorm followed another. (1989c, p. 177)

His descriptions of confrontations with the unconscious lead some to believe that Jung was substantially debilitated, even clinically impaired, during at least part of that time.[2] Indeed, Jung himself uses that kind of language: "At times [the inner pressure] became so strong that I suspected there was some psychic disturbance in myself" (1989c, p. 173). Whether or not the events in the several years following his rupture with Freud amounted to a breakdown, undoubtedly that period reflects an intense struggle by Jung to converse with and come to terms with the contents of the unconscious.

Jung's emergence both from his break with Freud and from his descent into the unconscious took place in 1916, a pivotal year in which he wrote three of his major early works: "The Transcendent Function" (1957/1960); "The Structure of the Unconscious" (1916/1953), which was later revised and became "Relations Between the Ego and the Unconscious" (1928/1953); and the anonymously published *VII Sermones ad Mortuos* (1925/1967). A year later he wrote another major work, "The Psychology of the Unconscious Processes" which later was revised and became "On the Psychology of the Unconscious" (1943/1953). Embedded in these works are the core of many of Jung's most important ideas more fully developed later. These foundational concepts, particularly the transcendent function, flowed directly from the conversation between conscious and unconscious materials to which Jung submitted. In this sense, "The Transcendent Function" essay is the transcendent function at work, a mediatory product flowing directly from a dialogue between conscious and unconscious forces in Jung that psychologically transformed him and prompted, at least in part, his paradigm-shifting theories and writings during that period.

THE 1916 AND 1958 PUBLISHED FORMS OF THE ESSAY

The version of "The Transcendent Function" that we see in Volume 8 of the *Collected Works* (Jung, 1957/1960) is not the original work that Jung wrote in 1916 but a revision he prepared forty-two years later. Jung wrote the essay in its original form in German in 1916 under the title "Die Transzendent Funktion." Inexplicably, the paper was not published in any form until 1957, when it was, according to Jung, "discovered by students of the C. G. Jung Institute, Zurich" (1957/1960, p. 67fn), translated into English by A. R. Pope (a renowned Jungian analyst in Zurich who died in 1998), and published under the name "The Transcendent Function" by the Students Association, C. G. Jung Institute, Zurich (Jung, 1957) in what Jung would later call "its first, provisional form" (1957/1960, p. 67fn). The original paper written in 1916 and translated by Dr. Pope in 1957 shall be referred to as the "1916 version." In 1958, Jung "considerably revised" (1957/1960, p. 67fn) the original German version for republication together with a prefatory note (1957/1960, p. 67fn). The prefatory note was partially rewritten by Jung and it, together with the work as revised in 1958, was then published in Volume 8 of the *Collected Works* in 1960. The revised paper that appears in the *Collected Works* shall be referred to as the "1958 version."

Given the importance of the transcendent function in Jung's psychology and the synchronistic timing of these two versions at the inception (soon after his break with Freud) and culmination (just three years before his death) of his writing, a comparison and analysis of these important works offers a unique opportunity. To my knowledge, no one has ever done any analysis of the differences between the 1916 and 1958 versions. To fully apprehend all of the nuances and provide a comprehensive study of this subject, a detailed comparison of the two works was conducted. In order that the reader can participate in the analysis a word-by-word comparison of the two versions is set forth in Appendix A; the lined-out text is language that was removed from the 1916 version when Jung revised it to create the 1958 version; the underlined text is the language Jung added in 1958.

A cursory review of Appendix A shows that Jung made substantial changes to the 1916 version when he created the 1958 version. There are numerous clarifications and stylistic changes that merely made the work's manifest meaning more understandable. However, there were important substantive changes as well. Though Jung stated in the prefatory note to the 1958 version that his changes were intended to "preserve the main trend of thought and the unavoidable limitedness of its horizon" (1957/1960, p. 67), some additions and omissions constitute significant conceptual shifts. The analysis will focus on the 1958 version both because it is more widely read and because it represents a more developed iteration of Jung's ideas. Reference will also be made, however, to the 1916 version where relevant. Though the more important revisions will be included in the actual text of the work, less important ones shall be included in footnotes or left to the reader's scrutiny.

EXPLORATION OF DETAILS OF "THE TRANSCENDENT FUNCTION" PAPER

The Prefatory Note

Written in final form a mere two years before his death in 1961, and fully forty-two years after the original version, the prefatory note provides important insight into Jung's thoughts about the significance of the paper and the concepts it embodies. In the opening passages, Jung indicates that the paper might give the reader "some idea of the efforts of understanding which were needed for the first attempts at a synthetic view of the psychic process of analytical treatment" (1957/1960, p. 67). One of the most significant departures of Jungian psychology from other approaches is its rejection of the notion that psychological manifestations can be reduced exclusively to the effects of events of early life, the so-called reductive view. Rather, the Jungian, synthetic view is that in addition to the push of early life experiences, psychological existence is also influenced by the pull of unconscious, purposive elements of the psyche that guide us forward. As Jung states later in the paper, "Constructive treatment of the unconscious, that is, the question of meaning and purpose, paves the way for the patient's insight into that process which I call the transcendent function" (p. 75). From the perspective of the synthetic view, psychology is not just about unearthing the traumas of childhood but also learning what psyche is guiding us toward:

> Jung is critical of the reductive method because the full meaning of the unconscious product (symptom, dream, image, slip of the tongue) is not disclosed. By connecting an unconscious product to the past, its present value to the individual may be lost. . . . Jung was more interested in where a person's life was leading him, rather than the supposed causes of his situation. His was a teleological point of view. Jung described his orientation as "synthetic," with the implication

> that it was what emerged from the starting point that was of primary significance. (Samuels, Shorter, and Plaut, 1986, p. 127)

Jung saw the unconscious as key not just to revealing and healing old wounds, but also to learning about one's destiny, the telos of one's life. In contrast to the reductive view which seeks to tie psychological phenomena to events of the past, the synthetic view implicates meaning, purpose, and destiny. Seen in this way, the unconscious takes on a mystical quality. As Jung states in the prefatory note:

> After forty-two years, the problem has lost nothing of its topicality. . . . This problem is identical with the universal question: How does one come to terms in practice with the unconscious? . . . Indirectly, it is the fundamental question, in practice, of all religions and all philosophies. For the unconscious is not this thing or that; it is the Unknown as it immediately affects us. (1957/1960, pp. 67–68)

Though Jung does not say so explicitly, the fact that he capitalizes "Unknown" and links it to "all religions and philosophies" leads me to conclude that he believes that the unconscious has a kind of divine quality, one that affects us in an unexplainable and numinous way.

Finally, the prefatory note informs the reader that Jung will be describing the method of "active imagination," which he calls "the most important auxiliary for the production of those contents of the unconscious which lie, as it were, immediately below the threshold of consciousness" (1957/1960, p. 68). Jung quickly cautions that because the method of active imagination accesses unconscious contents, it is "not a plaything for children" (p. 68), almost like a label on a modern-day consumer product. He gives fair warning that unconscious contents "may overpower the conscious mind and take possession of the personality. . . and may even lead to a genuine 'psychotic interval'" so that the method should "not be employed except under expert supervision" (p. 68).

In this short prefatory note, Jung gives us important information about the transcendent function, the method of active imagination, and the synthetic approach. Jung also puts the reader on notice that he is addressing not just techniques but rather what he sees as the heart of psyche: meaning and purpose, neither of which can be sought or gained without real risk.

Definitional Sections

Jung wastes no time in telling the reader what he means by the transcendent function. The first paragraph of the paper gives an opening definition of the concept:

> There is nothing mysterious or metaphysical about the term "transcendent function." It means a psychological function comparable in its way to a mathematical function of the same name, which is a function of real and imaginary numbers. The psychological "transcendent function" arises from the union of conscious and unconscious contents. (1957/1960, p. 69)

Here, in Jung's first description of the transcendent function, we see the specific reference to "the union of conscious and unconscious contents," the bringing together of what we perceive consciously and the unconscious contents of which we are unaware. Curiously, Jung goes out of his way to say that there is "nothing mysterious or metaphysical" about the transcendent function. But it *is* mysterious and metaphysical! The very idea of uniting conscious and unconscious material is abstract, subtle, abstruse, and otherworldly. Indeed, barely a page earlier, Jung calls coming to terms with the unconscious the "universal question" (1957/1960, p. 67), the "fundamental question . . . of all religions" (p. 68), and refers to the unconscious as the "Unknown" (p. 68). Methinks he doth protest too much! One might speculate that the "scientific" Jung was reacting to the "metaphysical" Jung in a denial of what was clearly an intuitive, abstract, even numinous concept.

One other early passage is helpful for definitional purposes. In his discussion of the relationship between the conscious and the unconscious, Jung says:

> The tendencies of the conscious and the unconscious are the two factors that together make up the transcendent function. It is called "transcendent" because it makes the transition from one attitude to another organically possible without loss of the unconscious. (1957/1960, p. 73)

The function is called "transcendent" because it allows an individual to transcend his or her attitude and arrive at a new one; it potentiates psychological growth. Furthermore, Jung tells us, the shift takes place organically. This prefigures another theme visited later: that the transcendent function (and the transformation it ushers in) is a natural process producing change in the normal course of psychic events.

Compensatory Relationship of the Unconscious to Consciousness

Essential to Jung's metapsychology and the transcendent function is the idea that the unconscious contains complementary or compensatory material to that of consciousness:

> Experience in analytical psychology has amply shown that the conscious and the unconscious seldom agree as to their contents and

their tendencies. This lack of parallelism is not just accidental or purposeless, but is due to the fact that *the unconscious behaves in a compensatory or complementary manner* [italics added] towards the conscious. (1957/1960, p. 69)

Jung cites four separate reasons for the complementary and compensatory relationship between consciousness and the unconscious:

(1) consciousness possesses a requisite level of intensity such that elements not meeting that level remain in the unconscious;

(2) consciousness has "directed functions" that inhibit all "incompatible material" thereby forcing it into the unconscious;

(3) consciousness embodies "the momentary process of adaptation" whereas the unconscious contains not only the present but also personal material from an individual's past along with "all the inherited behavior traces" of humanity;[3] and

(4) the unconscious contains all "the fantasy combinations" which have not yet become conscious but which "under suitable conditions will enter the light of consciousness." (p. 69)

Here Jung delineates the significant differences between his conception of the unconscious and Freud's view: Freud saw the unconscious as the repository for material that was too unpleasant, violent, or powerful to be held in consciousness, whereas Jung proclaimed the unconscious to be an independent psychic system in dynamic partnership with consciousness. Jung believed that consciousness contains directed, adaptive, and personal material, whereas the unconscious houses the less directed (intuitive), personal material from the past, behavior traces from the rest of humanity (the seedling for Jung's later work on the archetypes), and fantasy material. For the first time in depth psychology, we see here the idea of consciousness and the unconscious as co-equals in psyche. Consciousness allows us to function in our day-to-day lives, whereas the unconscious compensates and complements by providing symbol, fantasy, intuition, and collective images.

Jung gives special scrutiny to the "definiteness and directedness of the conscious mind" (1957/1960, p. 69) and asserts that it is in constant tension with what he calls "counter-positions" in the unconscious (1957/1960, p. 71; 1957, p. 7). Though Jung saw these qualities as necessary to adapt to the needs of the modern age,[4] he also identifies the crucial disadvantage of the so-called "directed process" (p. 70): it constantly makes a judgment which, by its nature, excludes what is not known, the unconscious, thereby making consciousness necessarily one-sided:

> The judgment in its turn is always based on experience, i.e., on what is already known. . . . It is never based on what is new, what is still unknown, and what under certain conditions might considerably enrich the directed process. . . . Through such acts of judgment the directed process necessarily becomes one-sided. . . . One-sidedness is an unavoidable and necessary characteristic of the directed process, for direction implies one-sidedness. It is an advantage and a drawback at the same time. (pp. 70–71)

Jung clearly delineates the significant detriment of the directed process: it closes us off from the new and unknown that reside in the unconscious.

Furthermore, Jung argues, the more the unconscious counter-position is pushed down, the greater its strength and the chances it will erupt into consciousness with unpleasant results.

> The counter-position in the unconscious is not dangerous so long as it does not possess any high energy-value. But if the tension increases as a result of too great one-sidedness, the counter-tendency breaks through into consciousness, usually just . . . when it is most important to maintain the conscious direction. . . . The further we are able to remove ourselves from the unconscious through directed functioning, the more readily a powerful counter-position can build up in the unconscious, and when this breaks out it may have disagreeable consequences. (1957/1960, p. 71)

Here Jung gives voice to what is now a widely accepted and oft-cited principle of depth psychology: when we ignore, subvert, or deny the unconscious through overemphasis on the directed, conscious process, the unconscious will manifest itself in unpleasant or even tragic ways. As Hillman (1975) states it: "An axiom of depth psychology asserts that what is not admitted into awareness irrupts in ungainly, obsessive ways, affecting consciousness with precisely the qualities it strives to exclude" (p. 46).

Thus, Jung lays out his conception of the relationship of consciousness and the unconscious: for every attitude or position in the conscious there is a complementary, compensatory, counter-position in the unconscious. Interestingly, Jung's language on this score shifts over time. Though he uses the phrase *compensatory or complementary* in the 1916 version of this essay, his later works emphasize the *opposites* in the conscious and unconscious. As Jung's thinking progressed, the importance of the opposites in psychic functioning increased. As that change took effect, Jung's writings began to emphasize the compensatory nature of the unconscious and to give less weight to, even exclude, the complementary nature, a subject we will visit in greater depth in the next chapter.

Omnipresence and Compensation of the Unconscious

Jung's next move in the paper is to make a case for the omnipresence of the unconscious in psychological life, thus further distancing himself from Freud. Jung asserts that analytic treatment does not stop intrusions from the unconscious: "We deem it unwise to expect an elimination or standstill of the unconscious after the so-called completion of the treatment" (1957/1960, p. 71). Indeed, he says, we can expect constant intrusions from the unconscious; it is the very nature of psychic life. In one of the significant 1958 additions, Jung states: "Freud's hope that the unconscious could be 'exhausted' has not been fulfilled. Dream-life and intrusions from the unconscious continue—*mutatis mutandis*—impeded" (p. 72). Freud's conception of the unconscious as the repository of repressed material meant that with sufficient analysis, the unconscious could theoretically all be made conscious and emptied out. In contrast, Jung saw the unconscious as an inexhaustible and omnipresent part of psychic life; it cannot be exhausted any more than can consciousness.

For Jung, this is a fundamental psychic truth: The unconscious is ever present, influencing conscious life. Even when something from the unconscious is made conscious, there emerges still another counter-position to what just became conscious. Instead of encouraging a falsely omnipotent attitude that analysis can give the patient a handle on the unconscious, Jung acknowledges the ubiquitous effects of the unconscious and exhorts an analytic stance that will assist the patient in learning how to continuously deal with it.

Jung (1957/1960) thus comes to the central focus of the essay, finding a way to bring consciousness into contact with the unconscious:

> The basic question for the therapist is not how to get rid of the momentary difficulty, but how future difficulties may be successfully countered. The question is: what kind of mental and moral attitude is it necessary to have towards the disturbing influences of the unconscious, and how can it be conveyed to the patient?
>
> The answer obviously consists in getting rid of the separation between conscious and unconscious. This cannot be done by condemning the contents of the unconscious in a one-sided way, but rather by recognizing their significance in compensating the one-sidedness of consciousness and by taking this significance into account. (p. 73)

Interestingly, the language just quoted was not a part of the 1916 version; it was added by Jung in 1958. Its addition stands as testimony to the importance of the role of the unconscious in compensating for the one-sidedness of consciousness and in the part the analyst plays to assist the patient in discovering that. It also tells us that even after four decades of developing further ideas, Jung's conviction that psychological health requires constant interplay between consciousness and the unconscious remained unshakable.

The Constructive Method: Importance of Purpose and Meaning

Jung not only believed in the omnipresence of the unconscious, but also that in it lies the core of new attitudes that seek to guide us in a teleological way. As indicated, Jung flatly disagreed with Freud's assertion that the unconscious only contains repressed material. He said, "The unconscious also contains all the material that has *not yet* reached the threshold of consciousness. These are the seeds of future conscious contents" (1928/1953, p. 128). This was the heart of Jung's belief in the synthetic or constructive method. Instead of reducing the unconscious to what it represents about early life, Jung beseeched that it be received for what might be constructed or synthesized about purpose, future, and destiny. "The unconscious is continually active, combining its material in ways *which serve the future* [italics added]. It produces . . . subliminal combinations that are prospective. . . . For these reasons, the unconscious could serve man as a unique guide" (1943/1953, p. 116). The transcendent function is closely tied to the constructive view of psyche. It assists us in moving from the old way in which our directed, one-sided consciousness has been guiding us to a new way of being, bringing us closer to the purpose to which we are being drawn. As Jung states in the 1958 version:

> It [the transcendent function] is called "transcendent" because it makes the transition from one attitude to another organically possible, without loss of the unconscious. The constructive or synthetic method of treatment presupposes insights which are at least potentially present in the patient and can therefore be made conscious. If the analyst knows nothing of these potentialities he cannot help the patient to develop them either. (1957/1960, pp. 73–74)

Instructively, the 1958 language shifted significantly from Jung's original 1916 language. An excerpt from Appendix A comparing the two versions follows (the lined-out text is language that was removed from the 1916 version when Jung revised it to create the 1958 version; the underlined text is the language Jung added in 1958):

> ~~The term]~~ <It is called> "transcendent" ~~[designates the fact that this function mediates]~~ <because it makes> the transition from one attitude to another ~~[. The constructive method however presupposes some conscious knowledge, which the patient too can be made to realize in the course of treatment, since the physician is aware in~~

> ~~principle of the potential existence of this knowledge. If the physician himself knows nothing about it, then in this respect]~~ <organically possible, without loss of the unconscious. The constructive or synthetic method of treatment presupposes insights which are at least potentially present in the patient and can therefore be made conscious. If the analyst knows nothing of these potentialities> he cannot help the patient <to develop them> either.

Two changes are significant. First, the idea that the transcendent function makes a transition from one attitude to another "organically possible, without loss of the unconscious." This language stresses the notion that the transcendent function is a normal part of psychic life that organically, naturally occurs through the interplay of consciousness and the unconscious. This topic will be discussed further since Jung is somewhat contradictory on this point. Second, Jung's refinements of the language regarding the nature of the constructive information available to the individual are significant. The use of the word *insights* in the 1958 version, absent from the 1916 version, underscores Jung's belief that information in the unconscious is purposeful.

Jung makes the latter point clear in the next page of the 1958 version. Emphasizing that both the constructive method and the transcendent function have at their core meaning and purpose, Jung states, "Constructive treatment of the unconscious, that is the question of meaning and purpose, paves the way for the patient's insight into that process which I call the transcendent function" (Jung, 1957/1960, p. 75). Once again, the 1958 language is significantly different from the 1916 version:

> ~~[Through constructive]~~ <Constructive> treatment of the unconscious ~~[the foundation is laid for]~~ <,that is, the question of meaning and purpose, paves the way for the patient's insight into that process which I call> the transcendent function.

Though meaning and purpose were always, at least in part, at the heart of how Jung saw the importance of the unconscious, these concepts apparently became clearer during Jung's life. Thus, when he drafted the 1958 revisions, Jung took the opportunity to clarify the centrality of meaning, purpose, the constructive method, and the transcendent function in his psychology.

The Role of the Analyst: Mediating the Transcendent Function

Jung posits that the analyst has a central role in assisting the patient in recognizing and integrating the contents of the unconscious: "In actual practice, the suitably trained analyst mediates the transcendent function for the patient, i.e., helps him to bring conscious and unconscious together and so arrive at a new attitude" (1957/1960, p. 75). Though this statement is clear on its face, closer scrutiny raises several questions. Is the analyst mediating the actual *contents* of the patient's transcendent function, in the sense of somehow psychically carrying the contents until the patient is able to absorb the new attitude? Or is the analyst mediating the *idea* of a new attitude or situation and in that sense holding some kind of potential space for the patient? Or, is the analyst mediating the transcendent function by *modeling* it for the patient, showing the patient that it is normal and positive to allow that kind of transition? Jung's words do not directly answer these questions, but the answer is probably a combination of each of these ways of mediation and/or different ways at different times. As Joseph (1997) states, the analyst "carries unrealized potentials for psychological transformation" by "being open to carrying whatever aspects of initiatory change the patient needs to encounter at a given moment" (p. 153). S. Powell (1985) states it somewhat differently when she says that "the symbolic attitude is mediated through the analyst until the patient is able to allow unconscious contents of the psyche to enter consciousness freely" (p. 51).

Addressing the subject of transference, Jung enunciates what might be called "constructive transference." The patient transfers to the analyst an as yet undeveloped function: accessing and integrating unconscious material to produce a transformation of attitude. Jung explains that the patient naturally attaches to the analyst since the analyst holds that which is integral to the patient's growth:

> In this function of the analyst [mediating the transcendent function for the patient] lies one of the many important meanings of the *transference*. The patient clings by means of the transference to the person who seems to promise him a renewal of attitude. . . . [T]here is a tendency to understand it in a reductive sense only, as an erotic infantile fantasy. . . . It has become a metaphorical expression of the not consciously realized need for help in a crisis. Historically it is correct to explain the erotic character of the transference in terms of the infantile *eros*. But in that way the meaning and purpose of the transference are not understood. . . . The understanding of the transference is to be sought not in its historical antecedents but in its purpose. (1957/1960, p. 74)

Jung's thinking about the role of transference within the analyst-analysand relationship gives relief to his discussion of the constructive method. He sees the unconscious as a deep source of insight which the patient may tap to apprehend the meaning of the patient's life. The analyst assists the patient both by holding the potential of that apprehension and by knowing that the transference has as much to do with the patient's deep drive to move to a new attitude as it does to the reductive, early-life experiences.

Artificially Inducing Unconscious Contents

Jung then ponders a logical inconsistency in his thinking: If the unconscious is organically at work providing the counter-position to consciousness, why should it be necessary to induce artificially a confrontation between conscious and unconscious contents? He asks, "why is it so absolutely necessary to up the unconscious contents" (1957/1960, p. 78); "why cannot the unconscious be left to its own devices" (p. 79)? First, Jung states what would become an important foundation of his metapsychology, the self-regulating nature of the psyche: "Since the psyche is a self-regulating system, just as the body is, the regulating counteraction will always develop in the unconscious" (p. 79). However, Jung cautions that the self-regulating mechanism can be defeated by overdevelopment of the conscious mind and that that has occurred in modern, Western civilization:

> Its [the unconscious's] regulating influence, however, is eliminated by critical attention and directed will, because the counteraction as such seems incompatible with the conscious direction. To this extent the psyche of civilized man is no longer a self-regulating system but could rather be compared to a machine whose speed-regulation is so insensitive that it can continue to function to the point of self injury. (1957/1960, p. 79)

Moreover, when the unconscious counteraction is suppressed, it not only loses its regulating influence but strengthens the directed function of the conscious mind:

> It then begins to have an accelerating and intensifying effect on the conscious process. It is as though the counteraction has lost its regulating influence, and hence its energy, altogether, for a condition then arises in which not only no inhibiting counteraction takes place, but in which its energy seems to add itself to that of the conscious direction. (1957/1960, p. 79)

Jung gives examples of this kind of suppression and the megalomania that results. He concludes that it is imperative we remember the importance of the regulating influences of the unconscious to the well-being of body, mind, and psyche:

> Anyone who has seen these things happen over and over again in every conceivable shade of dramatic intensity is bound to ponder. He becomes aware how easy it is to overlook the regulating influences, and that he should endeavor to pay attention to the unconscious regulation which is so necessary for our physical and emotional health. (1957/1960, p. 81)

By asserting that modern Western civilization, through its overdevelopment of the directed ego functions of the conscious mind, has created a dangerous psychic imbalance that inhibits the natural operation of the unconscious, Jung sets the stage for his discussion of the role of the transcendent function and active imagination in restoring equilibrium to the relationship between consciousness and the unconscious.

Producing Unconscious Material: Active Imagination

The initial stage in the actual mechanics of the transcendent function is the production of data from the unconscious: "First and foremost, we need the unconscious material" (Jung, 1957/1960, p. 77). Though Jung later places much greater emphasis on the use of dreams, at this early stage he concludes that they are not an appropriate source of unconscious material for purposes of the transcendent function. He states that although "the most readily accessible expression of unconscious processes is undoubtedly dreams" (p. 77) and that the "dream is, so to speak, a pure product of the unconscious" (p. 77), he also points out that "since the energy-tension in sleep is usually very low, dreams . . . are inferior expressions of unconscious contents" (p. 77) and are "unsuitable or difficult to make use of in developing the transcendent function" (p. 77). Jung's conclusion about the unsuitability of dreams paved the way for his development of active imagination, which he saw as more effective for the production of "spontaneous fantasies" (p. 78) that have "a more composed and coherent character" (p. 77). The technique, one that Jung calls an "artificial aid" (p. 81) for evoking unconscious material, can be used either in response to a patient's "depressed or disturbed state of mind for which no adequate cause can be found" (p. 81) or, in the absence of a specific symptom, "just a general, dull discontent, a feeling of resistance to everything, a sort of boredom or vague disgust, an indefinable but excruciating emptiness" (p. 83). Jung then gives voice to another tenet of his psychology: within the symptom lies the key to the patient's ability to respond.

> Naturally the patient can give any number of rationalistic reasons [for the depressed or disturbed state of mind]—the bad weather alone suffices as a reason. But none of them is really satisfying as an explanation, for a causal explanation of these states is usually satisfying only to the outsider. . . . The patient would like to know what it is all for and how to gain relief. *In the intensity of the emotional disturbance itself lies the value, the energy which he should have at his disposal in order to remedy the state of reduced adaptation.* (p. 82)

The goal is not to eliminate the symptom but rather to dive into the energy locked inside of it. The core of active imagination is finding a way into the symptom or emotional state. Only then can the symptom be seen constructively, as being involved in pulling one in a purposeful way. As a way to obtain direction from the symptom, Jung instructs that the patient contact the affect and record the fantasies and associations that emerge, following them wherever they may lead:

> He must make himself as conscious as possible of the mood he is in, sinking himself in it without reserve and noting down on paper all the fantasies and other associations that come up. Fantasy must be allowed the freest possible play, yet not in such a manner that it leaves the orbit of its object, namely the affect, by setting off a kind of "chain-reaction" association process. . . . Out of this preoccupation with the object there comes a more or less complete expression of the mood, which reproduces the content of the depression in some way, either concretely or symbolically. Since the depression was not manufactured by the conscious mind but is an unwelcome intrusion from the unconscious, the elaboration of the mood is, as it were, a picture of the contents and tendencies of the unconscious that were massed together in the depression. (1957/1960, p. 82)

The idea is to help the patient produce conscious representations (pictures, symbols, images, or associations) of unconscious contents that underlie the mood.

This section of the paper introduces Jung's seminal thinking on the fantasy-making capacity of the psyche and represents his leap into imaginal psychology. Jung's premise, explored in greater depth in his other writings, was that through imagery we can retrieve information from the unconscious. Since the texts of the 1916 and 1958 versions do not vary in any substantial way through these passages, we can surmise that this aspect of Jung's thinking was essentially formed in 1916. It is likely that the core concepts of imaginal psychology emerged directly from Jung's own descent into the unconscious.

Jung imagined that through this process unconscious contents became more powerful and moved closer to consciousness. He felt that by giving them psychic energy, the images would be vivified and emerge into the realm of consciousness where they would begin to prompt a shift:

> The whole procedure is a kind of enrichment and clarification of the affect, whereby the affect and its contents are brought nearer to consciousness, becoming at the same time more impressive and more understandable. This work by itself can have a favourable and vitalizing influence. At all events, it creates a new situation, since the previously unrelated affect has become a more or less clear and articulate idea, thanks to the assistance and co-operation of the conscious mind.

> This is the beginning of the transcendent function, i.e., of the collaboration of conscious and unconscious data. (1957/1960, p. 82)

Active imagination is used to coax material from the unconscious toward the threshold of consciousness and, in a sense, catalyze the transcendent function. The transcendent function, in turn, can act as a mediator to bring unconscious imagery into dialogue with consciousness. Though the 1916 and 1958 versions are similar through these passages, the sentence relating that a "new situation" was not part of the 1916 version. One can speculate that the revision was made to emphasize the transformational quality of the transcendent function.

Jung was also aware that each individual is different in the way that the unconscious might be contacted. Thus he emphasized that active imagination might take different form for different individuals. He advocated the use of drawing, painting, visualization, imaginal dialogue, clay work, and even movements, all depending on what prompts imagery most effectively. The use of techniques other than speaking for evoking unconscious material came from Jung's own experiences and remains an important part of Jungian work today.

Utilizing Unconscious Material: Creative Formulation and Understanding

Jung next discusses how one deals with the unconscious material prompted by active imagination. He identifies "two main tendencies" that emerge: the "way of creative formulation" and the "way of understanding" (1957/1960, p. 84). In the way of creative formulation, one responds in an intuitive or artistic way, processing the material by generating aesthetic motifs. In the way of understanding, the individual tends to respond in a more intellectual way, and "there is an intense struggle to understand the *meaning* of the unconscious product" (p. 84). Interestingly, "*meaning*" did not appear in the 1916 version. Rather, Jung describes the person as engaging in an "intensive, intellectual analysis whereby the motifs of the unconscious material are more or less intensively abstracted into ideas" (1957, p. 19). This revision confirms how meaning became a more integral part of the transcendent function to Jung over time.

Jung stresses that to fully engage unconscious material, one must seek to engage both the creative/aesthetic and the intellectual/understanding tendencies. The two compensate for each other and an overreliance on one will give a skewed result:

> *One tendency seems to be the regulating principle of the other;* both are bound together in a compensatory relationship. Experience bears out this formula. So far as it is possible at this stage to draw more general conclusions, we could say that aesthetic formulation needs understanding of the meaning, and understanding needs aesthetic

> formulation. The two supplement each other to form the transcendent function. (1957/1960, p. 85)

Dealing with unconscious material is an exercise that requires both understanding and analysis, on the one hand, and aesthetics, intuition, and creation, on the other; neither by itself is sufficient.[5] "The ideal case would be if these two aspects could exist side by side or rhythmically succeed each other; that is, if there were an alternation of creation and understanding" (p. 86).

Relation of Ego to Unconscious: Bringing Together the Opposites

After carefully laying the groundwork, Jung now makes the move into the core of the transcendent function. Once the imagery, symbolism, and affect of the unconscious material have been manifested, the conscious mind must interact with them. After watching Jung meticulously develop the seemingly irreconcilable likenesses of the omnipresent, compensatory, imagistic nature of the unconscious and the directed, definite, overdeveloped nature of consciousness, one wonders how he can possibly bring them together. He does so with the metaphor of a coming to terms of two antithetical positions out of which emerges "a third":

> Once the unconscious content has been given form and the meaning of the formulation is understood, the question arises as to how the ego will relate to this position, and how the ego and the unconscious are to come to terms. This is the second and more important stage of the procedure, the bringing together of opposites for the production of a third: the transcendent function. (1957/1960, p. 87)

This passage is quite important. It is the first time in this essay that Jung uses the phrase "the bringing together of opposites." Whereas earlier in the paper, Jung referred to the unconscious as "compensatory or complementary" (p. 69) to consciousness, and to the transcendent function as arising from "the union of conscious and unconscious contents" (p. 69), he now speaks in terms of "bringing together of opposites for production of a third." Significantly, neither the word "opposites" or "third" appears in the 1916 version. Indeed, the entire passage quoted above was added by Jung in 1958. As will be discussed further in chapter 3, the concepts of the "opposites" and the transcendent function yielding the "third" emerged strongly in several works between 1916 and 1958. Though we will revisit these themes in greater detail later, suffice it for now to say that Jung's theory of the opposites has become the subject of some debate and disagreement in the Jungian community.[6]

After formulating the second phase of the transcendent function, the bringing together of the opposites for the production of the third (the first being the emergence of the unconscious material), Jung adds another critical component. Though it may seem somewhat counterintuitive given the importance of the unconscious in Jung's psychology, he states categorically that it is the conscious ego that must control this stage: "At this stage it is no longer the unconscious that takes the lead, but the ego" (1957/1960, p. 87). Jung says this is crucial because of the danger of the ego being overwhelmed by the unconscious. He admonishes that just as it is imperative that the unconscious not be subverted by the directedness of consciousness, it is equally important that the ego not be overcome by the unconscious:

> The position of the ego must be maintained as being of equal value to the counter-position of the unconscious, and vice versa. This amounts to a very necessary warning: for just as the conscious mind of civilized man has a restrictive effect on the unconscious, so the rediscovered unconscious often has a really dangerous effect on the ego. In the same way that the ego suppressed the unconscious before, a liberated unconscious can thrust the ego aside and overwhelm it. There is a danger of the ego losing its head, so to speak. (pp. 87–88)

This material is critical. Despite all his work with the unconscious, Jung does not advocate the domination of consciousness by the unconscious but rather an equal partnership between the two. The opposites of consciousness and the unconscious are brought together to come to terms with one another.

Final Result: Dialogue Creating Emergence of the Third

With both the unconscious material having been acquired and the conscious ego fully engaged, the transcendent function culminates in a kind of conversation between the two. Jung envisions a dialogue in which both consciousness and the unconscious have an equal say:

> Thus, in coming to terms with the unconscious, not only is the standpoint of the ego justified, but the unconscious is granted the same authority. The ego takes the lead, but the unconscious must be allowed to have its say too. . . . It is exactly as if a dialogue were taking place between two human beings with equal rights, each of whom gives the other credit for a valid argument and considers it worth while to modify the conflicting standpoints by means of thorough comparison and discussion or else to distinguish them clearly from one another. (1957/1960, pp. 88–89)

The dialogue analogy is critical to Jung's conception of the transcendent function which he sees as a kind of information exchange between two equal entities. The fact that the 1916 and 1958 versions are substantially similar through these passages indicates that the colloquy metaphor was elemental to the transcendent function from the moment it was conceived and remained so.

A further conceptual leap is made as Jung analogizes between the ability to dialogue with the "other" intrapsychically (via the transcendent function) and interpersonally (in relationships). He underscores that the inability to listen to others will inhibit the ability to listen to the intraphysic other, and the inability to dialogue with the unconscious will impede human relationships:

> Everyone who proposes to come to terms with himself must reckon with this basic problem. For, to the degree that he does not admit the validity of the other person, he denies the "other" within himself the right to exist—and vice versa. The capacity for inner dialogue is a touchstone for outer objectivity. (1957/1960, p. 89)

In essence, Jung is telling us that the ability to dialogue with both the outer and inner other are key to his concepts of individuation and psychological well-being.

Jung finally arrives at the ultimate statement of the transcendent function which incorporates the idea of an exchange between consciousness and the unconscious, now labeled by Jung as opposites, out of which flows some new situation or thing.

> The shuttling to and fro of arguments and affects represents the transcendent function of opposites. The confrontation of the two positions generates a tension charged with energy and creates a living, third thing—not a logical stillbirth in accordance with the principle *tertium non datur* but a movement out of the suspension between opposites, a living birth that leads to a new level of being, a new situation. The transcendent function manifests itself as a quality of conjoined opposites. So long as these are kept apart—naturally for the purpose of avoiding conflict—they do not function and remain inert. (1957/1960, p. 90)

This important quote is instructive in several critical ways not the least of which is its substantial variation from the 1916 version. A comparison follows:

> ~~[The transcendent function lies between the conscious and the unconscious standpoint and is a living phenomenon, a way of life, which partly conforms with the unconscious as well as the conscious and partly does not. It is an individual-collective phenomenon which in principle agrees with the direction of life which anyone would follow, if he were to live in a completely unconscious, instinctive way.~~

> ~~This explains why primitive man so often appears as the symbol for the transcendent function. Back to nature in Rousseau's sense is impossible and would only be a futile regression. One can however go forwards and through psychological development again reach nature, but this time consciously taking account of instinct]~~ <The shuttling to and fro of arguments and affects represents the transcendent function of opposites. The confrontation of the two positions generates a tension charged with energy and creates a living, third thing—not a logical stillbirth in accordance with the principle tertium non datur but a movement out of the suspension between opposites, a living birth that leads to a new level of being, a new situation. The transcendent function manifests itself as a quality of conjoined opposites. So long as these are kept apart—naturally for the purpose of avoiding conflict—they do not function and remain inert.

As can be seen, the original essay was devoid of the phrase "shuttling to and fro," of the reference to the "opposites," of the allusion to "living birth that leads to a new level of being, a new situation," and of the analogy to the "conjoined opposites."

Jung's addition of the expression "shuttling to and fro" gives a sense of constant interplay or rhythm between the conscious and unconscious parts of psyche, a theme we will revisit later and one that was not present in the original essay. It reflects the notion, later expressed by Jung and others, that psychic life is comprised of a rhythmic movement between the differentiated, subjective, personal mode of consciousness and the undifferentiated, objective, imagistic state of the unconscious.[7] A second crucial addition to this important paragraph is Jung's use of the phrase, the "transcendent function *of the opposites* [italics added]" (1957/1960, p. 90). The change in language underscores Jung's belief that the conscious and unconscious positions represent antithetical perspectives. He reinforces this position by calling the interaction between the two a "confrontation" and by concluding that the transcendent function "manifests itself as a quality of conjoined opposites." He elaborates in the next paragraph where he states that the presence of unintegrated opposites indicates a loss of consciousness. Jung shows us here that dealing with and resolving opposites is central to his idea of individuation and wholeness.

Finally, Jung's 1958 revision labels the product of the transcendent function a "living, third thing." Though the 1916 version called the transcendent function "a living phenomenon, a way of life" (1957, p. 23), the later version makes it clear that something new and unknown emerges. In the 1958 version, Jung calls the result of the interaction between consciousness and the unconscious a "living, third thing" and a "living birth that leads to a new level of being, a new situation" (p. 90). This last aspect is perhaps the most significant.

For the first time in his writing, indeed in depth psychology, Jung asserts that the interaction between consciousness and unconscious yields something new and different, something more than a mixture of or compromise between the two, a third thing that transforms consciousness. Jung gives voice to a phenomenon that has been discussed in various terms ever since by depth psychologists: the idea of something new, a third, emerging from the holding of opposing or different forces.

Closing Passages: Liberation and the Courage to be Oneself

The final paragraph of the essay, missing from the 1916 version, finishes where the essay starts: by paying homage to the importance of the unconscious to psychological health. Jung says that the process of dealing with the counter-position of the unconscious implicates the entire psyche and that ultimately it expands consciousness.

> As the process of coming to terms with the counter-position has a total character, nothing is excluded. Everything takes part in the discussion, even if only fragments become conscious. Consciousness is continually widened through the confrontation with previously unconscious contents, or—to be more accurate—could be widened if it took the trouble to integrate them. (1957/1960, p. 91)

But Jung cautions us that the transcendent function is not an automatic thing; it takes courage, perseverance, and effort on the part of the individual: "Even if there is sufficient intelligence to understand the procedure, there may yet be a lack of courage and self-confidence, or one is too lazy, mentally and morally, or too cowardly, to make an effort" (1957/1960, p. 91). This raises an important response to the notion that the transcendent function is an innate psychic process. Here, at least, Jung sees the transcendent function as something that can be affected by a person's willingness and courage, a concept that is at odds with a purely "natural" transcendent function.

Jung's concluding remark, also not included in the 1916 essay, indicates both the way an individual can produce the transcendent function and how the transcendent function is integral to the individuation process:

> Where the necessary premises exist, the transcendent function not only forms a valuable addition to psychotherapeutic treatment, but gives the patient the inestimable advantage of assisting the analyst on his own resources, and of breaking a dependence which is often felt as humiliating. It is a way of attaining liberation by one's own efforts and of finding the courage to be oneself. (1957/1960, p. 91)

Thus, Jung brings the reader full circle. Having begun the essay with a discussion of how the unconscious complements and compensates for the directed processes of the conscious, he finishes by exhorting the reader that the transcendent function allows one to bring consciousness and the unconscious together to attain liberation and find the courage to be oneself.

SYNTHESIS: THE TRANSCENDENT FUNCTION AS REFLECTED IN THE ESSAY

Coming on the heels of Jung's own confrontation with the disturbing forces of the unconscious that followed his break with Freud, Jung's writing of "The Transcendent Function" in 1916 was both a formative event in the development of his psychology and, undoubtedly, a description of his own personal experience. Even that early version (written prior to any of Jung's works on the collective unconscious, the archetypes, the Self, and individuation) clearly established the outlines of his thinking about the omnipresence of the unconscious, its compensatory relationship to consciousness, and its synthetic nature. The 1916 writing also enunciated the concept of a dialogue between consciousness and the unconscious. Finally, it described the transcendent function that "lies between the conscious and the unconscious standpoint and is a living phenomenon, a way of life, which partly conforms with the unconscious as well as the conscious and partly does not" (p. 23).

While the original essay literally sat in a drawer, the concept of the transcendent function was discussed and developed further throughout Jung's works, letters, and seminars until the 1916 writing was finally published in 1957 and then immediately revised by Jung for inclusion in the *Collected Works*. The 1958 revisions evidence three primary developments in Jung's thinking: the greater centrality of the opposites, the increased emphasis on meaning and purpose, and the creation of a living, third thing, a new level of being. Together, the two versions of the essay give us a basic overview of Jung's view of the relationship between consciousness and the unconscious and the dialogue that occurs between them to produce an integration, a new level of consciousness along the path toward meaning and purpose. Left to be further explored in Jung's other works are important questions about the operation of the transcendent function, the way in which it prompts psychological growth, and its relationship with other Jungian concepts. We now turn to that exploration.

CHAPTER THREE

TRACING THE TRANSCENDENT FUNCTION THROUGH JUNG'S WORKS

"The Transcendent Function" was by no means Jung's full examination of the concept. Indeed, the essay left unanswered important questions: How exactly does the transcendent function work? How are fantasy and symbol implicated? Does the transcendent function operate on its own or can it be prompted? What changed for Jung between 1916 and 1958 to make the theory of the opposites so much more prevalent in his thinking? How does the transcendent function interact with Jung's concepts of psychological transformation, the synthetic view of psyche, and individuation? What is its relationship with other Jungian structures such as the Self and the archetypes? The answers to these questions can be extracted from the rich mines of Jung's other works. Paradoxically, what emerges is a picture of the transcendent function that is more perspicuous and at the same time ambiguous, more detailed yet somehow more difficult to fully apprehend. Despite Jung's efforts to explain the transcendent function further and to draw connections between it and other concepts, his other works evidence contradictions and ambiguities; they raise almost as many questions as they answer. Such quandaries may be inherent in the explication of a process like the transcendent function that attempts to explain something as inherently inexplicable as the transformation of consciousness itself. This chapter undertakes to address these issues by analyzing Jung's references to the transcendent function in his other writings and works.

The task is formidable. Jung refers to or discusses the transcendent function in eight written works, four letters, and five seminars. All of the references are listed in Appendix B together with the pages surrounding each reference to help the reader understand its context. Two of the eight written works were written within a year of the 1916 version of "The Transcendent Function": "The Structure of the Unconscious" (1916/1953), written in 1916, was later revised to become "Relations Between the Ego and the Unconscious" (1928/1953), and "The Psychology of the Unconscious Processes," written in 1917, was later revised to become "On the Psychology of the Unconscious" (1943/1953). A third, *Psychological Types* (1921/1971), was written within five years. It is in these three works that Jung discusses the transcendent function most extensively. Five other written works make less extensive reference to the concept.[1] In addition, Jung mentions or discusses the concept in four letters,[2] references that give fascinating texture to the more formal discussions in his written works. Finally, Jung mentions the transcendent function in five public seminars,[3] giving further rich relief to his thinking as he responds to the questions of colleagues and students.

Together, Jung's references to the transcendent function give us insight into the questions posed above. Two points should be kept in mind. First, each of these topics is extensive and the treatment here is not intended to be exhaustive. Rather, the aim is to sketch a topographical map of the Jungian terrain in which the transcendent function resides to get a sense of the role it plays in Jung's psychology. Second, this will not be a linear progression; indeed, a straight line cannot accurately reflect the relationship between and among these concepts. Instead, imagine Jung's ideas as a web with each idea inextricably intertwined with the others; each flows from, implicates, and relates to the others. By jumping onto this fascinating web of ideas, we will interact with it without fear of getting caught up or stuck, and thus will avoid attempting to reduce it to some final explanation.

THEMATIC ANALYSIS OF REFERENCES TO THE TRANSCENDENT FUNCTION

There are a number of ways one could review the extensive references to the transcendent function. One method would be to analyze the references chronologically, attempting to understand how the concept developed in Jung's thinking. Such a task would be difficult, if not impossible, because Jung both wrote papers that remained unpublished for long periods of time and made multiple revisions to works, making it difficult to know when he wrote specific passages. Thus, a thematic approach has been adopted. Each reference to the transcendent function is categorized as to theme, then all references to each theme are analyzed to ascertain Jung's thinking about the relationship between that theme and the transcendent function. This methodology proves fortuitous because it reveals an interwoven tapestry of Jungian ideas with the transcendent function at or near the center. It reveals that the transcendent function is implicated in or underlies key concepts in Jung's paradigm. Following is an explication of the themes and the underlying references to the transcendent function.

The Opposites: The Source and Development of Jung's Thinking

One can see directly from a reading of the essay that bears its name that the transcendent function implicates the concept of the opposites. The idea that psychological experience is profoundly affected by a struggle between opposites is at the heart of the Jungian paradigm. As one writer opines, "An acquaintance with the principle of opposition is essential to an understanding of [Jung's] point of view" because it lies "at the root of many of his hypotheses" (Samuels, Shorter, and Plaut, 1986, p. 102). Near the end of his life Jung himself stated, "the opposites are the ineradicable and indispensable pre-conditions to all psychic life" (1955–1956/1963, p. 170). As we saw in chapter 2, the transcendent function flows from opposing forces in consciousness and the unconscious; the idea of the opposites is the foundation upon which the edifice of the transcendent function is constructed. No comprehensive understanding of the latter is possible without an exploration of former. Notably, though the seeds for Jung's thinking on the opposites are contained in the 1916 version of "The Transcendent Function,"[4] the strength and prevalence of that theory grew in his subsequent writings such that it became central to his psychology generally and to the transcendent function in particular. Here we explore how that shift took place and how it affected Jung's thinking about the transcendent function.

Jung did not claim that he was the first to discuss the idea of the opposites in the human psyche. He noted that it went back at least as far as the ancient Greek philosopher Heraclitus, who enunciated the principle of *enantiodromia*, meaning "being torn asunder into pairs of opposites" (1943/1953, p. 73):

> Old Heraclitus . . . discovered the most marvellous of all psychological laws: the regulative function of opposites. He called it *enantiodromia*, a running contrariwise, by which he meant that sooner or later everything runs into its opposite. (1943/1953, p. 72)

In addition to the influence of Heraclitus, the analogy between Jung's opposites and Hegel's dialectical model (i.e., thesis and antithesis) has not gone unnoticed. Though Jung never referenced Hegel's dialectical logic,[5] Solomon (1992) compared the two models and even concluded that Jung's transcendent function was directly analogous to Hegel's synthesis. Others who contributed to Jung's conception of the opposites included Kant, Goethe, Schiller, and Nietzsche (Douglas, 1997, p. 22). It has even been suggested that the opposites inherent in Freud's dual-instinct theory, the conflicting combination of life and death instincts in every part of psychic life, also contributed to Jung's thinking (Frattaroli, 1997, p. 177).

Though Jung never explicitly acknowledged the source of his theory (Samuels, Shorter, and Plaut, 1986, p. 102), he came to see the opposites as akin to a law of nature. In fact, he eventually likened the law of psychic opposition to the first law of thermodynamics: that all energy is a function of two opposing forces.

> The concept of energy implies that of polarity, since a current of energy presupposes two different states, or poles, without which there can be no current. Every energetic phenomenon (and there is no phenomenon that is not energetic) consists of pairs of opposites: beginning and end, above and below, hot and cold, earlier and later, cause and effect, etc. (1921/1971, p. 202)

Jung came to believe that all psychic energy flows from the tension of opposing forces: "There is no energy unless there is a tension of opposites" (1943/1953, p. 53). He ultimately held that all life itself emerges from the opposites: "Life is born only of the spark of opposites" (p. 54).

Though it is difficult to pinpoint where the theory first emerged in Jung's writings, certainly one of the earliest references to the opposites is in "The Structure of the Unconscious" (1916/1953), which was originally written the same year as the first version of "The Transcendent Function." There, in wrestling with the distinctions between the personal and collective aspects of consciousness, he comments on the opposition between personal and collective forces:

> Just as the individual is not merely a unique and separate being, but is also a social being, so the human mind is not a self-contained and wholly individual phenomenon, but is a collective one. And just as certain social functions or instincts are opposed to the egocentric interests of the individual, so certain functions or tendencies of the human mind are opposed, by their collective nature, to the personal mental functions. (p. 275)

In the same work, Jung comments on the contradictory nature of the individual and collective parts of the human psyche and talks about their union using language that prefigures his later description of the transcendent function as "an irrational life-process" (1939/1959, p. 289):

> The human psyche is both individual and collective, and . . . its well-being depends on the natural cooperation of these two apparently contradictory sides. Their union is essentially an irrational life process that can . . . neither be brought about, nor understood, nor explained rationally. (1916/1953, p. 289)

Here we begin to see the weaving of the web of interrelated Jungian ideas: individual consciousness, the collective unconscious, and the dynamic opposition of the psyche and an irrational life process (the transcendent function) that brings the disparate elements together.

Jung's early work on the opposites inherent in the individual and collective natures of psyche was followed by equally important work on the opposites inherent in the relationship between conscious and unconscious that he first broached in *Psychological Types* (1921/1971). In what many consider Jung's most important contribution to general psychology, this volume on the personality types is mandatory reading for anyone wishing truly to understand Jung's theory of opposites and how the unconscious acts in a compensatory or opposing way to consciousness. Though we see the beginnings of Jung's thinking about the opposites in the 1916 version of "The Transcendent Function" (1957) and in "The Structure of the Unconscious" (1916/1953), it is in *Psychological Types* (1921/1971) that it is truly formed. There Jung, leaning heavily on the work of Friedrich Schiller, a late eighteenth-century German philosopher, outlines the long history of duality between abstract idea and physical thing, the so-called opposition of realism and nominalism (p. 26; see also 1943/1953, p. 54).[6] The debate between realism and nominalism was about whether there is a fundamental duality between form and matter, idea and thing, thought and feeling, subject and object, inner and outer—an important theme in Western consciousness. Out of this history, Jung posits two basic personality types (1921/1971, p. 4): the extrovert, whose primary orientation is outward toward the object, the psychological equivalent of the nominalist, and the introvert, whose primary orientation is away from the object and toward the subject (himself or herself), ideas, and his or her own psychological processes, the psychological equivalent of the realist. Introverts process the world around them with emphasis on form, idea, thought, subject, and inner reality, whereas extroverts use matter, thing, feeling, object, and outer reality.

The history that Jung presents of the duality between subject/object and idea/thing is critical to understanding his theory of the opposite nature of psychic processes and the emergence of the transcendent function. In his discussion of introversion and extroversion, Jung introduces key concepts that anticipate his formulation of the transcendent function, the mediating force between the conscious and unconscious. Discussing the opposition of realism and nominalism, Jung uses language that is remarkably similar to his later description of the transcendent function:

> There is no possibility, therefore, of finding any satisfactory, reconciling formula by pursuing the one or the other attitude. And yet, even if his mind could, man cannot remain thus divided, for the split is not a mere matter of some off-beat philosophy, but the daily repeated problem of his relation to himself and to the world. And because this is basically the problem at issue, the division cannot be resolved by a discussion of the nominalist and realist arguments. *For its solution a third, mediating standpoint is needed* [italics added]. *Esse in intellectu* lacks tangible reality, *esse in re* lacks mind. Idea and thing come together, however, in the human psyche,

> which holds the balance between them. . . . Living reality is the product of neither of the actual, objective behavior of things nor of the formulated idea exclusively, but rather of the combination of both in the living psychological process, through *esse in anima*. Only through the specific vital activity of the psyche does the sense-impression attain that intensity, and the idea that effective force, which are the two indispensable constituents of living reality. . . . It is, pre-eminently the creative activity from which the answers to all answerable questions come; it is the mother of all possibilities where, like all psychological opposites, the inner and outer worlds are joined together in living union. (1921/1971, pp. 51-52)

In this profoundly important passage, we begin to see ideas fundamental to Jung's psychology: psyche (or soul) as the "third, mediating standpoint" or terrain upon which the fundamental opposite worlds of inner and outer, idea and thing, can be "joined together in living union." Jung tells us here that the human psyche, through its creative forces, is able somehow to combine the seemingly opposite forces of idea and thing to create a third, living reality. Clearly, this language prefigures Jung's formulation of the transcendent function.

Thus, we see in two profound dualities the roots of Jung's foundational ideas on the dynamic opposition of the psyche: (1) the personal *vs.* collective aspects of the psyche that Jung conceived as opposites in his 1916 writing of "The Structure of the Unconscious" (1916/1953) and (2) the fundamental opposites of idea and thing, thought and feeling, subject and object, inner and outer, introvert and extrovert, that Jung identified in *Psychological Types* (1921/1971) based on the ancient history of the debate between realism and nominalism.

Many have critiqued Jung's foundational reliance on the psychic dynamism of the opposites as excessive and even theoretically wrong. Seen from a broad historical perspective, Jung's theory of the opposites constitutes the psychological manifestation of two millennia of dualistic thinking in Western consciousness. The ancient Greeks gave intellectual birth to the opposites in Western civilization when the realists and nominalists first distinguished idea from thing, inner from outer, subject from object. The opposites are also alive and well in the ideas of Descartes, who saw an emerging autonomous self as being fundamentally distinct from an objective external world that it seeks to understand, and whose thinking was presaged in earlier historical developments.[7] It has been argued that the latter half of the twentieth century ushered in the beginnings of a paradigm shift away from dualistic, either/or, oppositional thinking into a new way of conceiving humanity, psychology, indeed consciousness. Some have connected this shift to a "reintegration of the repressed feminine" (Tarnas, 1991, p. 444), others with the movement from monism and dualism to polytheism (see, e.g., Hillman, 1975, p. 170).[8]

In any event, Jung's theory of opposites is a key concept closely related to the transcendent function. Though he gives us no firm indication of the ultimate source of his theory, the thinking of Heraclitus, Plato, and others about the dualities between idea and thing, form and matter, inner and outer, subject and object, clearly affected Jung in a profound way. Jung also likely drew from the ideas of Hegel, Kant, Goethe, Schiller, Nietzsche, and even Freud in formulating his concept of the opposites as the source of all psychic energy. Jung's early work on the interplay between the personal and collective aspects of the psyche necessarily implicated the idea of opposites, as did his seminal ideas about typology. Eventually, Jung came to believe that all psychological life, indeed all life itself, arose from the tension of the opposites.

The Dynamic Opposition of Consciousness and the Unconscious

The concept that psychic life is divided into countless pairs of opposites (e.g., good/bad, light/dark, love/hate, life/death, inner/outer, idea/thing, etc.) only captures part of Jung's view of psyche. He further believed that one member of each pair resided in consciousness and the other in the unconscious, and each dynamically opposed the other in a kind of psychic debate. He posited that for every perspective held in consciousness, an opposite one in the unconscious sought to be heard, understood, and assimilated. Given this premise, one can see why the transcendent function, the mechanism through which consciousness and the unconscious dialogue, is so important to Jungian thought.

Though Jung had already formulated some of his ideas on the dynamic opposition of the psyche when he wrote the 1916 version of "The Transcendent Function," those ideas are further developed in a very extensive chapter 2 of *Psychological Types* (1921/1971). There, in an extensive discussion of Schiller's ideas on the "separation of the two functions" (p. 69), Jung argues that (1) each person is predisposed toward a dominant function in consciousness, either extroversion or introversion (p. 75), and (2) that that predisposition is then further developed or exaggerated by "cultural demands" so that the person can be of greater utility to the collective (p. 75). Thus, Jung bemoaned, cultural demands impel a differentiation of psychic functions and destroy the wholeness of the individual for the sake of collective:

> It is not man who counts, but his one differentiated function. Man no longer appears as man in our collective culture: he is merely represented by a function, what is more he identifies himself with this function and denies the relevance of the other inferior functions. (p. 72)

The result, according to Jung, is that the inferior function is driven into the unconscious (p. 74) where it remains trapped, thereby creating a psychic injury: "so the enslavement of the inferior functions is an ever-bleeding wound in the psyche of modern man" (p. 72).

This culturally mandated differentiation of functions enhances humanity's ability to operate as a collective entity but polarizes the functions in the individual. Jung quotes Schiller: "'There was no other way of developing the manifold capabilities of man than by placing them in opposition to one another'" (1921/1971, p. 73). Near the end of the discussion about Schiller, Jung details for the first time his seminal ideas about how the opposites can only be mediated through a symbol that emerges from the fantasy-making capacity of the psyche and concludes: "This function of mediation between the opposites I have termed the *transcendent function*, by which I mean . . . a combined function of conscious and unconscious elements" (p. 115).

Jung's ideas about the dynamic opposition of consciousness and the unconscious are also reflected in other writings that discuss the transcendent function. In "The Relations Between the Ego and the Unconscious" (1928/1953), Jung alludes to the "two opposing 'realities,' the world of the conscious and the world of the unconscious" (p. 218), notes the "sharp cleavages and antagonisms between conscious and unconscious" (p. 219), and concludes by referring to the transcendent function as the "fusion . . . of the differentiated with the inferior functions, of the conscious with the unconscious" (p. 220). In "On the Psychology of the Unconscious" (1943/1953), Jung refers to the transcendent function as "bridging the yawning gulf between conscious and unconscious" and describes it as "a natural process, a manifestation of the energy that springs from the tension of opposites" (p. 80). In *Mysterium Coniunctionis* (1955–1956/1963), Jung says: "This continual process of getting to know the counterposition in the unconscious I have called the 'transcendent function'" (p. 200). Elsewhere, Jung refers to "these unconscious compensations" (1939/1958, p. 488), "spontaneous unconscious compensation" (p. 500), and "cooperation of conscious reasoning and the data of the unconscious" (1955, p. 690).

All of these references evidence this fundamental concept in Jung's metapsychology: consciousness and the unconscious stand in dynamic opposition to one another. Whatever is being held in the rational, directed faculties of consciousness is being compensated for or opposed by a counter-position in the irrational, undirected unconscious, and the latter is constantly pushing against the former to reach an accommodation. These opposites in consciousness and the unconscious are the raw materials out of which the transcendent function is forged. Indeed, the dialogue between consciousness and the unconscious has been variously called "the transcendent function of the opposites" (1957/1960, p. 90), the "mutual confrontation of the opposites" (1939/1958, p. 489), and the "manifestation of the energy that springs from the tension of the opposites" (1943/1953, p. 81).

The final conceptual move in understanding Jung's theory of the opposites is that the opposites must be united. So long as psychic material remains split between consciousness and the unconscious, we are deprived of essential psychological resources. As Jung stated in *Psychological Types*, squelching the inferior functions results in a kind of psychological division:

> This one-sided development must inevitably lead to a reaction, since the suppressed inferior functions cannot be indefinitely excluded from participating in our life and development. The time will come when the division in the inner man must be abolished, in order that the undeveloped may be granted an opportunity to live. (1921/1971, p. 74)

Jung argues that to the extent the opposites remain separated, we remain split psychologically, unwhole and unrealized:

> In whatever form the opposites appear in the individual, at bottom it is always a matter of a consciousness lost and obstinately stuck in one-sidedness, confronted with the image of instinctive wholeness and freedom. This presents a picture of the anthropoid and archaic man with, on the one hand, his supposedly uninhibited world of instinct and, on the other, his often misunderstood world of spiritual ideas, who, compensating and correcting our one-sidedness, emerges from the darkness and shows us how and where we have deviated from the basic pattern and crippled ourselves psychically. (1957/1960, p. 90)

It is from emphasis on the union of the opposites that the importance of the transcendent function flows; it is the instrumentality through which the opposites are reconciled and through which growth emerges. Hence Jung labeled the transcendent function as that which allows "mediation between the opposites" (1921/1971, p. 115), "union of the opposites" (1928/1953, p. 223; 1939/1958, p. 501; 1939/1959, p. 289), that which "progressively unites the opposites" (1955, p. 690), and the "mode of apprehension . . . capable of uniting the opposites" (1943/1953, p. 109).

Surprisingly, though the opposites of consciousness and the unconscious are foundational to much of Jung's psychology, he is not entirely consistent on the subject. In fact, there are two areas of contradiction, or at least ambiguity. First, as discussed in chapter 2, Jung sometimes refers to the unconscious as complementary to rather than in opposition to consciousness (see, e.g., 1957, p. 5). In fact, in one writing Jung states flatly that "conscious and unconscious are not necessarily in opposition to one another, but complement one another to form a totality" (1928/1953, p. 177). In these and other places,

Jung essentially disagrees with his own assertion, that opposites are the basis of all psychic energy, and offers a notion that seems intuitively correct: psyche is comprised of disparate, but not necessarily opposite, states or elements whose interaction forms a whole. Though these latter descriptions of the relationship between consciousness and the unconscious do not represent the preponderance of Jung's writings, they anticipate what is a widely held question about, indeed criticism of, Jung's theory of opposites. Some post-Jungians have opined that his extreme expressions of the opposites reflect more a feature of Jung's personal psychology than a universal theory of psychology. Others assert that though psyche manifests multiple and dissimilar elements, they are not necessarily opposite. Corbett (1992), for example, offers a view, that though the transcendent function is a drive to unify and integrate, it is not about opposites but about psychological parts that are missing:

> Many post-Jungian writers have questioned the notion that the psyche is necessarily structured in sets of opposites. . . . Samuels (1985) pointed out that the perception of psychic functioning in terms of opposites ignores the concurrent mutual support, complementarity, incremental gradations of change and subtle transitions found within the psyche. . . . A different metaphor is needed to describe the movement of the unconscious into consciousness.
>
> This movement is motivated by a need to join with whatever is missing from ourselves, in order to enhance the wholeness and cohesiveness of the personality. The missing quality is not necessarily an "opposite" one. (pp. 395–96)

Samuels (1985) cites other writers who criticize Jung's theory of opposites as too encompassing or theoretically flawed. He concludes, "Concentration on the opposites leads to neglect of slight gradations and subtle transitions of difference; the concept is simply too global" (p. 114).

A second inconsistency in Jung's theory of the opposites concerns their location. The transcendent function is founded on opposites located one in consciousness and one in the unconscious. Yet in many key passages about the opposites, Jung makes reference to opposites both of which are fully available to the conscious mind. Though there are numerous examples of Jung's use of the opposites in this latter sense, a few are instructive here. In one place, in talking about the power of the child archetype on adults, Jung says, "The conflict [between the dependence of a child and its desire to be independent] is not to be overcome by that conscious mind remaining caught between the opposites" (Jung, 1941/1959, p. 168). Elsewhere, Jung discusses the struggles humanity has with pairs of moral values such as megalomania/inferiority and good/evil (Jung, 1928/1953, pp. 149–50), values of which we are clearly conscious. A quick review of the index to Jung's collected works reveals countless references to pairs of opposites (e.g., above/below, ascent/descent, birth/death, body/mind, cold/warm, fire/water, good/evil, light/heavy, right/wrong, same/different) that clearly manifest in the conscious mind. Finally, in discussing the role of the symbol in the operation of the transcendent function, Jung (1921/1971) describes how conscious and unconscious states can come into dialogue, and he refers to the opposites in consciousness, specifically in the conscious ego:

> For this collaboration of opposing states to be possible at all, they must first face one another in the fullest *conscious opposition* [italics added]. This necessarily entails a violent disunion with oneself, to the point where thesis and antithesis negate one another, while the ego is forced to acknowledge its absolute participation in both. (p. 478)

Jung's acknowledgment, indeed repeated illustrations, of opposites existing purely in the conscious mind (in addition to those that face each other across the boundary between both consciousness and unconscious) again makes intuitive sense. Considering the transcendent function in any way except a purely abstract, theoretical model, requires us to acknowledge that it must include opposites in consciousness as well as those in both consciousness and the unconscious. Indeed, if the one of the pair were located entirely in the unconscious (i.e., were it entirely unconscious), it would never compensate, oppose, or rise to consciousness. Its presence must manifest in some conscious way—as an inkling of a conscious attitude, a symptom, an affect, some distress, some feeling of dis-ease, a dream, or an illness—before it becomes an issue. Once it becomes distressing in some conscious way, then the opposites are in play and the transcendent function can operate upon them. In fact, that is the essence of Hegel's dialectic model: the constant posing of the opposite viewpoint (antithesis) as a counterbalance to the proposition being considered (thesis) yields the emergence of a reconciled, more balanced view (synthesis). Jung felt that the opposition comes primarily from the unconscious, but he often contradicts himself and gives clear examples where the opposites to which he refers are clearly extant in the conscious mind alone.

Moving away from the Jungian paradigm, opposites (or even more broadly, compensations and complements) are probably everywhere: in the conscious mind, between consciousness and the unconscious, and also in pairs in the unconscious. Put another way, for every conscious thought or attitude, one can probably locate several states in the conscious mind that are opposite or compensatory to or at least inform that thought or attitude. In addition, one could probably imagine thoughts, attitudes, feelings, or beliefs residing in the unconscious that are also implicated. Still, Jung's thesis that the unconscious compensates for or opposes consciousness feels accurate. What we add here, however, is that in practice the unconscious opposite is often (some might say almost always) manifested in various conscious ways in order to give notice of the conflict's existence. This point also clears up the confusion created when, frequently, the transcendent function is referred to by post-Jungians in situations where the opposition being faced is wholly conscious.

Where does this leave us regarding Jung's theory of the opposites? In most of his writings Jung suggests that consciousness and the unconscious are in dynamic opposition to one another, that each attitude or viewpoint in consciousness is mirrored by an opposing view in the unconscious. From that hypothesis flow the ideas that the separation of the opposites between consciousness and the unconscious results in a kind of psychological splitting and that wholeness requires a bringing together or reconciliation of the opposites; therein lies the importance of the transcendent function. Yet we have also unearthed two important inconsistencies, or at least ambiguities, in Jung's view of the opposites. First, they are not always exactly opposite and indeed may reflect a kind of psychic multiplicity seeking some sort of stasis. Second, contrary to his central assertion, Jung acknowledged that opposites exist not only between consciousness and the unconscious but often find manifestation entirely in consciousness.

The Role of Fantasy and Symbol

Jung's arrival at the concepts of the dynamic opposition of consciousness and the unconscious and of the bringing together of the opposites for psychological wholeness set the stage for his innovative theories about the role of fantasy[9] and symbol[10] in the operation of the transcendent function. Jung hypothesized that opposites cannot be reconciled rationally but rather can be united only irrationally through fantasy and the symbol-producing capacities of the unconscious. Thus, fantasy and symbol became critical to Jung's thinking about the transcendent function and to the psychological well-being it promotes.

To Jung, fantasy was not an abstract concept but a psychic reality by which he was personally affected in a profound way. In describing the impact of Philemon, an Egypto-Hellenistic pagan figure who appeared in his dreams and fantasies during the critical period after his break with Freud, Jung says:

> Philemon and other figures of my fantasies brought home to me the crucial insight that there are things in the psyche which I do not produce, but which produce themselves and have their own life. Philemon represented a force which was not myself. . . . It was he who taught me psychic objectivity, the reality of the psyche. Through him the distinction was clarified between myself and the object of my thought. (1989c, p. 183)

Jung came to learn firsthand the innate capacity and enormous power of the psyche. In the face of skepticism he was certain to receive from elsewhere in his professional circle, Jung forcefully avowed the importance of fantasy:

> The scientific credo of our time has developed a superstitious phobia about fantasy. But the real is what works. And the fantasies of the unconscious work, there can be no doubt about that. . . . Something works behind the veil of fantastic images, whether we give this something a good name or a bad. It is something real, and for this reason its manifestations must be taken seriously. (1928/1953, p. 217)

Beyond his general feeling that fantasy is a powerful and real force, Jung also specifically posited that in fantasy all opposites are joined:

> The psyche creates reality every day. The only expression I can use for this activity is *fantasy*. Fantasy is just as much feeling as thinking; as much intuition as sensation. There is no psychic function that, through fantasy, is not inextricably bound up with the other psychic functions. . . . Fantasy, therefore, seems to me the clearest expression of the specific activity of the psyche. It is, pre-eminently, the creative activity from which the answers to all answerable questions come; *it is the mother of all possibilities, where, like all psychological opposites, the inner and outer worlds are joined together in union* [italics added]. (1921/1971, p. 52)

One can see from the language of this passage the profound belief Jung placed in the power of fantasy. He maintained that fundamental opposites cannot be resolved by reason but only by fantasy and that in fantasy lies the nexus between all psychic functions. Furthermore, Jung tells us, because of its capacity to unite seemingly unlinkable opposites, fantasy is the "mother of all possibilities," a source of answers to the most difficult questions. Because these ideas are well accepted in most quarters of depth psychology now, it is difficult to fully apprehend how radical they were when Jung advocated them. More than a whimsical landscape of imagination and imagery, Jung conceived of fantasy as that terrain of psyche where the shackles of preconceived limits could be discarded and psyche could actually transform itself.

Symbol was equally important to Jung because he asserted that it was the mechanism through which fantasy made its journey from the unconscious to consciousness. Jung posited that through fantasy the unconscious produced symbols—images, motifs, notions—that can be accessed by consciousness to produce the transcendent function and create psychological change. Much of Jung's formative work on the role of fantasy and symbol in the transcendent function is based on the ideas of Schiller as set forth in chapter 2 of *Psychological Types*. Though many recommend that the reader start with chapter 10, "General Description of the Types" (see, e.g., Hopke, 1989, p. 51), Jung urged that the reader "who really wants to understand" the work immerse himself in chapters 2 and 5 (1921/1971, p. xv). Chapter 2 is a detailed discussion of Schiller's views, together with Jung's responses and elaborations, about the opposition between introversion (which places emphasis on thought, form, passivity, and inner processing) and extroversion (which gives primacy to sensation, matter, activity, and outer processing). Jung quotes Schiller as concluding that the two "can never be made one" (p. 103),[11] but that they can collaborate through a "reciprocal action between the two" (p. 103). We can see here the influence Schiller's writing may have had on Jung; Schiller's "reciprocal action between the two" sounds the same timbre as Jung's dialogue between the opposites of consciousness and the unconscious to create the transcendent function. Schiller, before Jung, saw that opposites could not be reconciled without some sort of extraordinary psychic activity.

However, Jung and Schiller give different formulations of the nature of psychic activity necessary to break the impasse of the opposites. As pointed out by Jung, Schiller posits that the deadlock is best approached through psyche's activity of thinking, what he calls "purely a task of reason" (1921/1971, p. 104). Jung takes strong exception to Schiller's conclusion, arguing that opposites are, by their very nature, not reconcilable through rationality or reason. In so doing, he employs a Latin phrase that often accompanies his discussions of the transcendent function, *tertium non datur*, which in essence means "there is no middle way" (Jung, 1943/1953, p. 77), and says that opposites can only be united irrationally:

> It is a pity that Schiller is so conditioned to . . . look upon the co-operation of the two instincts as a "task of reason," for opposites are not to be united rationally: *tertium non datur*—that is precisely why they are called opposites. . . . In practice, opposites can be united only in the form of a compromise, or *irrationally*, some new thing arising between them which, although different from both, yet has the power to take up their energies in equal measure as an expression of both and of neither. Such an expression cannot be contrived by reason, it can only be created through living. (1921/1971, p. 105)

One can see in this quote important tones of the transcendent function: some new thing arising irrationally between the opposites; something different from both opposites but standing as an expression of part of each of them, an expression of both and of neither; and something that can be created only through living. All of these elements were subsequently incorporated by Jung into his expression of the transcendent function.

We must pause here to explore another important area of ambiguity or inconsistency in Jung. He takes pains to inform us that reconciliation of opposites is not "purely a task of reason," as asserted by Schiller, but rather can be accomplished only "irrationally." Yet Jung's own definition of "irrational" asserts that something irrational is not *contrary* to reason but *beyond* it, so that it cannot be understood. In other words, something can be irrational and also based in reason though it may be so complex as to surpass our reasoning powers. Given this definition of irrational, isn't Jung merely saying that the way psyche resolves opposites is beyond our comprehension? Schiller might very well agree with that while maintaining that psyche is still performing a task based upon reason. In addition, didn't Jung tell us in "The Transcendent Function" that in coming to terms with the unconscious the "ego takes the lead" (1957/1960, p. 88)? By acknowledging that the ego takes the lead in the second phase of the transcendent function, Jung acknowledges that it is, at least partly, a task of reason. Furthermore, Jung implies that all rational things occur in consciousness and all irrational things occur in the unconscious. His bias in this direction is evident from the outset in his discussion of the one-sidedness, definiteness, and directedness of the conscious mind. But we know intuitively that there are both rational and irrational contents in consciousness and both as well in the unconscious.

This is not to say that Jung was not enunciating an important and novel idea: that we should rely on the irrational and the unconscious rather than the reasonable and the conscious to propel psyche. Yet his principle suffered from inconsistency around the role of ego and ambiguity about how reason might play into the process. To put it another way, is it possible that Schiller and Jung are in greater agreement than Jung realized or acknowledged? Both state that the tension of the opposites is the primary force and that the stalemate can only be broken through some reciprocal action (Schiller) or dialogue (Jung) between the two. Is Jung overstating the disagreement? What may be most important is Jung's perception that they disagreed. By reacting so strongly to the phrase "task of reason" and emphasizing the word "irrational," Jung articulates a position present throughout his works: that he places greater trust in fantasy, symbol, images, and the nonlinear functions of psyche than he does in reason, rationality, and the directed functions. Once again, this position flows from Jung's own process and psychology.

In any event, Jung goes on to say that the new, irrational thing that arises between the opposites is the symbol and that the symbol is generated by the fantasy-making capacity of psyche. Citing Schiller's notion that we can only unite the thinking (introverted) and sensing (extroverted) functions by being able to experience them at the same time, Jung explains that out of the experience of the opposites would flow a symbol that can unite the opposites:

> Thus, if a man were able to live both faculties or instincts at the same time, i.e., thinking by sensing and sensing by thinking, then, out of that experience . . . a *symbol* would arise which would express his accomplished destiny, i.e., his individual way on which the Yea and Nay are united. . . . The object of the mediating function . . . would be precisely a symbol in which the opposites are united. . . . The essence of the symbol consists in the fact that it represents in itself something that is not wholly understandable, and that it hints only intuitively at its possible meaning. The creation of a symbol is not a rational process, for a rational process could never produce an image that represents a content which is at its bottom incomprehensible. (1921/1971, pp. 105–06)

The symbol is explained here as emerging from the experience of the opposites. Notably, Jung calls the symbol the "object of the mediating function," that is, the object around which the mediating function operates. Thus, the symbol somehow carries pieces of both the opposites and becomes a mediating force between them. This is possible, as the passage tells us, because the symbol is born not of a rational process, since no rational process can unite what are inherently separate opposites, but rather from a place that is not wholly understandable.

But where does the symbol come from? Jung returns to Schiller and identifies what Schiller calls a "third instinct" (1921/1971, p. 106), between thought/form/passivity and sensation/matter/activity. Schiller felt that the third instinct was the "play instinct," while Jung terms it "fantasy activity":

> Schiller calls the symbol-creating function a third instinct, the *play* instinct; it bears no resemblance to the two opposing functions, but stands between them and does justice to both their natures. . . . *The third element, in which the opposites merge, is fantasy activity which is creative and receptive at once.* (1921/1971, pp. 106–07)

Here, Jung identifies fantasy as the symbol-creating function of psyche and describes it as the "third element, in which the opposites merge," a description clearly analogous to the language he uses to describe the transcendent function in various other places.

As we see from these critical passages, symbol and fantasy, mere parlor tricks in other orientations, are the building blocks of psychological growth and health in Jung's psychology. Through a discussion and extension of Schiller, Jung arrives at a central tenet of his psychology: fantasy activity in the unconscious generates symbols—images, motifs, patterns—that allow the fusion of material that would otherwise remain polarized. In so doing, Jung identifies fantasy and the symbols that arise from it as the raw materials that fuel the engine of the transcendent function.

Operation of the Transcendent Function

Having laid the groundwork with fantasy and symbol, we can now review the mechanics of the transcendent function. Jung describes this process in two places in *Psychological Types:* in chapter 2 ("Schiller's Ideas on the Type Problem") and in chapter 11 ("Definitions"). In chapter 2, he describes how the symbol emerges from fantasy activity and rises to consciousness, creating the possibility for uniting the opposites and effecting psychological change. The following, though extensive, is critical to a complete understanding of how Jung sees the symbol as uniting the opposites and producing the transcendent function. A full analysis follows the quote:

> The separation into pairs of opposites is entirely due to conscious differentiation; only consciousness can recognize the suitable and distinguish it from the unsuitable and worthless. . . . It would, therefore, be pointless to call upon consciousness to decide the conflict between the instincts. . . . The unconscious, then, might well be the authority we have to appeal to, since it is a neutral region of the psyche where everything that is divided and antagonistic in consciousness flows together into groupings. . . .
>
> Thus, besides the will, which is entirely dependent on its content, man has as a further auxiliary in the unconscious, that maternal womb of creative fantasy, which is able at any time to fashion symbols in the natural process of elementary psychic activity, symbols that can serve to determine the mediating will. I say "can" advisedly, because the symbol does not of its own accord step into the breach, but remains in the unconscious just so long as the energic value of the conscious contents exceeds that of the unconscious symbol.
>
> Under normal conditions, therefore, energy must be artificially supplied to the unconscious symbol in order to increase its value and bring it to consciousness. This comes about . . . through a differentiation of the self [footnote omitted] from the opposites. This differentiation amounts to a detachment of libido from both sides. . . . The will does not decide between the opposites, but purely for the self, that is, the disposable energy is withdrawn into the self. . . . The libido becomes wholly objectless, it is no longer related to anything that could be a content of consciousness, and it therefore sinks into the unconscious, where it automatically takes possession of the waiting fantasy material, which it . . . activates and forces to the surface.
>
> The constellated fantasy material contains images of the psychological development of the individuality in its successive states—a sort of preliminary sketch or representation of the onward way between the opposites. Although it may frequently happen that the

> discriminating activity of consciousness does not find much in these images that can be immediately understood, these intuitions nevertheless contain a living power which can have a determining effect on the will. But the determining of the will has repercussions on both sides, so that after a while the opposites recover their strength. The renewed conflict again demands the same treatment, and each time a further step along the way is made possible. This function of mediation between the opposites I have termed the *transcendent function,* by which I mean nothing mysterious, but merely a combined function of conscious and unconscious elements, or, as in mathematics, a common function of real and imaginary quantities [footnote omitted].
>
> Besides the will . . . we also have creative fantasy, an irrational, instinctive function which alone has the power to supply the will with a content of such a nature that it can unite the opposites. (1921/1971, pp. 113–15)

This important quotation must be parsed to allow a more detailed understanding. We can describe the multiple step process set forth by Jung in the following way:

1. Opposites are separated by virtue of the nature of consciousness.
2. Since consciousness itself is what creates the opposites, it would "be pointless" to call upon consciousness to resolve them.
3. Therefore, we must look to the unconscious, "that maternal womb of creative fantasy," for the resources to reconcile or unite the opposites.
4. A symbol capable of uniting opposites is born in the unconscious through fantasy, "in the natural process of elementary psychic activity."
5. The creation of the symbol creates the *possibility but not the certainty* of the symbol rising to consciousness; "the symbol does not of its own accord step into the breach."
6. To bring the symbol to consciousness, "energy must be artificially supplied to the unconscious symbol."
7. The supplying of energy to the symbol takes place through the "differentiation of the self from the opposites" in which the Self[12] chooses not to give energy (libido) to either of the opposites.
8. The energy (libido), instead of being directed to one of the opposites, "is withdrawn into the self."[13]
9. Once withdrawn from the opposite poles into the Self, the libido has no object in consciousness upon which to focus, it "becomes wholly objectless" and, therefore, "sinks into the unconscious" where it re-

trieves the symbol ("takes possession of the waiting fantasy material") which it "activates and forces to the surface."

10. Once the symbol is grasped in consciousness, the ego then glimpses a greater possible individuality through a union of the opposites, a "sort of preliminary sketch or representation of the onward way between the opposites," that can transform the conflict into a new way of being and some change may be effected.
11. The ego is able to absorb some but not all of the change implicated by the symbol/fantasy material and the opposites are partially reinstated.
12. The process begins all over again since the "renewed conflict again demands the same treatment."

Jung describes a repeating process by which the opposites are reconciled piece by piece through the production of a symbol from the fantasy function of psyche and the emergence of that symbol for partial absorption by the conscious ego of the deeper, unknown material to which the symbol points. The repeated, cyclical, rhythmic interplay between the opposites, fantasy, the symbol, and the ego engages the transcendent function, the *ad seriatim* union of the opposites, to produce a wholly new thing. The entire process might be thought of as a flowchart as follows:

opposites in consciousness and the unconscious	➔	symbol born in the unconcious through psyche's fantasy activity
possibility of symbol rising to consciousness	➔	artificial energy needed to make symbol conscious
Self chooses not to supply energy to either opposite	➔	energy withdrawn from opposites into Self
energy, now "objectless," sinks into unconscious	➔	symbol activated by energy and forced to consciousness
ego glimpses new way through union of opposites	➔	ego partially absorbs resolution of opposites
opposites recover strength and are partially restored	➔	process repeats, opposites gradually unite

The section of *Psychological Types* from which these passages have been extracted is critical to this book and to an understanding of Jung's psychology. One can see the important connections in Jung's thinking between the opposites, fantasy, symbol, the interaction of the Self and ego, the creation of the transcendent function, and the push toward wholeness and individuation.

The second place in *Psychological Types* where Jung describes the operation of the transcendent function through symbol and fantasy is in the eight-page section of chapter 11, "Definitions"[14] that defines "Symbol" (1921/1971, pp. 473–81). The part of the definition that applies to the transcendent function echoes many of the themes and details presented immediately above with some important additions and variations. First, in this section, Jung's description of the libido "sinking" into the unconscious to retrieve the symbol is devoid of the reference to the Self that was present in chapter 2: "All progress having been rendered temporarily impossible by the total division of the will [between the opposites], the libido streams backwards, as it were, to its source" (p. 479). No reason is given for the omission. It is mentioned here primarily because the reference in chapter 2 is the first anywhere to the Self. One might speculate that because the concept of the Self was not yet fully developed, neither was Jung's thinking about the role of the Self in the direction of libido.

Chapter 11 (1921/1971) also expands the nature of the symbol itself and why it is well suited to act as a conduit between consciousness and the unconscious:

> The symbol is always a product of an extremely complex nature. . . . It is, therefore, neither *rational* nor *irrational* (qq.v.). It certainly has a side that accords with reason, but it has another side that does not; for it is composed not only of rational but also of irrational data. . . . But precisely because the new symbol is born of man's highest spiritual aspirations and must at the same time spring from the deepest roots of his being, it cannot be a one-sided product of the most highly differentiated mental functions but must derive equally from the lowest and most primitive levels of the psyche. (p. 478)

The symbol is the quintessential example of something that is neither rational nor irrational, neither conscious nor unconscious, neither purely reason nor instinct. The symbol is a liminal entity standing with a foot in each of these opposite camps, a vehicle that allows us to move between and create dialogue among these territories that do not otherwise touch one another. Seen in this way, one might say that the production of the symbol, though part of the process we call the transcendent function, is also *itself a manifestation of it*; it arises out of and represents a uniting of the opposites of the conscious and unconscious, rational and irrational.

A further expansion in chapter 11 involves the way in which the ego struggles with the symbol, resists its unifying effects, and seeks to redivide the symbolic material back into the opposites with which the conscious ego is more comfortable:

> From the activity of the unconscious there now emerges a new content, constellated by thesis and antithesis in equal measure and standing in a *compensatory* (q.v.) relation to both. *It thus forms the middle ground on which the opposites can be united* [italics added]. If, for instance, we conceive the opposition to be sensuality versus spirituality, then the mediatory content born out of the unconscious provides a welcome means of expression for the spiritual thesis, because of its rich spiritual associations, and also for the sensual antithesis, because of its sensuous imagery. The ego, however, torn between thesis and antithesis finds the middle ground in its own counterpart, its sole and unique means of expression, and it eagerly seizes on this in order to be delivered from its division. The energy created by the tension of the opposites therefore flows into the mediatory product and protects it from the conflict which immediately breaks out again, for both the opposites are striving to get the new product on their side. Spirituality wants to make something spiritual out of it, and sensuality something sensual; the one wants to turn it into science or art, the other into sensual experience. The appropriation or dissolution of the mediatory product by either side is successful only if the ego is not completely divided but inclines more to one side or the other. But if one side succeeds in winning over and dissolving the mediatory product, the ego goes along with it, whereupon an identification of the ego with the most favoured function (v. *Inferior Function*) ensues. Consequently, the process of division will be repeated later on a higher plane. (1921/1971, pp. 479–80)

Jung here gives us rich detail on how the ego can provide such resistance to the symbolic material that no integration occurs. The mediatory product, the symbol, is dissolved if the ego chooses one opposite over the other; in that event, the same dynamic "battle" will be repeated.

The transformation, the operation of the transcendent function, occurs if the ego is stable enough to tolerate the tension of the opposites and neither of the opposites succeeds in winning over the mediatory product:

> If, however, as a result of the stability of the ego, neither side succeeds in dissolving the mediatory product, this is sufficient demonstration that it is superior to both. The stability of the ego and the superiority of the mediatory product to both thesis and antithesis are to my mind correlates, each conditioning the other. Sometimes it seems as though the stability of the inborn *individuality* (q.v.) were the decisive factor, sometimes as though the mediatory product possesses a superior power that determines the ego's absolute stability. In reality it may be that

> the stability of the one and the superior power of the other are the two sides of the same coin. (p. 481)

Jung here echoes an earlier theme: the operation of the transcendent function requires an equal partnership between symbolic material and the stability of the ego.

Finally, at the end of this long passage relating to symbols in the definitions section of *Psychological Types*, Jung summarizes the entire process of the symbol mediating a reconciliation between the opposites:

> If the mediatory product remains intact, it forms the raw material for a process not of dissolution but of construction, in which thesis and antithesis both play their part. In this way it becomes a new content that governs the whole attitude, putting an end to the division and forcing the energy of the opposites into a common channel. The standstill is overcome and life can flow on with renewed power towards new goals.
>
> I have called this process in its totality the *transcendent function*, "function" being here understood not as a basic function but as a complex function made up of other functions, and "transcendent" not as denoting a metaphysical quality but merely the fact that this function facilitates transition from one attitude to another. The raw material shaped by thesis and antithesis, and in the shaping of which the opposites are united, is the living symbol. Its profundity of meaning is inherent in the raw material itself, the very stuff of the psyche, transcending time and dissolution; and its configuration by the opposites ensures its sovereign power over all the psychic functions. (1921/1971, p. 480)

One is struck by the powerful language used by Jung here about the symbol, its transformational qualities, and the role it plays in the transcendent function. Indeed, in these important passages, Jung gives the symbol the credit for uniting the opposites and in providing the entire impetus for psychological growth.

Because of the profundity and complexity of these concepts, some readers are frustrated that Jung does not give more examples of how they actually work. In this regard, Jung's letters and seminars can be very helpful since they contain several references which help to flesh out those concepts. In a 1939 letter, in commenting on the emergence of personality characteristics that seem inconsistent with one's conscious personality, Jung gives an example from the Bible of how a symbol merges from the tension of opposites:

> Take the classic case of the temptation of Christ, for example. We say that the devil tempted him, but we could just as well say that an

> unconscious desire for power confronted him in the form of the devil. Both sides appear here: the light side and the dark. The devil wants to tempt Jesus to proclaim himself master of the world. Jesus wants not to succumb to the temptation; then, thanks to the function that results from every conflict, a symbol appears: it is the idea of the Kingdom of Heaven, a spiritual kingdom rather than a material one. Two things are united in this symbol, the spiritual attitude of Christ and the devilish desire for power. Thus the encounter of Christ with the devil is a classic example of the transcendent function. It appears here in the form of an involuntary personal experience. But it can be used as a method too; that is, when the contrary will of the unconscious is sought for and recognized in dreams and other unconscious products. In this way the conscious personality is brought face to face with the counter-position of the unconscious. The resulting conflict—thanks precisely to the transcendent function—leads to a symbol uniting the opposed positions. The symbol cannot be consciously chosen or constructed; it is a sort of intuition or revelation. Hence the transcendent function is only usable in part as a method, the other part always remains an involuntary experience. (1973a, pp. 267–68)

One can see in this passage Jung's application of several key concepts: the opposites resident in the conscious and unconscious (here, in the form of two conflicting personality traits, light and dark or spirit and power), the emergence of the symbol (here, the Kingdom of Heaven), the uniting of the two opposites (here, the Kingdom of Heaven unites the spiritual attitude of Christ and the devilish desire for power), and the transformation to a wholly new attitude or perspective (here, the idea of spirit and power united in a spiritual kingdom rather than a physical one).

In a seminar in analytical psychology in March, 1925, Jung and his colleagues discussed the case of a girl seeking to "find her true self" (1989a, p. 9). Her conscious personality was inferior, limited, "and meager in every sense" and as a result, her "unconscious . . . presented exactly the reverse picture" (p. 9) where she was surrounded, in visions and images, by "ghosts of very important people" (p. 9). Jung describes how the "tension between her real life and her unreal life increased" (p. 9) and how "when such an opposition as that occurs, something must happen that brings things together" (p. 10). After struggling with a series of ghosts of ever greater and superior stature, an older female character with great spiritual beauty emerged in her fantasy. Soon thereafter, the young woman effected extraordinary change in her life, apprenticing with a famous dressmaker, finally opening her own shop and becoming well known for making beautiful, original clothes. Jung details how the mediating symbol of the older female personality bridged the exaggerated inferior conscious and the inflated superior unconscious positions to create the transcendent function and transformation for the patient:

> The figure which she developed is the mediatory symbol. It is the living form into which she slowly developed. Thus there is created an attitude which liberates from the pairs of opposites. She detached herself from the cheapness of her surroundings on the one hand, and on the other from the ghosts which did not belong to her. One could say that nature working alone works along the lines of the mediatory or transcendent function. (p. 10)

Later in the seminar, Jung comes back to a discussion of the transcendent function and its dependence on the symbol, which he also calls the "living form," that emerges from fantasy. Jung noted that the symbol consists of both fantasy and real, irrational and rational, and that fantasy is the lynchpin of reconciling the opposites:

> Going back to the transcendent function, on the one side are to be found the real facts, on the other the imagination. This brings about the two poles. In the case of the girl, the ghosts went much too far on the side of imagination, and the reality side was much too small. When she put herself into reality she was a first-rate tailoress.
>
> Fantasy is the creative function—the living form is a result of fantasy. Fantasy is a pre-stage of the symbol, but it is an essential characteristic of the symbol that it is not mere fantasy. We count upon fantasy to take us out of the impasse; for though people are not always eager to recognize the conflicts that are upsetting their lives, the dreams are always at work trying to tell on the one hand of the conflict, and on the other hand of the creative fantasy that will lead the way out. (p. 11)

In *Psychological Types* and these other sources, Jung fulfills the assignment he gave himself in the 1916 version of "The Transcendent Function" (1957) to "describe the *contents* of the transcendent function" (p. 23). In contrast to the 1916 essay where he described only the "external forms and possibilities of the transcendent function" (p. 23), in these writings Jung describes in detail how fantasy and symbol are used by psyche to catalyze the transcendent function to move beyond the standstill inherent in the opposites, down the path of individuation.

Jung's Ambiguity about the Nature of the Transcendent Function

Even having explored the way the transcendent function operates, its exact nature remains somewhat elusive. That it involves a dialogue between consciousness and the unconscious through the instrumentalities of fantasy and symbol is clear. But what is the transcendent function exactly? Is it the expression of the *relationship* between consciousness and the unconscious when in dynamic opposition? Is it the *process* that ensues out of such opposition? Is it the *method* one uses to conduct the process? Is it the *final result*, the third thing that emerges? Or is it some combination of all these? Indeed, Jung's writings are unclear on this very point.

> Jung sometimes defined the transcendent function as a *function:* a specific action or, by analogy with the mathematical term, an expression of a relationship, a dependence between elements of different sets. But more often than not he referred to it as a *method,* a *process* or the *effect* brought about by these dynamics. (Dehing, 1992, p. 15)

Part of the problem is the ambiguity built into the word *function*. Its multiple meanings include the ideas of relationship between two variables, an action or activity (which would be consistent with the idea of a process or a method), and an effect generated by an activity.[15]

However, it is also evident that Jung used the expression inconsistently. In the opening paragraph of "The Transcendent Function," for example, Jung focuses on the relational aspect explaining that the transcendent function "means a psychological function" that "arises from the union of conscious and unconscious contents" (1957/1960, p. 69). In *Psychological Types* (1921/1971) he uses similar language calling the transcendent function "a combined function of conscious and unconscious elements" (p. 115). These and other references envision the transcendent function as an oppositional relationship between consciousness and the unconscious, a set of polarities or potentialities, like a battery loaded with charge awaiting an opportunity to be discharged. Yet confusingly Jung also uses the label *transcendent function* to refer to the actual process through which the polarities and potentialities are discharged. In "On the Psychology of the Unconscious" (1943/1953), for example, Jung calls the transcendent function a "process of coming to terms with the unconscious" (p. 80). Similarly, in *Mysterium Coniunctionis* (1955–1956/1963), he describes the transcendent function as the "continual process of getting to know the counterposition in the unconscious" (p. 200).

To complicate the picture, in addition to referring to the transcendent function as both a relationship and a process, Jung even sometimes refers to a it as a method. In one place, for example, Jung describes how, through the tension of the opposites, the unconscious compensates for consciousness, leading to change through the transcendent function:

> The whole process is called the "transcendent function." *It is a process and a method at the same time* [italics added]. The production of

> unconscious compensations is a spontaneous *process;* the conscious realization is a *method.* The function is called "transcendent" because it facilitates the transition from one psychic condition to another by means of the mutual confrontation of the opposites. (1939/1958, p. 489)

One can see from this passage how Jung could very easily traverse the boundaries between function, process, and method. The dialogue between consciousness and the unconscious *is* a function because it reflects a relationship between them. But what flows from that relationship is a process, and the conscious practice of it becomes a method. Elsewhere, in a letter describing how the temptation of Christ exemplifies the bringing together of the opposites of spirituality and power, Jung concludes that the transcendent function is both a personal experience and a method:

> Thus the encounter of Christ with the devil is a classic example of the transcendent function. It appears here in the form of an involuntary personal experience. But it can be used as a method too; that is, when the contrary will of the unconscious is sought for and recognized in dreams and other unconscious products. In this way the conscious personality is brought face to face with the counterposition of the unconscious. . . . Hence the transcendent function is only usable in part as a method, the other part always remains an involuntary experience. (1973a, p. 268)

In these passages, Jung states explicitly what is implicit in the idea of the transcendent function: it is both a process that can occur spontaneously and a method that can be prompted. Indeed, the essay "The Transcendent Function" is focused on both the abstract idea of the transcendent function and the practical method called "active imagination." Further, the transcendent function is often discussed by Jung in combination with the synthetic method (Dehing, 1992, p. 18).

Finally, Jung also uses transcendent function to refer to the result of the function, process, and method just outlined. That is, in addition to using the transcendent function to describe the function or relationship between consciousness and the unconscious, to identify what happens when the two dialogue with one another, and to refer to the method through which such an interaction can be accomplished, Jung even sometimes calls the new, third thing that emerges the transcendent function. In describing a patient's enormous shifts through joining the conscious with the unconscious, for example, Jung concludes, "The result . . . is the transcendent function born of the union of the opposites" (1928/1953, p. 223). Emphasizing the importance of bringing unconscious material into consciousness to effect "a settlement with the activated residues" of our history, he states, "This settlement makes the crossing of previous boundaries altogether feasible and is therefore appropriately called the transcendent function" (1943/1953, p. 99). Finally, in working with a patient's dream during a seminar, Jung refers to an animal in the dream as symbolizing the reconciliation of the opposites: "From this reconciliation a new thing is always created, a new thing is realized. That is the transcendent function" (1984, p. 648).

Thus, Jung did indeed use the term *transcendent function* in several different ways. Though this can be somewhat confusing, at least one author opined that Jung's ambiguity was intentional, that it represented his refusal to be boxed in by the limitations of strictly delineated definitions when attempting to describe nonlinear and multifaceted psychic phenomena:

> It is characteristic of Jung to define his important terms ambiguously; the transcendent function is no exception. . . . Jung was never much concerned about strict definition. In spite of this—or perhaps because of this—his accumulated definitions denote an intuitive concept embracing and containing process and effect, function and method, showing now one facet of the concept, now another. (Sandner, 1992, p. 31)

Seen in this way, Jung's multiple use of and ambiguity around the term *transcendent function* merely reflects its several different aspects.

Jung is also not entirely consistent as to whether or not the transcendent function is a natural process. In some of his writings he states that it is akin to an autonomous activity outside of a person's control; in other writings he implies that a person can have an impact on the operation of the transcendent function, either encouraging it or blocking it. One can intuitively see the two different sides of this discussion. On the one hand, one might say, individuation is an archetypal process pulling all people toward a purpose that can only be realized by integration of the material in the unconscious; envisioned in this way, the transcendent function is a natural and ongoing process along that path. On the other hand, some might respond, consciousness and the unconscious are separated by opposites the very nature of which are difficult if not impossible to reconcile; seen in this way, one might posit that the transcendent function is in no way assured to happen and that it therefore needs artificial help. Jung acknowledges these different perspectives and speaks about the transcendent function in both these ways.

For the most part, Jung comes out on the side that the transcendent function is a natural part of psychic rhythm, that it happens constantly whether we like it or not and whether we catalyze it or not. He states:

> The transcendent function . . . is a natural process, a manifestation of the energy that springs from the tension of the opposites. . . . The

> natural process by which the opposites are united came to serve me as the model and basis for a method. (1943/1953, p. 80)

We see here the essence of Jung's "natural process": the opposites create a tension from which energy springs and the transcendent function is the natural result of that energy. As Jung elaborated in a letter, "The transcendent function is not something one does oneself; it comes rather from experiencing the conflict of the opposites" (1973a, p. 269). We can also see how this view dovetails with Jung's ideas regarding the synthetic method, purpose, and individuation. Jung ties these ideas together later in the same work:

> The transcendent function does not proceed without aim or purpose, but leads to the revelation of the essential man. *It is in the first place a purely natural process, which may in some cases pursue its course without the knowledge or assistance of the individual, and can sometimes forcibly accomplish itself in the face of opposition* [italics added]. The meaning and purpose of the process is the realization, in all its aspects, of the personality hidden away in the embryonic germplasm; the production and unfolding of the original potential wholeness. (1943/1953, p. 110)

The same theme is echoed in another letter Jung states that the transcendent function "is a natural and spontaneous phenomenon, part of the process of individuation" (1955, p. 690). In these passages we see Jung's assertion that the transcendent function is a purely natural process, one that proceeds without a person even knowing about it; it may even impose itself on a person who opposes it. These annunciations express the view that the transcendent function is not something a person controls but is an innate, psychic process. Seen in this way, one might call the transcendent function autonomous, even archetypal,[16] that it is part of a universal human instinct to be whole.

Yet there are places where Jung offers a very different vision of the transcendent function, one in which there are things a person can do to encourage or impede the occurrence or frequency of the transcendent function. In the closing passages of "The Transcendent Function," for example, Jung comments on how coming to terms with the counter-position in the unconscious continually widens consciousness; then he pauses and adds an important qualifier:

> Consciousness is continually widened through the confrontation with previously unconscious contents, or—to be more accurate—could be widened if it took the trouble to integrate them. That is naturally not always the case. Even if there is sufficient intelligence to understand the procedure, there may yet be a lack of courage and self-

> confidence, or one is too lazy, mentally and morally, or too cowardly, to make an effort. (1957/1960, p. 91)

Here, in his own rejoinder to the idea that the transcendent function is a purely natural process, Jung states plainly that it may or may not occur and that one's courage, self-confidence, and psychological preparedness influence one's ability to experience the transcendent function. Jung makes similar comments elsewhere. For example, speaking about how the analytical technique can make unconscious compensations conscious, Jung states that "the unconscious process itself hardly ever reaches consciousness without technical aid" (1939/1959, p. 488).

Is the transcendent function a natural process that moves forward in each of us independent of our disposition or efforts, or is it something we invoke and guide in some sense? As with many of Jung's ideas, this question cannot be answered in an either/or way. Paradoxically, the transcendent function can be viewed through either of these two lenses. As one writer states it, "Jung defined the transcendent function as *both* [italics added] an instinctive process and as something requiring conscious development" (Salman, 1992, p. 145). In other words, the transcendent function is both natural (instinctive) and can be prompted or assisted (developed); these two aspects sometimes occur together, sometimes independently, and sometimes in rhythm with one another. Most people would likely agree that there are times, in fact many times, when psychological change occurs seemingly in spite of and against the will of the person to whom the changes are occurring. Such recurrences illustrate Jung's seminal idea that the unconscious is autonomous, and instinctual, and motivates change in us even when we do not want it. Yet it seems also to be the case that a person can encourage or impede the transcendent function by their psychological openness, willingness, courage, and tenacity. This paradox and its implications will be explored further in chapter 7 as we ponder whether the transcendent function can be increased in relationships, in culture, and in our daily lives.

Individuation: Constructive View, Meaning and Transformation

Jung's writings subsequent to "The Transcendent Function" evidence a coalescence of his thinking about psychological change, meaning, purpose, and the synthetic view of psyche, which all led to his enunciating the principle he called "individuation." He believed that the psychological change produced by the transcendent function, rather than being random, was guided in a teleological way to make each person the unique individual he was intended to be.

By 1916, the core of these ideas was formed but undeveloped. The original version of "The Transcendent Function" established the transcendent function as the workhorse of psychological change: "The term *transcendent* designates the fact that this function *mediates the transition from one attitude to another*" (1957, p. 9). Jung even asserted that the transcendent function literally changes the personality:

> I will refrain from discussing the nature of this *change of personality* [italics added], since I only want to emphasize the fact that an important change does take place. I have called this change, which is the aim of our analysis of the unconscious, the transcendent function. (1928/1953, p. 219)

The 1916 essay also firmly established the teleological, purposive view of the unconscious, in contrast to the Freudian view that it is merely the receptacle where uncomfortable, repressed information is dumped.

As this purposive view of psyche developed into an even more central pillar of Jung's paradigm, he developed the concept of individuation, the idea that psyche aims each of us in a particular, teleological direction:

> The psyche consists of two incongruous halves which together should form a whole. . . . Conscious and unconscious do not make a whole when one of them is suppressed and injured by the other. . . . Both are aspects of life. Consciousness should defend its reason and protect itself, and the chaotic life of the unconscious should be given the chance of having its way too. . . . This means open conflict and open collaboration at once. That, evidently, is the way human life should be. It is the old game of hammer and anvil: between them the patient iron is forged into an indestructible whole, an "individual."
>
> This, roughly, is what I mean by the *individuation process* [italics added]. As the name shows, it is a process or course of development arising out of the conflict between the two fundamental psychic facts. . . . How the harmonizing of conscious and unconscious data is to be undertaken cannot be indicated in the form of a recipe. It is an irrational life-process. . . . Out of this union emerge new situations and new conscious attitudes. I have therefore called the union of the opposites the "transcendent function." This rounding out of the personality into a whole may well be the goal of any psychotherapy that claims to be more than a mere cure of symptoms. (1939/1959, pp. 287–89)

This passage evidences the connections between the opposites, the transcendent function, meaning/purpose, the synthetic view of psyche, and individuation. These ideas obviously overlap and intertwine. The transcendent function does not proceed without aim; its role in resolving and uniting the opposites is part of a larger, guided process in psyche toward wholeness, a thumbnail sketch of which might look like this:

(1) the opposites resident in consciousness and the unconscious create a psychic tension from which all psychological life flows;

(2) the polarity inherent in the dynamic opposition of consciousness and the unconscious creates an energy flow that will lead to a dialogue between them;

(3) given proper circumstances, the transcendent function will manifest as a quality of conjoined opposites, a new, third thing that is not a mixture of the opposites but transcends them while uniting them and expressing them both in some way;

(4) the psychic changes effected by the transcendent function create shifts that make the personality less fragmented and split, more unified and complete;

(5) the process, which Jung called "individuation," repeats in a never-ending cycle leading the person to ever greater degrees of wholeness;

(6) the transcendent function and individuation are not random processes without direction but are guided in some way toward what the individual was meant to be;

(7) psychological growth is pushed inexorably and synthetically forward toward individuation (i.e., each modicum of growth contributes to the construction or synthesis of a prospective final goal) as opposed to being explained reductively by the events of early life (i.e., each psychological event is reduced causally to an earlier trauma or episode).

The critical link drawn by Jung between the transcendent function and the individuation process is simple: a person cannot grow toward wholeness without reconciling the polarities of consciousness and the unconscious. Jung repeats the same idea elsewhere. For example, in *Symbols of Transformation* (1952/1956), Jung describes how the crucifixion of Christ, a symbol that brings together masculine consciousness and the feminine unconscious, "signifies the conjunction of the conscious and unconscious, the transcendent function characteristic of the individuation process" (p. 433). Similarly, in a letter written in 1954, Jung asserts that the only hope of understanding the eternal rift between good and evil is through a collaboration between conscious and unconscious: "The cooperation of conscious reasoning and the data of the unconscious is called the 'transcendent function' [footnote omitted]. This function progressively unites the opposites . . . [and is] part of the process of individuation" (1955, p. 690).

That the individuation process is guided purposively is emphasized in a number of references. Describing, for example, the obstinacy evident in a patient's dream, Jung states:

> I naturally asked myself what was the source of this obstinacy and what was its purpose? That it must have some purposive meaning I was convinced, *for there is no truly living thing that does not have a final meaning* [italics added], that can in other words be explained as a mere left-over from antecedent facts. (1928/1953, p. 133)

Jung not only felt that purpose and meaning guide the psyche generally but that they also guide the transcendent function and the individuation process:

> The transcendent function does not proceed without aim and purpose, but leads to the revelation of the essential man. . . . The meaning and purpose of the process is the realization, in all its aspects, of the personality originally hidden away in the embryonic germ-plasm; the production and unfolding of the original, potential wholeness. The symbols used by the unconscious to this end are the same as those which mankind has always used to express wholeness, completeness, and perfection: symbols, as a rule, of the quaternity and the circle. For these reasons I have termed this the *individuation process.* (1943/1953, p. 110)

This passage reflects the inescapable connections between meaning and purpose, the transcendent function, and the individuation process. The transcendent function does not proceed without aim but rather purposefully toward "the revelation of the essential man." The meaning and purpose of the transcendent function is the potential totality that paradoxically lies at the end of the process but also was there all along, "the original, potential wholeness," the "personality originally hidden away in the embryonic germ-plasm." Corbett (1992) eloquently summarizes the connections between the transcendent function, individuation, and meaning:

> The transcendent function describes the capacity of the psyche to change and grow toward individuation when consciousness and the unconscious join, revealing the essential person. . . . This movement [from unconscious to conscious] is motivated by a need to join with whatever is missing from ourselves in order to enhance the wholeness and cohesiveness of the personality. . . . The transcendent function enables such movement toward wholeness to occur. . . . Its function is to express the *telos*—goal of the personality. (pp. 395–96)

As we complete this section, we see the centrality of meaning and purpose to Jung and Jungian psychology. Certainly one of the reasons that some are drawn to this branch of the tree of psychology is because it, unlike many others, brings together the ideas of psychological development and meaning

Rather than reducing psyche to the desiccated realms of physiological, neurological, behavioral, and reductive explanations, Jungian psychology posits that psyche and soul necessarily implicate telos and purpose.

The Archetypes of the Collective Unconscious

Jung's writings also evidence noteworthy connections between the transcendent function and his seminal thinking about the archetypes of the collective unconscious. In contrast to Freud, who saw the unconscious as entirely personal to each individual, a repository for repressed early life experiences, Jung posited that there is another layer, area, or terrain of the unconscious, what he called the "collective unconscious" or "objective psyche," that is shared by all human beings and contains "the phylogenetic and instinctual bases of the human race" (Samuels, Shorter, and Plaut, 1986, p. 155). As Jung himself states it:

> We have to distinguish between a personal unconscious and an *impersonal* or *transpersonal unconscious*. We speak of the latter also as the *collective unconscious* [footnote—The collective unconscious stands for the objective psyche, the personal unconscious for the subjective psyche], because it is detached from anything personal and is common to all men, since its contents can be found everywhere, which is naturally not the case with the personal contents. (1943/1953, p. 66)

Further, Jung theorized that the collective unconscious contained what he called "archetypes" and described as "components in the form of inherited categories" (1928/1953, p. 138), ways of organizing human experience into categories or patterns that are universal, timeless, and ubiquitous. Jung conceptualized such categories and patterns as inner figures—he mentioned "the shadow, the animal, the wise old man, the anima, the animus, the mother, the child" (1943/1953, p. 110)—and behaviors—"especially those that cluster around the basic and universal experiences of life such as birth, marriage, motherhood, death, and separation" (Samuels, Shorter, and Plaut, 1986, p. 26). Jung hypothesized that such figures and behaviors were "the legacy of ancestral life" (1943/1953, p. 77) inherited by all humans and were, therefore, recognized and reflected in the customs and images of all cultures:

> There are present in every individual, besides his personal memories, the great "primordial" images, . . . the inherited possibilities of human imagination as it was from time immemorial. The fact of this inheritance explains the truly amazing phenomenon that certain motifs from myths and legends repeat themselves the world over in identical forms. . . . I have called these images and motifs "archetypes," also "dominants" of the unconscious. (1943/1953, pp. 65–66)

Elsewhere, archetypes have been described as "the inherited part of the psyche; structuring patterns of psychological performance linked to instinct" (Samuels, Shorter, and Plaut, 1986, p. 26) and "a fundamental organizing principle which originates from the objective psyche, beyond the level of the empirical personality" (Corbett, 1996, p. 15).

Given the role of the transcendent function in bringing contents of the unconscious, including the archetypes, into conversation with consciousness, it would stand to reason that there must be a link between the transcendent function and the archetypes. Indeed, in a section of "On the Psychology of the Unconscious" (1943/1953) called "The Archetypes of the Collective Unconscious" (pp. 90–113), Jung brings the transcendent function and the archetypes together in two ways. First, he proposes that recognizing the autonomy and being open to the influence of the archetypal figures in the collective unconscious prompts the transcendent function:

> So long as the collective unconscious and the individual psyche are coupled together without being differentiated, no progress can be made. . . . If on the other hand we take the figures of the unconscious as collective psychic phenomena or functions, this hypothesis in no way violates our intellectual conscience. It offers a rationally acceptable solution, and at the same time a possible method of effecting a settlement with the activated residues of our racial history. This settlement makes the crossing of previous boundaries altogether feasible and is therefore appropriately called the *transcendent function*. It is synonymous with the progressive development toward a new attitude. (1943/1953, pp. 98–99)

Here Jung tells us that it is coming to terms with archetypal figures themselves ("effecting a *settlement* [italics added] with the activated residues of our racial history"), a recognition of an other, that allows the transcendent function, the shift in attitude. Though this would seem to be a straightforward point, it bears emphasis here, particularly in light of the deeper perspectives we will engage later. Psychological change does not occur through an effort of subjective, "I-controlled" will but rather through a recognition that "I" am part of a larger psychic object which guides me. In Jungian terms, it is the very acknowledgment of the collective unconscious and the autonomous patterns that personify it that catalyzes the possibility of the transcendent function, a change in consciousness. Jung echoes this theme in a 1955 letter where he states that it is through the "careful consideration of the *numina*" of the archetypes that "unconscious data are integrated into conscious life (as the 'transcendent function')" (1973c, p. 283).

A second reference in "On the Psychology of the Unconscious" (1943/1953) makes this point in an even stronger way when Jung identifies the archetypes themselves as mediators of the transcendent function out of which the opposites can be united:

> The archetypes are of course always at work everywhere. . . . At the climacteric . . . it is necessary to give special attention to the images of the collective unconscious, because they are the source from which hints may be drawn for the solution of the problem of opposites. From the conscious elaboration of this material *the transcendent function reveals itself as a mode of apprehension mediated by the archetypes and capable of uniting the opposites* [italics added]. By "apprehension" I do not mean simply intellectual understanding, but understanding through experience. An archetype, as we have said, is a dynamic image, a fragment of the objective psyche, which can be truly understood only if experienced as an autonomous entity. (p. 109)

This passage is crucial to show the development of Jung's thinking. Here Jung is identifying the transcendent function as essentially *an experience of the archetypes*,[17] an understanding through experience of a dynamic image from the objective psyche. In one of his seminars, Jung described in powerful detail how the archetypes erupt and interrupt the relative quiet of directed consciousness, thereby prompting the transcendent function:

> Say you have been very one-sided and lived in a two-dimensional world only, behind walls, thinking that you were perfectly safe; then suddenly the sea breaks in: you are inundated by an archetypal world and you are in complete confusion. Then out of that confusion suddenly arises a reconciling symbol—we cannot say "the" in spite of the fact that it is always the same—it is *an* archetypal symbol or *a* reconciling symbol which unites the vital need of man with the archetypal conditions. So you have made a step forward in consciousness, have reached a higher level; therefore it is of course a transcendent function because you transcended from one level to another. It is as if you had crossed the great flood, the inundation, or the great river, and arrived on the other bank, and so you have transcended the obstacle. (1988a, p. 975)

In a sense, the transcendent function and the archetypes are different expressions of the same thing, dialogue between conscious and unconscious, one in process form and one in personified form. To put it differently, whenever contact is made with an archetypal image, the transcendent function (or at least the potential for it) will likely ensue, whenever the transcendent function is at work, consciousness is interacting in some way with archetypal material.

Significantly, "The Transcendent Function," Jung's first attempt to describe how consciousness and the unconscious dialogue in order to effect psychological transformation, focused exclusively on the process itself and was devoid of reference to the collective unconscious and the archetypes. Granted, those concepts were not yet fully formed. However, that poses a foundational question: Is it possible that the archetypes came to Jung, in part, as a convenient way to more fully describe the transcendent function? Put another way, is the transcendent function the core process and the archetypes a reification of the unconscious part of the dialogue Jung was describing between consciousness and the unconscious? Are the archetypes Jung's attempts to give voice to or personify the operation of the transcendent function? These questions will be explored as we proceed further.

Anima and Animus: Mediators between Consciousness and the Unconscious

The link between the transcendent function and the archetypes explored in the last section is more specifically manifested in the connection Jung draws between the transcendent function and the anima/animus. According to Jung, the anima is an important archetypal structure that holds the feminine aspects of man; its counterpart, the animus, similarly holds the masculine aspects of women. Jung believed that each person has contrasexual attitudes and feelings actively at work in the unconscious and that the development of a whole personality required those to become assimilated into consciousness.

> The anima archetype is the feminine side of the male psyche; the animus archetype is the masculine side of the female psyche. Every person has qualities of the opposite sex, not only in the biological sense that man and woman secrete both male and female sex hormones but also in a psychological sense of attitudes and feelings. . . .
>
> If the personality is to be well adjusted and harmoniously balanced, the feminine side of a man's personality and the masculine side of a woman's personality must be allowed to express themselves in consciousness and behavior. (Hall and Nordby, 1973, pp. 46–47)

In the Jungian paradigm, anima and animus play a compensatory role to the persona, the archetypal, outward face of the psyche. An individual's persona, or public mask aimed at conforming with the collective, is counterbalanced by the anima or animus which demands interaction with the unconscious. In describing the way in which the anima performs this function in a man, Homans (1995) states:

> Jung believed that the anima and the persona were related in a balanced or compensatory fashion. The persona is a psychological

> structure composed of patterns of conformity to social norms. . . . If the conscious ego identifies fully with the persona, then the individual becomes only a role, fully adapted to society and fully rational, and as a consequence the dimension of inner living—the unconscious—is repressed. But Jung believed that no matter how rigid the persona of a man might be, there still existed for him an invisible system of relations with the unconscious. (p. 105)

As the concepts of anima and animus evolved in Jung's thinking, they came to represent not just contrasexual aspects but more expansive connections to the unknown or the other within the unconscious. As one author put it:

> The animus of the woman is not so much the repressed Masculine as it is the repressed Other, the unconscious Other that she has been prevented from living out. The anima of the man may function in a similar way. There is a mystery about the unknown, and the unknown is often the unconscious Other within. . . . The potential of man's anima and woman's animus is that they can be guides to the depths of the unconscious. (J. Singer, 1972, pp. 193–94)

Elsewhere the anima/animus are described as the archetypal energy in the unconscious that embody what Jung called "the not-I" (Samuels, Shorter, and Plaut, 1986, p. 22). Jung himself acknowledged the broad and profound role of the animus and anima when he called the former "the *archetype of meaning*" (1934/1959, p. 32) and the latter "the *archetype of life itself*" (p. 32). Thus, anima and animus have a central role in Jungian psychology because of their role in guiding us to the depths of the unconscious where we can make contact with and come to terms with the unknown or other within. Indeed, Homans (1995) goes further and asserts that the anima (and animus) are the symbols of the existence of the unconscious itself and, when properly assimilated, represent the very relations between consciousness and the unconscious:

> Hence, the anima is at one level an archetypal figure with which the ego must contend, but at a more abstract, theoretical level the anima is also a symbol or the existence of the unconscious. To come to terms with the anima is, therefore, to become aware that there is an unconscious. Just as the personal structures adapt to outer, social reality, so the anima structures adapt to inner, psychological reality. *Accordingly, when the archetype of the anima is assimilated, an autonomous complex is transformed into a function of the relation between conscious and unconscious* [italics added]. The individual has to come to terms with the existence of the unconscious. (pp. 105–06)

Finally, the bringing together of consciousness and the unconscious through the operation and assimilation of the anima and animus fosters individuation, the telos of Jungian work. As Bradway (1982) states:

> The conscious approach to and acknowledgment of the anima and animus provide experiences that carry one into contact with inner conflicts as well as with one's own vital resources. *The anima and animus thus provide for consciousness a bridge or link with the unconscious and therefore contribute to the individuation process, which requires the bringing of unconscious components into consciousness* [italics added]. (p. 278)

From these descriptions, one can readily see the close link between the anima and animus and the transcendent function. Each is integrally involved in establishing a relationship or dialogue between consciousness and the unconscious; each has as a central purpose bringing a compensatory balance of the unconscious to consciousness; each plays a part in fostering an interaction between consciousness and the unconscious to potentiate individuation. Indeed, from this perspective, it might be difficult to exactly identify the difference between them. We might say that the assimilation of the anima/animus makes the transcendent function possible; or that the operation of the transcendent function fosters the assimilation of the anima/animus; or that the anima/animus is an archetype and the transcendent function is an archetypal process both of which are fundamentally involved in the same activity; or some combination of all these. In any event, the conceptual connection is clear.

Jung makes several references in his works that solidify the multiple links between anima/animus and the transcendent function we have drawn above. In "The Relations Between the Ego and the Unconscious" (1928/1953), for example, Jung begins a section by stating that, "I owe it to the reader to give him a detailed example of the specific activity of animus and anima" (p. 212). He then gives two detailed descriptions, one about a female patient and one about a male, of the specific ways in which animus and anima, respectively, operated to bring the unconscious into conversation with consciousness. In summarizing the effect of assimilation of the anima/animus, Jung says:

> Continual conscious realization of unconscious fantasies [of the anima and animus], together with active participation in the fantastic events, has, as I have witnessed in a very large number of cases, the effect . . . of bringing about a change of personality. . . .
>
> For the moment I will refrain from discussing the nature of this change of personality, since I only want to emphasize the fact that an important change does take place. I have called this change, which is the aim of our analysis of the unconscious, the transcendent

> function. This remarkable capacity of the human psyche for change, expressed in the transcendent function, is the principal object of late medieval alchemical philosophy, where it was expressed in terms of alchemical symbolism. . . . The secret of alchemy was in fact the transcendent function, the transformation of personality through the blending and fusion of the noble with the base components, of the differentiated with the inferior functions, of the conscious with the unconscious. (pp. 219–20)

In this quote, we can see the explicit link drawn by Jung between anima/animus and the transcendent function. He asserts that through continual work with the anima/animus, the transcendent function occurs; that is, that assimilation of the anima/animus prompts the transcendent function, the change in personality. In this excerpt Jung envisions that the anima/animus prompt the process of the dialogue between consciousness and the unconscious and the transcendent function is the final outcome of that process. Elsewhere, Jung describes the anima/animus in terms that are remarkably akin to the language he uses to describe the transcendent function. He states, for example, that "the anima plays the role of the mediatrix between the unconscious and the conscious" (1958/1964, p. 378), language that is strikingly similar to his descriptions of the transcendent function. Further, in a letter to an anonymous recipient in March, 1958, Jung says, "The anima is a representative of the unconscious and hence a mediatrix" (1973d, p. 422), again using the mediating language that he generally reserves for the transcendent function. Finally, in describing the function of the anima, Jung uses language that is virtually identical to the language he uses elsewhere to describe the transcendent function:

> Because the things of the inner world influence us all the more powerfully for being unconscious, it is essential for anyone who intends to make progress . . . to objectivate the effects of the anima and then try to understand what contents underlie those effects . . . From a consideration of the claims of the inner and outer worlds, or rather, from the conflict between them, the possible and the necessary follows. Unfortunately, our Western mind, lacking all culture in this respect, has never yet devised a concept, nor even a name for the *union of the opposites through the middle path,* that most fundamental item of inward experience, which could respectably be set against the Chinese concept of Tao. (1928/1953, p. 205)

Thus, as the previous section illustrated the connections between the concept of the archetypes and the transcendent function, this section shows the close links between the transcendent function and Jung's concept of the anima/animus. Both are centrally involved in bringing about the dialogue between consciousness and the unconscious, in mediating between consciousness and the unconscious to allow a union of the opposites or middle path, and in promoting individuation. The next section analyzes similar parallels between the transcendent function and another archetype, the Self.

The Self as Progeny of the Transcendent Function

Numerous references through Jung's works raise the issue of the relationship between the transcendent function and the Self. Again, some brief foundational work regarding the Self in Jungian psychology is necessary. Jung's Self has several different aspects. First, the Self represents the center of all consciousness, both conscious and unconscious, as opposed to the ego, which represents the center of the conscious part of psyche. As Jung (1929/1967) states it:

> If the unconscious can be recognized as a co-determining factor along with consciousness . . . then the centre of gravity of the total personality shifts its position. It is then no longer in the ego, which is merely the centre of consciousness, but in the hypothetical point between conscious and unconscious. This new centre might be called the self. (p. 45)

Similarly, J. Singer (1972) says that the "self embraces the whole of psychic totality, incorporating both consciousness and the unconscious; it is also the center of this totality" (p. 218). Yet, in addition to being the center of the totality of consciousness, the Self is also an archetype, the archetype of unity and totality (Storr, 1983, p. 20) that represents the potential of a person's entire personality being developed. Samuels, Shorter, and Plaut (1986) describe the Self this way:

> An archetypal image of man's fullest potential and unity of the personality as a whole. The self as a unifying principle within the human psyche occupies the central position of authority in relationship to psychological life and, therefore, the destiny of the individual. (p. 135)

Lastly, integral to Jung's formulation of the Self is the idea that it is transpersonal, beyond the individual, or as one called it "half immanent and half transcendent" (J. Singer, 1972, p. 238):

> That which is immanent in it is the aspect through which the self is related to human understanding, even within the limitations of its finitude. That which is transcendent in it is the aspect through which the self is related to the unconscious, to the impenetrable, to the infinite and the unreachable. (p. 239)

This implies that the Self has aspects which may be called divine. In fact, Jung calls the Self a "God-image" (1951/1959, p. 22; 1954/1958, p. 469). Another writer states flatly, "The self . . . is the God within" (Storr, 1983, p. 20).

Because of the multiple nature of the Self, its relationship with the transcendent function is multifaceted. As the archetype of unity and totality, the Self is the "instigator of the process of individuation" (Singer, 1972, p. 218), a process to which the transcendent function is integral. Viewed from this standpoint, one might say that the Self is the force guiding individuation through the instrumentality of the transcendent function. Referring to this kind of relationship, one commentator described the transcendent function as "the spontaneous activity from the Self" (Schellenbaum, 1992, p. 414). However, the Self might also be thought of as the goal towards which individuation and the transcendent function are striving. Jung, for example, calls the transcendent function the "*transitus* to the self" (1973b, p. 168).

The issue of whether the Self guides the transcendent function or the transcendent function leads to the Self raises an intriguing possibility: that the Self and the transcendent function are different iterations of the same concept, a union of consciousness and unconscious. This notion has been mentioned in several places. Urban (1992) refers to the transcendent function as an "essential aspect" of the Self (p. 421). Hillman, writing in the preface to the 1957 publication of Jung's 1916 version of "The Transcendent Function," states: "The term 'transcendent function', used here for the 'union of conscious and unconscious', is not so much in use today, having been replaced in a wider sense by the concept of the self" (Jung, 1957, p. 3). Horne (1998) states that in the Self "Jung reifies the transcendent function as a center of influence distinct from the ego" (p. 26). Indeed, there is some evidence for this proposition in Jung's works. Near the end of his life, Jung referred several times to the union of conscious and unconscious as the Self, where earlier he had used the term transcendent function (see, e.g., 1928/1953, p. 219; 1973b, p. 166). In a 1954 letter, Jung all but admits that the transcendent function and the Self are two forms of the same concept. He states: "The opposites are united by a neutral or ambivalent bridge, a symbol expressing either side in such a way that they can function together" (1973b, p. 166); the accompanying footnote states, "The bridge is the 'uniting symbol,' which represents psychic totality, the self" (p. 166, fn 11) and refers to the definition of the transcendent function given in the definitions section of *Psychological Types*. The Self as a reification of the transcendent function reprises the theme introduced in the previous section. The transcendent function was Jung's first conception of the interaction between consciousness and the unconscious. The structures he enunciated thereafter may very well be further refinements or explanations of the core process he called the transcendent function.

Jung's Inconsistencies Surrounding Dreams and the Divine

Two other areas that deserve mention are the curious inconsistencies in Jung's thinking about dreams and the divine. As mentioned in chapter 2, when Jung wrote the original version of "The Transcendent Function," he concluded that dreams were not an appropriate source of unconscious material for use in working with it. This was not because Jung believed at that time that dreams did not adequately express unconscious contents; in fact, he acknowledged that the "dream is, so to speak, a pure product of the unconscious" (1957/1960, p. 77). Rather, he felt that dreams did not carry enough tension to prompt the transcendent function (p. 77).[18] The idea that dreams would be unsuitable to prompt a dialogue between consciousness and the unconscious seems shocking to a present-day Jungian. As if to directly answer his own assertions that dream images are unsuitable for use with the transcendent function, other writings of Jung tell us how valuable they are. In "On the Psychology of the Unconscious"(1943/1953), for example, in describing the synthetic method and the importance of the transcendent function to it, Jung says:

> It [the transcendent function] is a natural process, a manifestation of the energy that springs from the tension of the opposites, and it consists of a series of fantasy-occurrences which appear spontaneously in dreams and visions. (p. 80)

In another discussion, Jung calls a patient's series of dreams "a *guiding function*" (1928/1953, p. 134), cites the transcendent function, and describes the dreams as "self-representations of unconscious developments which allowed the psyche of the patient gradually to grow out of the pointless personal tie" (p. 134). His other works also show repeated links between the dream and the transcendent function (see, e.g., discussions in 1984, 1988a, 1988b, 1989b).

Jung is also contradictory about whether the transcendent function has some metaphysical or divine quality. He proclaims in several key places that the transcendent function does *not* have such implications. Indeed, in the very first sentence of both versions of "The Transcendent Function," Jung asserts categorically, "There is nothing mysterious or metaphysical about the term 'transcendent function'" (1957, p. 5; 1957/1960, p. 69). Jung uses almost identical language in *Psychological Types* (1921/1971, p. 115). Yet in other places Jung links the transcendent function with the divine generally and God specifically. In one place, for example, Jung states: "It [the transcendent function] also shows that the phenomenon of spontaneous compensation, being beyond the control of man, is quite in accord with the formula 'grace' or the 'will of God'" (1939/1958, p. 506). Elsewhere, Jung asserts that from the transcendent function "a creative solution emerges which is produced by the constellated archetype and possesses that compelling authority not unjustly characterized as the voice of God" (1958/1964, p. 455). In these and other references[19] Jung makes clear that he *does* see something spiritual or divine in the transcendent function. Despite his protestations to the contrary, Jung clearly pondered the notion that the transcendent function has a core quality that is metaphysical, divine, or spiritual in nature.

The Shadow: Relationship to the Transcendent Function

Of the many references Jung makes to the transcendent function and its connections to other structures, he never connects it to the shadow. This is curious because this Jungian archetype seems to cry out for commentary about its relation to the transcendent function. To Jung, the basic idea of shadow was the unacknowledged, hence unconscious, dark side of the personality that is blocked out by the accepted, conscious side: "ego stands to shadow as light to shade" (Samuels, Shorter, and Plaut, 1986, p. 138). Jung succinctly described shadow as "the thing [a person] has no wish to be" (1946/1954, p. 262). Elsewhere (1937/1958), he said:

> Everyone carries a shadow, and the less it is embodied in the individual's conscious life, the blacker and denser it is. If an inferiority is conscious, one always has a chance to correct it. . . . But if it is repressed or isolated from consciousness, it never gets corrected, and is liable to burst forth suddenly in a moment of awareness. At all counts, it forms an unconscious snag, thwarting our most well-meant intentions. (p. 76)

In Jung's psychology, though the shadow can never be eradicated, coming to terms with it is an integral step along the path of individuation. Until we can recognize and integrate that which is unacceptable to us inside of ourselves, we cannot grow to our full potential.

It is surprising that we do not find a single mention of the shadow in connection with the transcendent function. One would think that one of the central roles of the transcendent function is to assist in accessing and integrating disowned parts of ourselves, the shadow. Yet the two concepts are never mentioned together. Though, as previously discussed, Jung does link the transcendent function with the archetypes generally, he makes no separate mention of the shadow. It may be that Jung saw this archetypal figure as no more important than any other and, thus, gave it no special treatment. Or it may be that Jung saw the transcendent function as more directly related to the Self. But the shadow does have a role in the Jungian paradigm that would merit connecting it to the transcendent function: it represents that which is inherently foreign or opposite to one's conscious nature, "the 'other person' in one, one's own dark side" (Samuels, Shorter, and Plaut, 1986, p. 138). Given that the shadow embodies all that is unacceptable to the conscious ego, that it resides as an archetypal energy in the unconscious, and that the role of the transcendent function is to unite opposites, these two concepts are clearly related. The transcendent function is the mechanism through which the shadow will be brought into conversation with the ego and the opposites in each brought together.

Here, again, we might wonder whether the shadow, like the archetypes discussed above, personifies or flows from the transcendent function. This structure, which carries instinctual opposites in the unconscious, might merely be Jung's image of how the energies and images of the unconscious are voiced. The shadow is clearly implicated by, though never discussed in connection with, the transcendent function.

INTEGRATING THE REFERENCES TO THE TRANSCENDENT FUNCTION

Imagining that Jung would further develop the ideas he introduced in "The Transcendent Function," this chapter set about extracting the deeper ore from his other works. What began as a mining expedition has become an archeological dig. In our endeavor to unearth explanatory information about the transcendent function, we stumbled upon an entire subterranean village full of relationships with their attendant complexities and contradictions. Like trying to understand an excavated civilization, certain clues are clear and consistent, others confusing, ambiguous, and even conflicting. The original essay introduced us to relatively unequivocal core ideas: the dynamic opposition between conscious and unconscious, the transcendent function as the bridge between them, and the synthetic view of psyche. The picture becomes murkier in Jung's later descriptions and references. Let us try to sort through and synthesize this material.

Jung's discussions about the transcendent function in subsequent works can be summarized in four broad areas. First, those later writings give us important clues about the source of his seminal idea of the transcendent function. We saw how his work with fundamental antitheses of idea/thing, form/matter, and introversion/extroversion in *Psychological Types* (1921/1971) led to his deeper belief in the dynamic opposition in the psyche. The greater Jung's conviction in the opposites inherent in psychological life, the greater became his need to formulate the transcendent function that bridges them. Propelled by Schiller's theory that some third instinct bridges the chasm between opposites (what Schiller called the "play instinct"), Jung posited the central role of fantasy and symbol, the foundation of his imaginal psychology.

Second, Jung's subsequent writings delved deeply into the actual mechanics of the transcendent function. In two separate places in *Psychological Types* (1921/1971) Jung explains, in a step-by-step fashion, how the tension of the opposites in consciousness and the unconscious, if held properly by the individual, leads to a dialogue mediated through fantasy and symbol, out of which flows the potential for the emergence of a third thing, a changed situation, a new attitude. This process is then repeated over and over again as the individual proceeds down the road of psychological growth uniting more and more opposites and facing new sets of opposites.

Third, a review of the subsequent works unearthed significant contradictions, or at least ambiguities, in Jung's thinking about the transcendent function, among which are the following:

- Jung was not consistent on the opposites, sometimes saying that the unconscious opposes consciousness, other times saying it was complementary or compensatory;
- Jung was unclear as to whether opposites always reside in consciousness *vs.* the unconscious or whether, at times, they also manifest entirely in a conscious way;
- In some places Jung said that reason was insufficient to bridge the opposites and that they could only be reconciled "irrationally," while in others he emphasized the control of the directed ego in the process;
- Jung was inconsistent on whether the transcendent function describes the relationship between conscious and unconscious, the process of bringing them into contact, the method used to create a dialogue, or the final product that emerges;
- Sometimes Jung said that the transcendent function is a natural process which proceeds independently of, even despite, the efforts of a person, while at others he said that it could be prompted or inhibited;
- In some places Jung describes the Self as guiding the process of individuation and the transcendent function, in others the Self is their goal or the final outcome;
- Jung sometimes states that dreams are unsuitable for work with the transcendent function, while in many other places shows how dreams are invaluable;
- Jung denies that the transcendent function is metaphysical or spiritual in nature, yet makes many references to it being connected to, even guided by, the Divine.

Belying the apparent simplicity and clarity of the transcendent function enunciated in the original essay, these inconsistencies lead inescapably to several hypotheses: the transcendent function is more complex than the original essay apprehended; the transcendent function changes over time in Jung's thinking;

the transcendent function has different faces, one moment appearing in one guise, the next in another; the transcendent function defies clarity because it embodies an archetypal kind of exchange between conscious and unconscious which, like any archetype, cannot be described exactly in the abstract but rather can only be discussed as it manifests in a particular instance; or that some combination of these is at work.

Finally, Jung's writings drew critical links between the transcendent function and other key elements of his psychology: the opposites, the synthetic view of psyche, the collective unconscious, the archetypes, the anima/animus, the Self, and individuation. This chapter conceptualized these connections as a web. Each concept is tied to and inextricably intertwined with the others, making it difficult to touch one without implicating the others. This exploration of the connections reveals the central role that the transcendent function played in Jung's thinking and in the way he conceptualized the workings of psyche. That centrality is the subject of the next chapter.

CHAPTER FOUR

THE TRANSCENDENT FUNCTION AS THE CORE OF JUNG'S WORK

The concluding point of the previous chapter, that the transcendent function is linked with virtually all the concepts that are at the core of Jung's psychology, brings this work to a new level. Up to now, we have been viewing the transcendent function as one of a number of distinct pieces of Jung's paradigm. What emerged from the analysis of the references in the last chapter is that the transcendent function is implicated by and inextricably intertwined with most, if not all, of Jung's other seminal ideas. The idea of archetypes, for example, for which Jung is perhaps most identified in the world of psychology, is fundamentally dependent on the transcendent function since no communication or settlement is possible with the energies, images, and messages they represent without the mediation of the transcendent function. Similarly, the concept of the Self, the central organizing archetype that guides us toward individuation, is either synonymous with or, at the very least, grows out of the idea of the transcendent function. Individuation, Jung's seminal idea about a purposive psyche pulling us forward in a teleological way, cannot occur without the constant and repeated operation of the transcendent function. Analogous kinds of critical links have been drawn between the transcendent function and the opposites, fantasy, symbol, all core Jungian ideas.

If the Jungian paradigm is pictured as a web of intertwined concepts, each of which somehow implicates the others, it would be no exaggeration to say that the transcendent function lies at or near the center of that web. Indeed, it may very well be the core concept from which the others flow. At least one other author agrees with this assertion. Horne (1998) states bluntly:

> Assimilation of the anima/animus to create a bridge or link between consciousness and the unconscious is very closely connected conceptually with the transcendent function. This notion of libido as "pur-

> posive" was only the first step in a series of theoretical insights that led Jung to the transcendent function, the heart of his paradigm, and likely the most fundamental source of his separation from Freud. (1998, p. 25)

Given this centrality, it is mystifying that there has not been more written about the transcendent function. Though frequently mentioned in writings on Jung's psychology, it is rarely identified as a core concept. Even when the transcendent function was the focus of the Twelfth International Congress for Analytical Psychology in Chicago in August, 1992, the papers presented there (Mattoon, 1993) did not generally capture its centrality. Frankly, its importance did not emerge to this author until after doing the research for this work. It was only in so doing that it became clear how fundamental the transcendent function was to Jung's thinking.

THE TRANSCENDENT FUNCTION AS JUNG'S ROOT METAPHOR

Let us take a further step. Taking the analysis in the preceding chapter and this one together leads us to a powerful proposition: that beyond its stated role in uniting the opposites, the transcendent function is Jung's root metaphor for psyche itself or for becoming psychological and is the wellspring from whence flowed much of the rest of Jung's imaginal, depth psychology. Put another way, the transcendent function is Jung's attempt to describe the most fundamental depth psychological activity, the interchange of information and images between consciousness and the unconscious, and everything else that Jung proposed represented merely a refinement or differentiation of that phenomenon. Enunciated immediately after Jung emerged from his own confrontation with the unconscious, the writing of the transcendent function in 1916 was an attempt to give voice to his own indescribable experience of coming to terms with the unknown in the unconscious. At the time Jung wrote the original version of "The Transcendent Function," he had not conceived of or written about the archetypes, the Self, the shadow, the anima/animus, or individuation, and had certainly not fully developed his theories regarding dreams, the opposites, fantasy and symbol, and the synthetic view of psyche. What emerged first for Jung was the transcendent function, the concept and practice of a dialogue between consciousness and the unconscious through which psyche transforms itself in some imaginal way; the concomitant structures and theories developed out of that basic premise. Horne offers a similar view when he calls the transcendent function "the heart of [Jung's] paradigm" (1998, p. 25). This is why we see the transcendent function emerge in the development and discussion of each of the other key concepts in Jung's writings. The other foundational concepts in Jung's psy chology all flesh out the way consciousness and the unconscious speak to one another. The transcendent function became the undifferentiated core of Jung's psychology out of which the other concepts differentiate or emerge. Indeed, it may have been the working of the transcendent function for Jung personally that allowed him to access the unconscious in a way that led to the formulation of the other aspects of his psychology.

Perhaps this also explains, at least in part, some of the ambiguities and inconsistencies in Jung's descriptions of the transcendent function. To put it another way, since the transcendent function is a root metaphor, it is not susceptible to a single description but has various facets. The dialogue between consciousness and the unconscious is too broad a concept to be described in a singular way. As Jung brought the transcendent function into the discussion of other topics in his psychology, its different aspects were revealed. Thus, instead of seeing Jung's various descriptions of the transcendent function as ambiguities or inconsistencies, we can see them as his attempts to explicate and more fully explore the multiple expressions of a broad, root metaphor, like an attempt to describe the various faces of a unique, priceless gem.

Reenvisioned from this perspective, we begin to see two distinct, and conceptually different, images of the transcendent functions:

(1) the "narrow" transcendent function, the function or process *within* Jung's pantheon of psychic structures, generally seen as the uniting of the opposites of consciousness and the unconscious from which a new attitude emerges; and

(2) the "expansive" transcendent function, the *root metaphor* for psyche or being psychological that subsumes Jung's pantheon and that apprehends the most fundamental psychic activity of interacting with the unknown or "other."

As Jung wrote in the prefatory note to the revised version of "The Transcendent Function" (1957/1960), "For the unconscious is not this thing or that; it is the Unknown as it immediately affects us" (p. 68). This statement, written just two years before Jung's death, is illustrative of the expansive view of the transcendent function. Or, as he states elsewhere, also written near the end of his life, the transcendent function results in a psychic shift, "But an alteration is possible only if the existence of the 'other' is admitted" (1955, p. 200).

IMPLICATIONS OF THE EXPANSIVE TRANSCENDENT FUNCTION BEYOND JUNG

The expansive transcendent function is an idea with obvious implications beyond Jung and his psychology. Seen in this way, the transcendent function replicates psyche itself and being psychological. The transcendent function is present as a root metaphor whenever we engage the unknown or "other" in an effort to deepen and become more psychological. As Beebe (1992) says, "Jung's identification of the transcendent function must be seen not merely as an event in his own history, however, but as a moment in the history of the evolution of the psychological attitude, a moment that is recapitulated whenever anyone manages to become psychological" (p. 118). The idea of the transcendent function as a root metaphor is crucial to and frames the remainder of this book. What are the key components of the transcendent function? If it is a metaphor, one might imagine things like it in other schools of psychology. Does it find expression in other theories? And if it is a metaphor, what is it trying to show us about psyche? What does it tell us about becoming psychological? Is the transcendent function reflective of some other archetypal expression of psyche? How does the transcendent function as a root metaphor appear more broadly in our lives?

The formulation of the expansive transcendent function and the transcendent function as a metaphor plunge this work into deeper territory. If the transcendent function is a root metaphor for psyche itself or for becoming psychological, then two crucial things follow. First, it would stand to reason that we might be able to identify concepts in the thinking and writing of others that are similar, parallel, or analogous to core ideas of the transcendent function. Indeed, psychic struggle between consciousness and the unconscious or between polarized segments of consciousness, mechanisms that mediate such antitheses, transformation through the liminal spaces between such opposing forces, and a third thing emerging from the struggle of the two can be found in other areas of psychology. Second, and more importantly, ultimately the transcendent function may be the expression of a larger psychological endeavor to reconcile fundamental ontological quandaries. The present work asserts that the transcendent function is an archetypal process expressing the autochthonous urge of psyche to plunge through binary oppositions in order to find the relations between apparently antithetical elements.

THE CORE OF THE TRANSCENDENT FUNCTION

In order to explore the deeper roots of the transcendent function, we must identify and analyze the ideas at its core. It is by no means monolithic. In fact, the heart of the transcendent function involves three separate ideas. First, it is a mediatory phenomenon. Jung's specific formulation of the transcendent function is that it mediates between consciousness and the unconscious. Viewed more expansively, it mediates not only between consciousness and the unconscious but also between "I" and "other," "me" and "not-me," known and unknown. It is this mediating endeavor of the transcendent function, often referred to as "holding the tension of the opposites," that allows us to suspend the "either/or" choice between antitheses (or apparent antitheses) and entertain the notion that there might be a "neither/nor" space between them. It enables us to encounter the unconscious, unknown, or other and have an exchange with it (and/or them). Second, the transcendent function has a transitional character. Through a bridging of consciousness and the unconscious, I and other, me and not-me, by allowing the neither/nor, a transition is potentiated, a new conscious attitude is made possible. We must be clear here. The mediatory aspect of the transcendent function does not guarantee transition; it potentiates it. Though Jung felt that the dialogue between consciousness and the unconscious often leads to transition, he was also clear that antitheses may be also be mediated so that they merely coexist and no transition occurs.

A third idea central to the transcendent function (particularly when viewed from the expansive perspective) is transformation, the so-called "third thing" (1957/1960, p. 90). Jung's writings make it clear that the transcendent function's role goes beyond mediation and transition. It is teleological in nature, part of the individuation process, guiding the individual to the person he or she is meant to be. This transformational aspect confronts the individual with something larger than the ego, something even numinous and holy. The kind of shift prompted by the transformational aspect of the transcendent function might be thought of as more profound and purposeful than a mere transition to a new conscious attitude.

These three different core ideas of the transcendent function are obviously related. Transition and transformation cannot occur without mediation. On the other hand, mediation can occur without either of the other two eventuating. Or mediation can lead to transition in conscious attitude without any deeper transformation. These distinctions will become more evident as we investigate the parallels between the transcendent function and concepts from other areas of psychology.

For purposes of the investigation below, the interplay of the basic elements and the multiple nature of the transcendent function might be represented schematically as follows:

living, third thing
(new attitude)
(transformation, individuation)

consciousness;	→	transcendent function	←	unconscious
I; me		(via fantasy and symbol)		other/not-me
known		(neither/nor space)		unknown

The schematic is intended to show the opposites of consciousness/the unconscious, I/other, me/not-me, known/unknown (i.e., the either/or), being suspended or held in the neither/nor field of the transcendent function, followed by a movement upward (or forward) to the new attitude or third thing. The process has four distinct elements: the two opposing forces (the either/or), the mediating transcendent function (the neither/nor space where the antitheses are suspended), and the new situation, the living third thing that is the result of the transitional and transformational role of the transcendent function.[1]

THE TRANSCENDENCE OF THE TRANSCENDENT FUNCTION

In this pivotal chapter, we pursue two simultaneous movements: one that identifies the transcendent function as the core of Jung's psychology and one that paints it with broader, even archetypal strokes. It is this second image that has led us to imply, indeed state directly, that the concepts that make up the transcendent function might be found in the ideas of others. That is the focus of the next chapter where the transcendent function will be compared and contrasted with a number of other ideas, both from other schools of depth psychology and from non-depth paradigms. This comparative analysis comes directly from my own experience and interest. Early in the course of graduate studies I read "The Transcendent Function" and was moved deeply by it. It prompted in me not only an intellectual attraction but deeply psychological, emotional, even physiological responses as well. Subsequently, as I studied and became acquainted with various psychological theories and constructs, resonances with the transcendent function were apparent. The material that follows in chapter 5 is an analysis of those resonances. The danger in a comparative study is that the transcendent function will become diluted or weakened so that we become confused about its very nature. However, my goal is just the opposite. Showing how the transcendent function and its components appear in the theories of others is designed to deepen our understanding of it and them. In order to be explicit, however, about the core of the transcendent function, I have identified and diagramed it in the previous section of this chapter.

Paradoxically, though the elements of the transcendent function can be found in the theories of other, there are ways in which the transcendent function fundamentally differs from or transcends them. The transcendent part of the transcendent function is the third idea that forms its core: transformation. What separates Jung's thinking from the others is the idea that the confrontation between or holding of the opposites potentiates a transformation, a new, third thing. Other theories are similar in their mediatory and transitional aspects but do not plunge as deeply as does Jung into the area of transformation.

Furthermore, Jung's formulation of the transcendent function as the engine of individuation is singular in the emergence of something that transcends ego, that is purposeful, and that has a certain numinosity. If one compares it to Hegel's dialectic, for example, which some have incorrectly labeled as identical to the transcendent function, the unique nature of the transcendent function becomes apparent. Hegel posited that through the opposition thesis and antitheses, a synthesis emerges. But Jung would see that formulation as limited and inaccurate when it comes to psychic growth. He sees the emergent product not as an amalgam of the two but something new, a third thing that transcends, not mixes the opposing parts of the psyche. That is why fantasy and symbol are so critical to the Jungian formulation, for it is only through them that psyche can break free of the limits and bondage of the opposites and experience a quantum leap to something new. This concept is difficult to grasp but is critical to a complete understanding of the transcendent function.

The reason that the operation of the transcendent function has such mysterious, numinous, even holy overtones is that it does not produce a linear, rational result. It is something wholly different. It is this irrational leap of faith, the transformational jump in consciousness, added to the mediatory and transitional qualities that separates the transcendent function from the other theories we will compare it to in the following chapter.

Thus, in this pivotal chapter we are left with some key polarities: the transcendent function as a component of Jung's thinking *vs.* the core of his paradigm; the narrow transcendent function *vs.* the expansive transcendent function; the proposition that there are similarities between the concepts which form the transcendent function and the theories of others *vs.* the idea that the transcendent function transcends them. Yet the whole idea of the transcendent function is that such polarities are not either/or propositions but rather ones to be held so that through the tension of holding them, something new can emerge. That is the goal of the final three chapters.

CHAPTER FIVE

THE TRANSCENDENT FUNCTION AND THE THEORIES OF OTHERS

Though Jung may have been the first to explore this kind of mediatory and transitional activity in such detail, others enunciate ideas and structures that reflect aspects of the transcendent function, particularly when viewed in its more expansive form. This should not be surprising. Much of psychology struggles with fundamental opposites such as self/other, me/not-me, known/unknown, inner/outer, conscious/unconscious. Despite differences in orientation, many schools endeavor to bring these dualities into conversation. Depth psychology specifically is fundamentally grounded in finding mediatory vehicles to expose contents of the unconscious so that consciousness can transition. No effective theory of psychology can exist without a concept that carries some of the properties of the transcendent function. The following sections explore ideas and structures that in some way reflect aspects of the transcendent function.

This chapter is not intended to imply that the transcendent function is the same as or even directly analogous to the theories and structures discussed here. Indeed, Jung is unique and extraordinary in his formulation of these matters. His thinking regarding the dynamic opposition of the psyche, the role of fantasy and symbol in mediating such antitheses, the emergence of something larger than the ego that is purposeful, even numinous and holy, and the potentiating of a transformation are all seminal and singular. Indeed, some might say that without the characteristics just enunciated, the transcendent function is not present. That is a fair statement. However, parts of those ideas and the basic notion of a psychological function mediating between consciousness and the unconscious or between different parts of consciousness can be found in the writings of others. An analysis of the similarities and differences between other ideas and the transcendent function can serve as the vessel through which the differences can be held to allow deeper material to emerge. Such a comparison can help us understand the transcendent function, place it within the context of other theories, and ultimately comprehend in a more profound way its importance to the psychological endeavor.

WINNICOTT: TRANSITIONAL OBJECTS AS MEDIATING ELEMENTS

A close analogy to Jung's transcendent function is found in the ideas of D. W. Winnicott. Grounded in the idea that the dependence relationship between child and mother is crucial, Winnicott posited that if the mother's care is not "good enough," the child may not fulfill its inborn drive to develop in a particular way. He laid out three phases of developmental dependence: absolute dependence in which the infant cannot differentiate itself from the environment and is unable to distinguish between "me" and "not me" (Summers, 1994, p. 139); relative dependence (commencing at about six months) in which the infant becomes aware of objects, recognizes an "out there," realizes there is a "me" separate from "not me," and feels anxious about both the separation from mother and its own survival; and toward independence in which the infant actually begins to separate.

Winnicott theorized that critical to the child's adapting to the realization/fear of separation in the relative dependence stage are what he called "transitional objects" and "transitional phenomena" (see, e.g., Winnicott, 1953, 1971). He posited that objects such as blankets and stuffed animals, which symbolically contain part of the child and part of mother, are used by the child as a bridge out of absolute dependence into relative dependence. The transitioning experience occurs as a result of the "me-yet-not-me" character of the transitional object (Eigen, 1991, p. 67); the child lets go of dependence on mother by bonding with an object that represents both mother and itself:

> Transitional objects. . . . are not mother or self, although feelings of mother and self are invested in them. They are "something else"—something other than mother and me, although filled with the latter two. They are something less than mother and me, and something more. (p. 68)

Winnicott also asserted that certain phenomena and activities—cooing, babbling, thumb-sucking, rocking, repeating songs, fantasizing, and dreaming—also serve the child in having a me-yet-not-me, transitional experience (Cwik, 1991, p. 100; Eigen, 1991, p. 69; Summers, 1994, p. 148).

In addition to soothing the child's separation anxiety and beginning the process of building a sense of self,[1] Winnicott saw transitional objects/phenomena as critical in introducing the child to play, creativity, and an intermediate area of experience between reality and fantasy:

> The paradox of the transitional object is that it is neither real nor delusional. It is *illusory*, an intermediate area of experience lying between reality and fantasy [citations omitted]. According to Winnicott (1971), the transitional object begins the world of illusion and prepares the way for play in childhood. Child's play, according to Winnicott, is based on giving an illusory meaning to something real. (Summers, 1994, p. 149)

Winnicott viewed the intermediate area between reality and fantasy as necessary not only to child development but also to adult mental health,[2] particularly in locating what he called the "True Self." He felt that without being able to experience the liminal space between reality and fantasy, a person would develop a false self, either overly concretized in reality or separated from reality in fantasy. Thus, Winnicott saw transitional objects and phenomena both as early developmental tools and as ongoing mechanisms that create an intermediate area between reality and fantasy, self and other, inner and outer, a liminal space that has a crucial role in mental health.

One can see here the direct analogy to the transcendent function. Winnicott's formulation of transitional objects/phenomena and the importance of play are analogous to Jung's formulation of the transcendent function and the importance of symbol and fantasy. The transcendent function is a transitional phenomenon and transitional phenomena are examples of the transcendent function. Both describe a mediatory space where opposites are suspended or united; Winnicott's play and Jung's fantasy are the terrain upon which the phenomena occur. Both serve as bridges between ontological antagonisms such as self/other, subject/object, inner/outer through a liminal experience that allows the opposites to be held side by side. As Barkin (1978) says, "By definition, then, the transitional object is neither inner nor outer but rather partakes of both, i.e, is at the border between them, in an intermediate area" (p. 515).

The nexus between these two concepts can also be seen in the direct connection drawn between fantasy and play in Jung's early writings about the transcendent function. In chapter 2 of *Psychological Types*, for example, where Jung explains how the transcendent function operates through symbol and fantasy, he refers to Schiller's theory that the fundamental opposites of form/matter, thinking/feeling, spirituality/sensuality, could only be united by "a third instinct, the *play* instinct" (1921/1971, p. 106). Jung chooses to call the third instinct "*fantasy activity, which is creative and receptive at once*" (pp. 106–07) and says "this is the function Schiller calls the play instinct" (p. 107). Indeed, Steelman (1991) believed that Jung's work on fantasy anticipated Winnicott's ideas about play by several decades (p. 156). Winnicott's play and Jung's fantasy are analogous territories where liminal experiences can happen.

Another key parallel between Winnicott's transitional phenomena and Jung's transcendent function is the crucial role each has in bringing a person to his or her unique individuality. Just as Jung drew connections between the transcendent function, individuation, and the Self, so Winnicott interrelated transitional phenomena, play, and finding one's True Self.

> What a distance traversed in Winnicott's paper on transitional experiencing! From a discussion of concrete objects clung to by infants to a missing sense of realness in an adult patient. . . . His example of an adult woman's missing sense of realness announces the central theme of his mature clinical writings: the search for a real or True Self. What he is most vexed with in his adult patients is their missing sense of realness, their failure to link up with, sustain, and live from True Self feeling. Some live in a fantasy world, some in a world that is too realistic. . . . The experience of the between, the intermediate area, the wonder of illusion, is deficient. *The first possession* with which Winnicott was concerned was the patient's own, most real and True Self. (Eigen, 1991, p. 73)

For both Jung and Winnicott, the mediatory and transitional experiences they posited have central roles in the development of the individual. Using the diagrammatic schema used above, Winnicott's concept can be analogized to the transcendent function as follows:

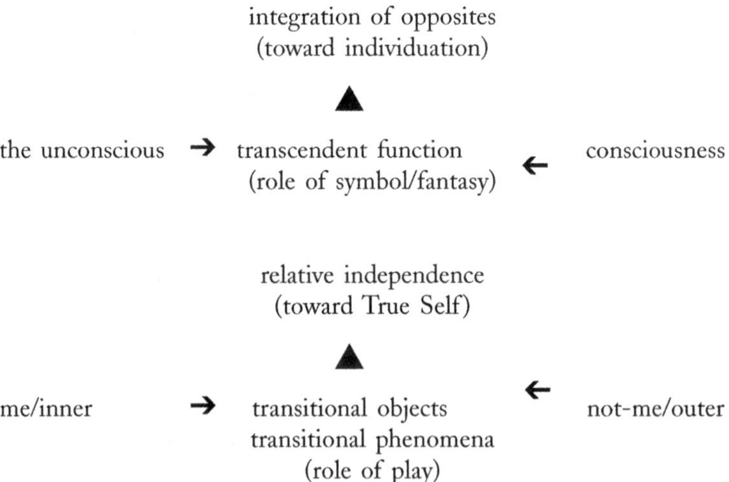

On the other hand, the concepts of Jung and Winnicott have some important differences. Jung's transcendent function is a part of his all-encompassing theory of opposites; fantasy and symbol are constantly at work attempting to reconcile innumerable pairs of opposites. Winnicott's transitional phenomena are much more focused on a few, though important, pairs of opposites: inner/outer, subject/object, reality/fantasy. In addition, though Winnicott stated that transitional objects/phenomena have significance throughout one's life, his theory is largely developmental while Jung's transcendent function is more explicitly ubiquitous to psyche. Further, Jung's transcendent function is essentially teleological; it unites opposites as part of a grander plan of individuation guided by the Self. Winnicott's theories about transitional phenomena and play are less purposeful, more phenomenological; they focus more on being able to fully experience rather than on moving toward some grander purpose. Finally, the transitional object/phenomenon is devoid of the kind of numinous and transformative qualities that Jung attributed to the transcendent function. One might say that Winnicott's theory contains the mediatory and transitional aspects of the transcendent function but lacks its transformative character. Nevertheless, Winnicott's theories of transitional objects and phenomena evince analogies to the transcendent function. Both in their mediating/transitional functions and in their roles of assisting the emergence of the individual, these vehicles show important similarities.

THE ANALYTIC FIELD: THE THIRD AS MEDIATING AGENT

An interesting and important application of the transcendent function emerges in the recent work on the presence of a "field" between or around the analyst and analysand. The psychoanalytic view, focusing on personal history, espouses that the field is created by the interaction of the subjectivity of the analyst and analysand. Ogden (1994) summarizes this view by describing the "analytic third":

> The analytic process reflects the interplay of three subjectivities: the subjectivity of the analyst, of the analysand, and of the analytic third. The analytic third is the creation of the analyst and analysand, and at the same time the analyst and the analysand (qua analyst and analysand) are created by the analytic third. (There is no analyst, no analysand, no analysis in the absence of the third.) (p. 93)

Analytical psychology holds that there is a similar kind of field but that it is created at the intersection of the analysand's individual subjectivity and the archetypal processes of the collective unconscious. Schwartz-Salant (1995) postulates an "interactive field" combining the subjective dimensions of the psychoanalytic field and the objective dimensions of the field in analytical psychology:

> In this conception of a field, personal, historical acquisitions—object relations—mix and combine with an objective substratum, Jung's collective unconscious. One becomes aware that the field has its own

> dynamics, which are separate from and independent of the individuals. Yet the discovery of these dynamics is only possible by experiencing them through the individual and combined subjectivities of both people. . . . Such a notion of the field—an understanding of which actively includes both subjective and objective dimensions—can be called the *interactive field* [footnote omitted]. The interactive field is *in between* the field of the collective unconscious and the realm of subjectivity, while at the same time including them both. (p. 2)

In the omitted footnote, Schwartz-Salant comments that his interactive field concept is really just an amplification of Jung's idea of the field as enunciated in his quaternity model of transference (Jung, 1946/1954) in which the conscious positions of both people and their unconscious components all have an impact on the analysis.

These iterations of the analytical field are integral to the clinical practice of depth psychology. They reflect the perspective that the analytic situation is cocreated by its participants and has a separate presence. As Schwartz-Salant (1995) states, "The field becomes a *presence* that both people are inside of and, simultaneously, observers of" (p. 5). This view of the analytic situation focuses the analyst's attention not on solving the analysand's problems but rather on contacting and harnessing the power of a third presence. Both the analyst and analysand experience and receive information from the field. From this perspective, healing comes not from the analyst to the analysand but from the analytic third to both.

In the same way that the transcendent function is a living, third thing that emerges from the dialogue between the conscious and unconscious, the analytic third is an autonomous entity that emerges from a psychic dialogue between the analyst and analysand. The two are also similar in the way in which they both demand surrender of attachment to preconceived structures. Just as the transcendent function only takes effect when the Self is able to withdraw attachment from both the opposites, allowing it to sink into the unconscious to retrieve the reconciling symbol, the analytic field is evident only when the analyst and analysand relinquish the need to know or understand, even to know or understand whether the material is emerging from the analysand or analyst. As Schwartz-Salant (1995) describes:

> One must be willing to sacrifice the power of knowing "whose content" one is dealing with and instead imagine that the content . . . exists in the field itself and does not necessarily belong to either person. The content can be imaginally thrust into the field that analyst and analysand occupy together so that it becomes a "third thing" (p. 5)

Another parallel can be seen in the way a union or reconciliation emerges. The transcendent function yields a uniting of the opposites; the analytic field produces a kind of union between the analyst and analysand. Schwartz-Salant (1995) identifies the joining or *coniunctio* that occurs interactive field:

> It is what occurs for the participants afterwards that distinguishes the notion of the interactive field. For example, a state of joining can be experienced by both parties—not a fusing that blurs boundaries, but a rhythmical process in which the field itself is felt to have its own dynamic. . . . This experience is akin to what the ancients called the sacred marriage, and what in alchemy is known as the *coniunctio.* Experiencing it opens one to the sense of mystery that can be transformative, much as a vision or "big" dream can be fateful. (p. 6)

The last sentence points to the final point of comparison. Like the transcendent function, the ultimate impact of the analytic field is the transformation of internal structures. Just as the transcendent function's telos is a shift or change of attitude, the analytic third ushers into reality potentials that were previously unintegrated:

> Experiencing the field and being changed by its process is a way of transforming internal structures. New forms that order affects, which were previously overwhelming and fragmenting, can come into existence. (Schwartz-Salant, 1995, p. 9)

Thus, we see in the concept of the analytic third forms and structures that are very similar to the transcendent function. Both emerge from a kind of tension of polarities, both provide ways to step outside of the bonds of previous conceptions, both operate to create a kind of *coniuncto,* and both are integrally involved in transformation. Indeed, one might postulate that the analytic field is an instance of the transcendent function emerging in the analytic situation.

FREUD AND EGO PSYCHOLOGY: THE EGO AS A MEDIATING STRUCTURE

At first blush, comparisons between Jung and Freud on the idea of the transcendent function might appear inapposite. As the core of Jung's prospective view of psychic energy that rejects Freud's purely reductive view, the transcendent function stands as the "most fundamental source of his separation from Freud" (Horne, 1998, p. 25). Paradoxically, there are important parallels between the roles of the transcendent function in Jungian psychology and the ego in Freudian psychology. Freud's structural theory posits three psychic agencies: the id, containing the inherited instincts (primarily sexuality and aggression); the ego, comprising a group of functions orienting the individual to the outside world; and the superego, a special agency containing the individual's basic moral training and ideal aspirations. In contrast to Freud's earlier topographical model which gave exclusive primacy to drives,[3] the structural model gives equal emphasis to the forces opposing the drives. With this theoretical shift, the ego assumed a central role in psychic functioning: balancing the drives of the id on the one hand and the demands of the external world and the ideals of the superego on the other (Freud, 1940/1949, p. 15). Put simply, the structural model posits that psychological health depends on the ability of the ego to manage these conflicting demands (Summers, 1994, p. 4).

Though very different from the transcendent function, the mechanisms of ego psychology have some similarities. First, the ego's function is to mediate between the demands of the unconscious id and the consciousness of the external world in the Freudian, structural model much as the transcendent function's role is to mediate the opposites of the unconscious and consciousness in the Jungian, constructive model. A second interesting parallel is in the nature of the mediatory functions in each: the ego, like the symbol that is the core of the transcendent function, resides in both consciousness and the unconscious,[4] allowing it (like the symbol) to act as a reconciling bridge between consciousness and the unconscious. Viewed schematically, the similarities can be represented as follows:

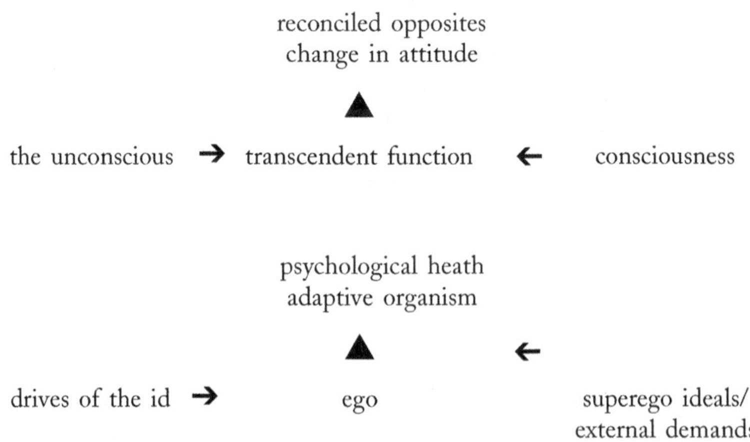

Still, there are crucial differences and distinctions. Though the ego has a mediating function, Freud sees it as more a psychic manager or adaptive mechanism than an agency of transition or transformation. This likely flows from a fundamental difference in the psychologies of the two men: Jung's was synthetic and prospective while Freud's was regressive and reductive. It is not surprising that a mediation between Jung's opposites would dictate a prospective, transformative step forward while between Freud's would produce more of a management or coping function. Secondly, Freud's ego is not specifically stated to be mediating between consciousness and the unconscious but between the drives of the id on the one hand and external reality and the superego on the other. Since external reality and the superego have both conscious and unconscious components aspects, the analogy with Jung's model is not exact. A further distinction is that Freud, like Schiller, sees the mediatory function being centered in the reasoning ego; Jung rejects the proposition that uniting opposites is a "task of reason" and says they can only be united "irrationally" (Jung, 1921/1971, p. 105) through fantasy and symbol. Most importantly, Jung's transcendent function potentiates a consciousness-changing event, the emergence of a new, third thing, while Freud's ego merely effects a compromise between consciousness and the unconscious. Nevertheless, the similarity in the two paradigms is striking since the central thrust of the mediatory function in both is between the untamed passions/drives of the unconscious and the reality of consciousness.

OTHER DEPTH ANALOGIES: KOHUT, KLEIN, FORDHAM, AND HILLMAN

The theories of Hans Kohut, Michael Fordham, Melanie Klein, and James Hillman all reflect structures or concepts in which pieces of the transcendent function can be seen. Kohut's self psychology (also sometimes called the theory of narcissistic development), for example, posits a process of development of the self that depends heavily on a mediating and transitional structure he called the "selfobject." Unlike Jung's Self which is present and complete from conception,[5] Kohut's self is "the way a person experiences himself as himself" (Kohut, 1977, p. xv)[6] and is built up gradually by accretion through interactions, both positive and negative, with those around the infant. To the extent the child receives mirroring, attuned, or affirming responses, the self structure accretes and builds; if, however, the infant receives disconcerting, aggressive, or abusive reactions, a deficit in self ensues, more or less like holes in Swiss cheese. Selfobjects, which are key to the development of the Kohutian self, are loosely speaking the people (generally family members) with whom the infant interacts, creating accretions to or deficits in the self structure. However, technically speaking, the selfobject is not the object at all but rather the infant's intrapsychic representation of the object; for example, it is not the physical being called mother but rather the emotional and psychological image that the baby carries of mother. As Corbett (1989) states it: "Kohut stresses that the selfobject is an intrapsychic phenomenon, not simply an interpersonal process" (p. 28).

The selfobject plays a developmental role bearing similarities to parts of the transcendent function and Winnicott's transitional object: it mediates ontological opposites (reality/illusion, inner/outer) to allow a transition to a third thing, the accreted part of the self structure. Like the transcendent function, the selfobject creates a neither/nor solution to an either/or problem; it creates a mediatory realm of experience where an exchange between "me" and "other" can take place with the result being a new thing, here progress toward the developing self. In Winnicottian terms, the selfobject is neither the actual object (e.g., mother) nor the child's mere projections but something in between, the child's psychological experience of himself or herself, like the transitional object. The selfobject is a symbolic (Jungian), me-not-me (Winnicottian) experience that brings fantasy/reality, inner/outer, together for the developing self.[7] Here we do not suggest that the selfobject is either identical to or directly analogous to the transcendent function, only that it plays a role in Kohut's model of the developing personality (providing a bridge between the fundamental antitheses of reality/illusion, inner/outer, and me/not-me) that is similar in concept to the transcendent function.

Melanie Klein's object relations theory of development also has interesting parallels to the transcendent function. Though the details of her theory are far beyond the scope of this work,[8] suffice it to say for our purposes that at its core is the developmental movement from the "paranoid position" to the "depressive position" (Summers, 1994, p. 74). The paranoid position dominates the first three to six months of life and is characterized by the infant splitting both objects (outside) and its own ego (inside) into good and bad to protect against its own aggressive, destructive drives. Movement to the depressive position occurs if early positive experiences and the child's innate libido are strong enough to produce a solid "internalized good object" (Summers, 1994, p. 88); the emerging ego begins to conceptualize that the good and bad objects it had previously split are indeed one and the same. In Kleinian parlance, the infant goes from experiences of "part objects" to "whole objects" (p. 89) and moves from a place of victim to more of a "feeling of power" (p.89), believing that it is now capable of doing injury. Klein called this stage the depressive position because the infant now realizes it can injure its loved ones.

Though quite different from the Jungian paradigm, the depressive position has elements in common with the transcendent function. Just as opposites are united by the transcendent function, the antitheses of good and bad in the paranoid position are brought together in the depressive position. Though Klein did not enunciate any clear mechanism for how one moves beyond the paranoid stage and into the depressive, it is clear that the transition involves a key psychological integration. Like the transcendent function, the depressive position mediates a fundamental either/or quandary and moves it to a space where both coexist.

The British analyst Michael Fordham, whose ideas are sometimes characterized as a Jungian-Kleinian hybrid, formulated important theories about the development of the Self in the infant (see, e.g., Fordham, 1969, 1985). He believed that the infant begins with what he called the "primal self"[9] in a state of integrated wholeness that is then periodically shattered by experiences of "deintegration" (Fordham called it "deintegration" because the original integration is disturbed). The exigencies of physical reality intervene—the infant becomes hungry, needs its diaper changed, requires soothing, or experiences pain. The infant is then fed, soothed, and comforted and falls asleep, thereby returning it to the state of wholeness/integration or "reintegration." This constantly repeating deintegration-reintegration cycle was posited by Fordham to describe how the Self guides a process of differentiation, organization, development, and individuation.

The deintegration-reintegration cycle, like the transcendent function, mediates between conscious and unconscious states and helps a person move from fragmented or opposite states to integrated ones. Also analogous is the rhythm and repetition evident in both models. Jung was clear that the product of the transcendent function is not a final integration but rather is immediately confronted by a new opposite, a deintegration of sorts, and the process starts over again; Fordham's model is also explicitly cyclical in nature. Solomon (1992) noted that the deintegration-reintegration cycle and the transcendent function were both "expressions in psychological language with origins in dialectical philosophy" (p. 132). As he states further:

> I and the Other can be thought of as elements, each of which internalizes its own experience of a joint interaction; a similar bipolar configuration is considered to occur in the rhythmic back and forth movement between deintegration and reintegration. This movement occurs externally between persons and internally between parts of persons. (p. 132)

Just as the transcendent function mediates between the conscious "I" and the unconscious "Other," the deintegration-reintegration process mediates between the primal Self and the "not-Self" experiences that have not yet been incorporated.

Finally, James Hillman's omnipresent concept of soul in archetypal psychology also has parallels with the transcendent function.[10] Archetypal psychology considers the archetype to be always phenomenal, manifested in time, space, and experience. In this paradigm, soul is not a thing but rather a kind of process where mere physical events are deepened into experiences,[11] where meaning becomes possible, where the desiccated surface of occurrence is turned, exposing the moist, fertile soil of participation, imagination, metaphor, play, and fantasy. Soul is what allows us to truly experience our existence in a deep and meaningful way:

> By *soul* I mean, first of all, a perspective rather than a substance, a viewpoint toward things rather than a thing itself. This perspective is reflective; it mediates events and makes differences between ourselves and everything that happens. Between us and events, between the doer and the deed, there is a reflective moment—and soul-making means differentiating this middle ground. (Hillman, 1975, p. xvi)

Soul, like the transcendent function, mediates and constitutes a middle ground. In the same way that the transcendent function creates a connection between directed consciousness and the compensatory unconscious, soul opens the link between the physicality of an event and the meaning of it; the transcendent function leads to a new attitude while soul leads to a new experience of the event. Soul is what transforms the touching of pieces of facial flesh between two people into a kiss, what makes the sound of rhyming words into a poem. Just as the transcendent function leads to a transformation of psychological state or attitude, soul leads to a transformation of experience from a physical one to a psychological one.

NON-DEPTH ANALOGIES: GESTALT, CLIENT-CENTERED, AND COGNITIVE THERAPIES

Gestalt therapy, eschewing the explanations and interpretations that are more the staple of analysis, gives primacy to what is directly perceived, felt, and acted. Its goals are to increase patient awareness and insight, thereby enhancing self-acceptance and esteem. Gestalt holds that all experience occurs in a field, a foreground of present occurrences overlaid against a background of habits, beliefs, and assumptions. Clinical work seeks to help the patient learn to perceive the entire field with all its parts "here-and-now" in order to make the experience more present, profound, and meaningful. Though the terminology and orientation are different, the idea of the here-and-now in Gestalt therapy has analogies to the transcendent function. The here-and-now is a way of attempting to unify two disparate elements: the background (what the patient is unaware of in terms of feelings, beliefs, values, etc.) and the foreground (what the patient is aware of in the situation). The analogy to the transcendent function may be understood at a deeper level by examining the role of "lived dialogue," a mode of Gestalt therapy that allows patients to speak with different psychic part of themselves (e.g., their "inner child," "procrastinator," "perfectionist," "rebellious teenager," etc.). In the same way that the transcendent function gives one the experience of "other," lived dialogue in Gestalt gives the patient a me-not-me experience. Lived dialogue also encourages modes of dialogue that are nonverbal such as dancing, singing, acting, or drawing, directly analogous to the kind Jung advocated in connection with the transcendent function.

The client-centered therapy pioneered by Carl Rogers has at its core the belief in "an *actualizing tendency* present in every living organism . . . a trust in a constructive directional flow toward the realization of each individual's full potential" (Raskin and Rogers, 1989, p. 155). Fundamental to its practice is the notion of "unconditional positive regard," a kind of supercharged empathy by the therapist who engages in continuously mirroring the patient's thoughts, feeling, insights, and conclusions. The theory is essentially that through the unconditional positive regard, the patient's innate actualizing tendency will be supported and the patient will be guided to a healthy disposition. In this paradigm, unconditional positive regard performs a role that may be said to be similar to the transcendent function: it is a mediatory and transitional phenomenon. It is intended to serve as a carrier or intermediate space for the patient. It transports the psychic structure of the patient from one of deficit and conflict to one of congruence and self-regard. In the same way that the Jungian analyst mediates the transcendent function for the analysand until the latter can perform the task alone, the client-centered therapist carries the unconditional positive regard for the patient until he or she can actualize it.[12]

Finally, even cognitive behavioral therapy evidences concepts analogous to the transcendent function. Proceeding from the simple assumption that how one thinks is the primary determinant in how one feels and behaves, cognitive behavioral seeks to correct the faulty information-gathering processes of the patient in order to correct the assumptions that lead to maladaptive behaviors and emotions. The therapist engages in a Socratic dialogue to help the patient see that such behaviors and emotions are based largely on "automatic thoughts," "core beliefs," or "schemas" (Beck and Weishaar, 1989, p. 300), various erroneous assumptions, images, and rules of life of which the patient is unaware. Though very different in thrust, the focus on thought in cognitive behavioral therapy is analogous to Jung's transcendent function. The painful affect and maladaptive behavior in consciousness are brought together with the automatic thoughts and core beliefs in the unconscious through the mediating vehicle of the thought out of which a transition or a shift in attitude or emotion is expected. We should be careful to point out that cognitive behavioral therapy is certainly not aiming at the unconscious to the same degree as Jungian psychology. Furthermore, cognitive behavioral therapy's mediatory and transitional vehicle is a rational, directed process, not an imagistic, imaginal, or symbolic one.

THE THIRD AS A UNIVERSAL PSYCHOLOGICAL CONSTRUCT

This part of the book has sought to broaden the landscape of the transcendent function. Comparing and contrasting the transcendent function with concepts from other schools of psychology yields interesting results. First, it helps us see how Jung's idea of a psychological function that mediates polarized segments of psyche toward a transition is reflected in one way or another in other areas: Winnicott's transitional object/phenomena, Freud's ego, Kohut's selfobject, Klein's depressive position, Fordham's deintegration-reintegration cycle, Hillman's soul, and the other non-depth analogies we explored. Second, the comparisons help us see how fundamental to all of psychology the idea of a dialogue with unconscious, unacknowledged, unaccepted, and/or unknown material is; fundamentally, all psychological growth has its routes in such a conversation. It also helps us see that Jung's idea about how psychological change happens, is a universal, even archetypal one and it buttresses the earlier analysis that put forth the expansive view of the transcendent function as being psychological in general. It appears that throughout the field of psychology, those theorizing about the way psyche works identify functions that mediate between different psychic structures or states or that allow psyche to transform from one state to another. Psyche uses these mediatory structures to seek the way between dualities.

On the other hand, this chapter also clarified and crystallized how unique and singular Jung's idea of the transcendent function is. It is broader, deeper, and more transformational than any of the concepts to which it was compared here. Jung remains distinctive and extraordinary in his linking of the dynamic opposition of conscious/unconscious, the role of fantasy and symbol, the dialogue between conscious/unconscious, the emphasis on purpose and meaning, and the value of psychological transformation in the context of becoming the person one is meant to become. While other concepts we have explored deal in more limited ways with the concepts of psychological growth and transition, the transcendent function is a more comprehensive, more purposeful, more profound, indeed more psychological model of how psychological transformation occurs. It seeks to explain the way that psyche is always in dialogue with itself in an archetypal process, to transform, to move more profoundly into itself by constantly engaging in dialogue with the unconscious. The deeper roots of this movement will be the focus of the next chapter.

CHAPTER SIX

THE DEEPER ROOTS OF THE TRANSCENDENT FUNCTION

The transcendent function is a phenomenon ubiquitous to human experience that implicates opposition/duality, liminality, descent, initiation, and transformation. It reflects and flows from the archetypal tendency of psyche to seek connections and dialogue in order to effect its innate and continual urge to move deeper into itself, to experience itself psychologically. From the first time I learned about the transcendent function, it seemed apparent that it reflected a more universal idea present in psyche. Though the outlines of that idea were ill-defined, it persistently gnawed at me and was a substantial part of the impetus for this book. Concepts in other schools of psychology seemed to parallel the activity and/or principle of the transcendent function; an image began to emerge of a process that flows from other ideas universal to human psychology. Given its ubiquity, I began to conceptualize archetypal processes that may be reflected by the transcendent function. Used in this way, the term *archetypal process* envisions Jung's description of archetype as "typical forms of behaviour which, once they become conscious, naturally present themselves *as ideas and images*" (1947/1960, p. 227). Viewed thusly, the transcendent function becomes an expression of deeper, archetypal patterns of psyche. This section explores such patterns.

THE BINARY OPPOSITION INHERENT IN CONSCIOUSNESS

The opposites as a natural part of psychic energy were discussed at length in chapter 3. The tendency to separate reality into pairs of opposites is pervasive in the human experience. Dualities such as life/death, light/dark, spirit/matter, inner/outer, good/bad, and love/hate have deep significance to the human endeavor. Jung posited that these opposites are the very engine of psyche. The essence of the transcendent function is the bridging and uniting of them. Similarly, the other mediatory and transitional phenomena examined in chapter 5 also relate, each in its own way, to opposites and bringing them together.[1]

We have no certain explanation as to why opposites play such a fundamental part in psychological life. Though still far from being conclusively established, there is evidence that at least part of the answer lies in basic brain chemistry. Neurons, the cells that make up the brain, are essentially on-off switches; they are either stimulated enough by the electric charge coming across the synapse from the neighboring neuron to fire a signal to the next neuron or they are not. Thus, brain chemistry is essentially an either/or process. Through various and countless combinations of these neuronal units, our basic thinking process may, as a result, have a similar dualistic structure (see, e.g. Pinker, 1997). Further speculation about the physiological basis for the opposites may be found in the two-hemisphere structure of the human brain. The so-called bilateral brain[2] has been shown to house essentially opposite functions in the two hemispheres; the left brain tends to perform logical, reasoning functions in a digital, computer-like way while the right brain acts in an analogical or metaphorical style (p. 234). Furthermore, the left hemisphere focuses more on the ego/me/self perceptions and the parts of things while the right hemisphere creates the experience of "otherness" (opposition from the self) and sees parts as having meaning only within a context (see, e.g., Jaynes, 1976, pp. 100–25). Though the science of brain chemistry and physiology is still evolving, the early evidence in this area tends to confirm that the opposites are a biological and physiological reality.

Many have written on how the opposites are inherent in consciousness even if they are not manifestations of the way the brain functions. Jung, for example, believed that the very act of becoming conscious brings with it binary opposition: "The separation into pairs of opposites is entirely due to conscious differentiation; only consciousness can recognize the suitable and distinguish it from the unsuitable and worthless" (1921/1971, p. 112). Dehing notes that "the very development of ego-consciousness necessarily leads us to divide our subjective experience into poles: for example, good and bad, love and hate, life and death" (1992, p. 27). Corbett states it somewhat differently: "The movement from unconscious to consciousness involves a movement from undifferentiation to apparent plurality. An unbroken totality becomes the fragmented condition of everyday consciousness which divides everything into parts" (1996, p. 137). Others (e.g., Romanyshyn, 1996) have argued that the opposites may spring from ontological duality of spirit and matter in human existence. This line of thinking holds that the opposites are a reflection of those two distinct sides of being human with which we perpetually struggle. From an Eastern perspective, the opposites inherent in spirit and matter is the "primal delusion" (R. Powell, 1982, p. 6) of humanity; humans are born out of nonduality, "out of the Void," into a world that emphasizes "thingness" and "selfhood" and "separateness" (p. 5) and humanity's belief that its material existence is separate from the spiritual source from whence everything comes is the source of all suffering.

Given that dualities are universal to human consciousness, the transcendent function is the *sine qua non* of healthy psychological functioning, for without it the opposites would never be bridged. By providing connective tissue between dualities, the transcendent function manifests the urge of the psyche to move beyond opposition. Psyche wants no part of the split between spirit and matter; indeed, it is the hinge that allows us to hold them together. Though humans have a difficult time reconciling the splits between the realms of spirit and ideas, on the one hand, and matter and things on the other, psyche does not. As Jung (1921/1971) states:

> Idea and thing come together, however, in the human psyche, which holds the balance between them. . . . Living reality is the product of neither of the actual objective behaviour of things nor of the formulated idea exclusively, but rather of the combination of both in the living psychological process, through *esse in anima*. (pp. 51–52)

Though ego consciousness demands separation between opposites, psyche does not. It is in the autonomous images/fantasies of psyche that opposites co-exist peacefully without explanation.

BRIDGING THE CHASM BETWEEN SUBJECT AND OBJECT

Whether our experience is purely subjective and personal or is a product of some greater set of objectivities is a debate that is likely as old as consciousness itself. Going back at least as far as the debate in ancient Greece between realism and nominalism discussed in chapter 3, the interplay between subject and object has vexed thinkers in virtually every era. In modernity, the most important move in this regard is the fundamental subject-object bifurcation inherent in the theories of Descartes and Kant. The transcendent function and its analogs represent, in part, psychology's struggle with this duality. The subject-object split is seen in almost every psychology today, particularly in the way each school endeavors to deal with self/other, idea/thing, inner/outer, and thought/feeling. Indeed, the transcendent function and its analogs are the frontline infantry in psychology's battle with this ontological quandary.

The transcendent function was, in large part, Jung's attempt to deal with the fundamental split between the subjectivity of the conscious ego and the objectivity of the unconscious (the objective psyche). Some have even hypothesized that Jung's notions of the objective psyche and psychoid archetypes are attempts on Jung's part to identify a psychological locale where subject and object are one (see, e.g. Giegerich, 1987, p. 108). To many, the reason that Jungian psychology is so intriguing is its avowal that subjective experience takes place within a larger field (the psychoid realm) and that the entire universe is the subject of which we are all small parts. That idea resonates deeply for some because it helps to explain data (feelings, senses, and intuitions) that seem to come from somewhere other than the perceiver's subjectivity. Giegerich (1987) argues that despite his efforts to bridge the gap between subject and object, Jung remained trapped by the very subject-object assumptions he was trying to overcome. That is, even though Jung's ideas about the psychoid archetype and the subjective universe are unique, they still "have the logical form of ontic ideas: *our* ideas *about* existing factors or aspects" (p. 114). In other words, we are still the "subject" hypothesizing ideas about something else, inherently implicating the subject-object split:

> It is obvious that this logical form *is* the splitting of subject (we as the ones having the idea) and object (what our idea refers to). When we adopt the idea of the subjective universe, we by doing so fall into and enact the subject-object alienation that we intend to overcome. (p. 114)

Interestingly, the transcendent function analogs described in chapter 5 display similar attributes, each in its own way struggling with and/or mediating between subject and object.[3]

The most radical attempts to dispose of the subject-object issue are postmodernism[4] and its cousin, archetypal psychology. The most extreme postmodernists, called "skeptical post-modernists" (Rosenau, 1992, p. 15), contend that there is no subjectivity, no center of experience.

> They consider the subject to be a fossil relic of the past, of modernity, an invention of liberal humanism, the source of the unacceptable object-subject dichotomy. They argue that personal identity of this sort, if it ever existed, was only an illusion, and it is no longer possible, today, in a post-modern context. (pp. 42–43)

Skeptical postmodernists consider the subject (or self) to be a mere position in language, a point of reference that is secondary to the essence of what is occurring. Without the subject, skeptical postmodernists contend, the subject-object distinction is extinguished:

> Erasing the subject, then, also suspends any division of the world into subjects and objects. It explodes the object-subject dichotomy, thwarts the authority of the one over the other, suspends the arbitrary power relations associated with the subject category, and thus abolishes this implicit hierarchy. (p. 49)

Even within postmodernism, however, the subject-object dichotomy persists. The more moderate theorists, called "affirmative post-modernists" (p. 15) concede that the subject must exist in order to even have a discussion. Though the affirmative postmodernists propose a liberated subject, "a decentered subject, an 'emergent' subject, unrecognizable by the modernists" (p. 57), subjectivity is necessary nevertheless. And, of course, with the subject comes the subject-object dichotomy.

Archetypal psychology evidences a similar desire to eliminate the subject-object distinction. Exhorting the avoidance of interpretation and a commitment to the image-making agency of soul, archetypal psychology urges us to abandon subjectivity and recognize that all we see is a manifestation of an archetypal unity. The subjectivity of "me" and the objectivity of "other" is removed; "I" am merely an expression of soul, a personification of psyche:

> Not I personify, but the anima personifies me, or soul-makes herself through me, giving my life her sense—her intense daydream is my "me-ness"; and "I" a psychic vessel whose existence is a psychic metaphor, an "as-if being," in which every single being is a literalism except the belief of soul whose faith posits me and makes me possible as a personification of psyche. (Hillman, 1975, p. 51)

Thus, archetypal psychology, similar to postmodernism, sees subject and object as mere illusions that humans use to make sense of soul's daydream that is being lived out through us.

Though the dichotomy between subject and object has been part of Western consciousness for at least two millennia, the transcendent function may be seen as psyche's way of telling us that the chasm should be bridged or, even more radically, that it may be an illusion. Not only does psyche seek the relationship and dialogues between seeming opposites, it also eschews the distinction between subject and object. Psychic activity is not constricted by the artificial bounds of linear logic and reason. Based in its own vocation of fantasy, psyche is unburdened by the shackles of the subject/object distinction. As Jung (1921/1971) says:

> The psyche creates reality every day. The only expression I can use for this activity is *fantasy*. . . . Fantasy, therefore, seems to me to be the clearest expression of the specific activity of the psyche. . . . Fantasy it was and ever is which fashions the bridge between the irreconcilable claims of subject and object. . . . In fantasy alone both mechanism are united. (p. 52)

Psyche may itself be the subject of which we all form a part. As Hillman (1975) admonishes:

> What we learn from dreams is what psychic nature really is—the nature of psychic reality: not I, but we; not one but many. . . . By employing as model of psychic actuality, and by conceiving a theory of personality based upon the dream, we are imagining the psyche's basic structure to be an *inscape of personified images*. The full consequences of this structure imply that the psyche presents its own imaginal dimensions, operates freely without words, and is constituted of multiple personalities. We can describe the psyche as a polycentric realm of non-verbal, nonspatial images. (p. 33)

The transcendent function seeks to bridge or remove the gap between subject and object. In this way, it allows psyche to move deeper, to find relationships in place of differences.

LIMINALITY AND INITIATION: AN ARCHETYPAL BETWEEN-NESS

The transcendent function operates in the space between psychologically disparate states. This "between-ness" serves an invaluable psychological purpose: to transition psyche from a conflicted set of circumstances to one that allows us to resolve (or to at least more comfortably tolerate) the conflict. The transcendent function serves as a psychic usher guiding us through doorways along the hallways of psychological growth. Viewed in this way, the transcendent function falls into an archetypal pattern that implicates liminality and initiation. It serves as psyche's ever present mechanism constantly shepherding us deeper through a series of mini-initiations requiring us to slip between seemingly irreconcilable states.

Much of seminal work on liminality was done by two anthropologists, Arnold van Gennep and Victor Turner. Van Gennep (1960) first coined the term as the middle of three stages of primitive initiation ceremonies: separation, liminality (or transition), and incorporation (or aggregation). A person is separated from one status in a culture, placed in "an intermediate state of liminality 'betwixt and between'" and, after an initiation process, is returned to the social structure in a new status or role (Hall, 1991, pp. 34–35). Van Gennep's liminality was extremely important to sociology and anthropology because it posited as normal that society has both bounded and unbounded dimension; previous theory had consistently focused almost exclusively on the boundedness of the social structure (Turner, 1974, p. 269). Turner (1987) expanded van Gennep's concept by pointing out that liminality "may be institutionalized as a state in itself" (Hall, 1991, p. 35), an ongoing state of unboundedness that engages in any significant shift, in any "change from one state to another" (Turner, 1987, p. 5).

Turner delved deeply into the symbolism of the liminal stage. He described the person going through a liminal experience as structurally invisible because he or she belongs neither to the old status nor to the new, likening the experience to going through a death and rebirth:

> The structural "invisibility" of liminal *personae* has a twofold character. They are at once no longer classified and not yet classified. In so far as they are no longer classified, the symbols that represent them are, in many societies, drawn from the biology of death, decomposition, catabolism, and other physical processes that have a negative tinge. . . . The other aspect, that they are not yet classified, is often expressed in symbols modeled on processes of gestation and parturition. The [initiants] are likened to or treated as embryos, newborn infants, or sucklings. (1987, pp. 6–7)

This passage illustrates the paradoxical nature of liminality: death of the old coexisting with birth of the new. The liminal experience is one where psyche straddles the boundary, with *both* death and birth and with *neither* death nor birth:

> The essential feature of these [liminal] symbolizations is that the neophytes are neither living nor dead from one aspect, and both living and dead from another. Their condition is one of *ambiguity and paradox* [italics added], a confusion of all customary categories. Jakob Boehme, the German mystic whose obscure writings gave Hegel his celebrated dialectical "triad," liked to say that "in Yea and Nay all things consist." Liminality may perhaps be regarded as the Nay to all positive structural assertions, but as in some sense the source of them all, and, more than that, as a realm of pure possibility whence novel configurations of ideas and relations may arise. (Turner, 1987, p. 7)

The liminal is the territory not only where both death and birth coexist but becomes an archetypal place of pure possibility that is the potential source of all sorts of original and new ideas. A space that can simultaneously hold opposites as polarized as death and birth where neither one nor the other prevails can, indeed, be the space of pure possibility:

> Undoing, dissolution, decomposition are accompanied by growth, transformation, and the reformulation of old elements into new patterns. . . . This coincidence of opposite processes and notions in a single representation characterizes the peculiar unity of the liminal: that which is neither this nor that, and yet is both. (Turner, 1987, p. 9)

Liminality is a phenomenon that allows us to enter a neither/nor space that allows the reformulation of the old into the new.

One can see how the transcendent function fits nicely within the rubric of liminality. Indeed, the language used to describe liminality is virtually identical to that used by Jung in connection with the transcendent function, particularly when Turner talks of the "coincidence of the opposites" and "that which is neither this nor that, and yet is both" (1987, p. 9). One might say that the transcendent function is the psychological manifestation of and catalyst for liminality. As one writer put it, "what Turner's concept of social *liminality* does for status in a society, Jung psychological concept of *transcendent function* does for the movement of the person through the life process of individuation" (Hall, 1991, p. 34). The transcendent function operates to provide a series of transitional experiences that move the person in stages through various transformations in attitude.

Psychologically speaking, liminality's symbolism of death and birth signifies the omnipresent cycle of the demise of one psychological position and the ascent of a new one. In Jungian terms, it is the perpetual pattern of the crossing of previously psychological boundaries enforced by the ego (self) as guided by the Self:

> From an archetypal viewpoint, liminality does not imply the universal archetypal experience of death, but rather the more complicated archetypal patterns of death and transformation, death and rebirth, or death and resurrection. Considered clinically, liminality implies regression of the self in service of the Self. . . . Psychologically, liminality is the sense of crossing and re-crossing borders. (Hall, 1991, pp. 45–46)

Hall further describes how the Self uses the transcendent function as a liminal phenomenon to "produce a unification of opposites" (p. 46) which effects "a change in the tacit self-image from which the conflict is viewed" (p. 47). He concludes:

> This change in self-image is initiated, mediated, and contained by the transcendent functional activity of the Archetypal Self. . . . The transcendent function parallels in the intrapsychic realm the change in role described by Turner within societies. (p. 47)

Liminality is the archetypal wellspring from which the transcendent function emerges.

A similar connection can be made to the closely related idea of initiation. Initiation is a process that has been specifically labeled as archetypal and connected directly to liminality (Henderson, 1967). Indeed, with his studies about the liminal stage of initiation ceremonies, van Gennep was said to have spurred the psychological discovery of the archetypal initiation process in the twentieth century (p. 9). Henderson argues that initiation experiences, so common to primitive and tribal life, are not a regular part of modern life. Coupled with the fragmentation of group identity and any real sense of community in the hustle and bustle of modern times, initiatory rituals and transitions lie dormant in the unconscious and call to us at critical times throughout our lives:

> Since modern man cannot return to his origins in any collective sense, he apparently is tempted and even forced to return to them in an individual way at certain critical times in his personal development. And in this resides the relevance today of reinforming ourselves of the nature of primitive forms of initiation. (Henderson, 1967, p. 14)

Jung was also very aware of initiation and its importance as an archetypal force. Discussing psyche's attempt to integrate the contents of the collective unconscious, Jung analogizes coming to terms with the fantasies of the unconscious to the archetypal process of initiation:

> We could therefore most fittingly describe these . . . fantasies as processes of initiation, since these form the closest analogy. All primitive groups and tribes that are in any way organized have their rites of initiation, often very highly developed, which play an extraordinarily important part in their social and religious life. . . . They are clearly transformation mysteries of the greatest spiritual significance. . . . The fact is that the whole symbolism of initiation rises up clear and unmistakable, in the unconscious contents. (1928/1953, pp. 230–31)

Finally, Henderson (1967) enunciates the themes that are the thrust of this section on liminality and initiation: the analytic situation is fundamentally initiatory at its core and it takes the patient through a series of initiations or liminal experiences that replicate the life process. He concludes that through the initiation archetype we are pursuing individuation: "The completion of this process, again through the mediation of the archetype of initiation, appears to be synonymous with the psychological concept of individuation" (p. 18).

One can see how initiation underlies the transcendent function. Death/rebirth and transformation are at the heart of both. Jung (1939/1958) recognized a connection between initiation and the transcendent function in "Psychological Commentary on *The Tibetan Book of the Great Liberation*" where he said:

> Many initiation ceremonies stage a . . . return to the womb of rebirth. Rebirth symbolism simply describes the union of opposites—conscious and unconscious—by means of concretistic analogies. Underlying all rebirth symbolism is the transcendent function. (p. 508)

Liminality and initiation are both processes ubiquitous to our existence. They are implicated whenever change, particularly psychological transformation, occurs. These concepts are extremely important since they represent a "between" stage that leads to something new. Put another way, liminality and initiation are archetypal processes that represent a movement between seemingly inviolable borders. The transcendent function is a psychological expression of those archetypal processes.

HERMES: THE ARCHETYPAL MESSENGER BETWEEN REALMS

Another archetypal source for the transcendent function may be found in the Greek god Hermes. Though a full treatment of Hermes is beyond the scope of this work, indeed it has been the subject of many volumes (see, e.g., Kerényi, 1944/1976; López-Pedraza, 1989), a brief visit with Hermes is instructive here. The Greeks credited Hermes with the discovery of language and writing, and he is associated with "the function of transmuting what is beyond human understanding into a form that human intelligence can grasp" (Palmer, 1969, p. 13). This last aspect of Hermes is important to both hermeneutics and the transcendent function; in both, transmuting what is beyond human understanding into something that can be grasped is crucial.

In the myth, Hermes is born of a Maia, a Titan goddess, and Zeus, an Olympian god. He brings together the primordial, primitive nature of the Titans, who preceded the Olympians, and the Olympians, who represent more a sense of a higher, spirit nature. Hermes has to do with between-ness, the bringing together of different realms. This quality of Hermes is critical since the transcendent function requires an archetypal energy to bring together different realms. After stealing his brother Apollo's cattle, Hermes impishly denies wrongdoing. In frustration, Apollo takes the issue to Zeus, father of the two, where Hermes repeats the same falsehoods. Zeus, amused and impressed by his son's audacity, appoints Hermes messenger between and among Olympus, humanity, and the underworld, hence Hermes's winged sandals and his ability to fly.

Archetypally, Hermes is the messenger between realms. He personifies the exchange of information in liminal and initiatory phenomena and is capable of simultaneously visiting two disparate places, crossing the boundary that seemed uncrossable. One writer terms Hermes the "connection-maker"

(López-Pedraza, 1989, p. 8). Hermes is thought both to connect the gods and goddesses together and to humanity (López-Pedraza, 1989, p. 8) and also to be a messenger to the underworld (Downing, 1993, p. 52). This aspect of Hermes, the ability to simultaneously hold multiple levels of consciousness, is crucial to the transcendent function. Several post-Jungian writers have used this hermetic imagery when describing the transcendent function: a "bridge between two worlds" (Agnel, 1992, p. 105); "a capacity to move back and forth between layers of meaning" (Young-Eisendrath, 1992, p. 153); "the messenger between gods and men" (Williams, 1983, p. 65).

A further aspect of Hermes flows from the source of his name, the *herm*, a heap of stones marking a boundary or crossroad (Downing, 1993, p. 56). Thus, Hermes is often known as the god of boundaries or crossroads, both physical and psychological. This dovetails nicely with Hermes as representing the liminal, the ability to hold multiple levels of meaning, the connection-maker. But in addition to representing the boundary or crossroad, Hermes also signifies the ability to make transition and transformation. As Downing (1993) states:

> He is the herm. He is also the crossroad itself. Every threshold is Hermes. . . . He is *there* at all transitions, marking them as sacred, as eventful, as epiphany. Our awareness of Hermes opens us to the sacredness of such moments, of those in-between times that are strangely frightening and that we so often try to hurry past. (p. 56)

One can see why Hermes is so important to the discussion of liminality. He is the god who not only represents the liminal but manifests it. He is not only the god of boundaries, he actually *is* the boundary. Whenever we look at a liminal or transitional phenomenon, we stare into the visage of Hermes. Hermes is the archetype that stands for change itself and is present whenever change is (Paris, 1990, p. 110). Hermes not only marks the boundary but is a messenger between the disparate realms. It is he who makes exchange possible between the world and the underworld, between consciousness and the unconscious, indeed between any two realms.

The transcendent function is a psychological manifestation of the archetypal experience of Hermes. It, like he, allows us to cross and recross boundaries, to simultaneously hold multiple levels of consciousness. Undoubtedly a search of Hermes' toolkit would reveal the transcendent function. It is an expression, instrumentality, and manifestation of his energy.

THE THIRD: FOUNDATIONS OF THE NUMBER THREE

The transcendent function represents a third, a hinge through which two disparate elements are mediated. Indeed, Jung refers to the "third thing"

(1957/1960, p. 90) in describing the transcendent function. That the third is referenced and implicated by the transcendent function is not coincidental since the number three is rich in associations relating to synthesis, balance, and completion (Biedermann, 1989, pp. 240, 252–53). The transcendent function is a psychological expression of the synthesis and balance inherent in the number three itself.

Triads of all sorts exist to express the idea of balance, synthesis, or perfection: thesis-antithesis-synthesis in philosophy, centripetal force-centrifugal force-equilibrium in cosmology, proton-electron-neutron and mass-power-velocity in physics, past-present-future and beginning-middle-end in ontology, spirit-body-soul in alchemy, and acid-base-salt in chemistry. Some have argued that synthesis comes in the form of threes because nature is ordered in threes—wave-radiation-condensation, water-air-earth, solid-liquid-gas, mineral-plant-animal—and that, as a result, humans have a kind of tripolar consciousness (Schimmel, 1993, p. 59).

Triads also seem to be pervasive in religion. This began with ancient beliefs: Anu-Enlil-Ea, the three primary Sumerian deities; Sin-Shamash-Ishtar, the astral trinity of Babylon; Isis-Osiris-Horus, the three dominant gods of Egypt. The pattern is also seen in modern religion: the Trinity (Father-Son-Holy Spirit) in Christianity; the Trimurti (Brahma-Shiva-Vishnu) in Hinduism, the three bodies (tri-kaya) of knowledge (dharma-kaya or true being, nirmana-kaya or earthly mode, and sambogha-kaya or the blessed mode of community believers) in Buddhism.

The idea of perfection as inherent in the number three is apparent in the thinking of the ancient Greeks Pythagoras and Plato. Pythagorean theory, here quoted by Jung (1948/1958), held that the number three stands for perfection and completion:

> "One is the first from which all other numbers arise, and in which the opposite qualities of numbers, the odd and the even, must therefore be united; two is the first even number; three the first that is uneven and perfect, because in it we first find beginning, middle, and end." (p. 118)

The Pythagorean notion of three as completion was expanded upon by Plato in his work *Timeaus* where he argued that three constituted totality and unity. Jung (1948/1958) quotes Plato:

> "Hence the god, when he began to put together the body of the universe, set about making it of fire and earth. But two things alone cannot be satisfactorily united without a third: for there must be some bond between them drawing them together. And of all bonds the best is that which makes itself and the terms it connects a unity

> in the fullest sense; and it is of the nature of a continued geometrical proportion to effect this most perfectly." (p. 119)

In the Pythagorean and Platonic paradigms, three, paradoxically, becomes an expression of one. Put another way, one devolves into "one" and the "other" (i.e., two); three, then, unites the one and the other. This is the logical and abstract precursor to the idea of the Holy Trinity (see, e.g., Jung, 1948/1958, pp. 118–19). In a discussion of this theory by Jung (1948/1958), one sees parallels to the language of the transcendent function.

> The "One" . . . seeks to hold to its one-and-alone existence, while the "Other" ever strives to be another opposed to the One. . . . Thus, there arises a tension of opposites between the One and the Other. But every tension of opposites culminates in a release out of which comes the "third." In the third, the tension is resolved and the lost unity is restored. (p. 119)

Here we see the deeper roots of the third in Jung's thinking in the transcendent function. Jung struggled with the interplay of the One, representing a primal even divine unity, the One opposed by the Other, which he saw as the fundamental opposition of the universe, and some reconciling third. This interplay became reified and formalized in Jung's theory of the transcendent function.

Interestingly, though Jung saw the opposites as united in the third, he did not agree with the Pythagorean and Platonic views of three as representing totality and an ultimate wholeness. For Jung, that meaning was connected with the number four. His writings are replete with references to four and the quaternity as the symbols of unity and wholeness. Jung says at one point, "The number three is not a natural expression of wholeness, since four represents the minimum number of determinants in a whole judgment" (1944/1953, p. 26). He expands upon this thought later:

> Three is not a natural coefficient of order, but an artificial one. There are four elements, four prime qualities, four colours, four castes, four ways of spiritual development in Buddhism, etc. So, too, there are four aspects of psychological orientation [sensation, thinking, feeling, intuition]. . . . The fourfold aspect is the minimum requirement for a complete judgment. The ideal of completeness is the circle or sphere, but its natural minimal division is the quaternity. (1948/1958, p. 167)

Jung believed that while the third and three are important to the process of uniting the opposites (the two), the transformation of the three leads to the wholeness of the four.

The number three and the third have a long cultural, religious, and mythical history. In some paradigms, three is symbolic of unity and perfection, and in others of transformation, movement, and balance. Jung was not only aware of such history but explicitly referenced and discussed it in his works, and it undoubtedly played a significant part in his ideation and imagery. The transcendent function has a three-part kind of structure because it is a reflection of the archetypal synthesis and balance for which psyche strives. Archetypally, the three is an answer to the "twoness" of the binary opposition inherent in consciousness. That is, if the brain or psychological functioning separates things into opposing pairs, the third is the natural attempt to bring them into interaction with one another. This interplay between separation and bringing together is what we turn to next.

RHYTHM OF CONSCIOUSNESS BETWEEN DIFFERENTIATION AND UNITY

We tend to describe psychological phenomena and structures in static terms, possibly as a defense against the overwhelming feeling that might be caused were we to acknowledge how fluid, changing, and even unstable they really are. Viewed more dynamically, what emerges is a pattern of oscillation between two polarized or disparate psychological states described variously as conscious/unconscious, subjective/objective, personal/impersonal, inner/outer, differentiated/unified, separated/merged. Jung makes several references to a rhythm between consciousness and the unconscious through the transcendent function. In "The Transcendent Function" essay itself (1957/1960), Jung describes the operation of the transcendent function as "the shuttling to and fro of arguments and affects" (p. 90). Elsewhere, he describes how opposites are united, but only temporarily or partially, and then manifest themselves again: "The renewed conflict demands the same treatment" (1921/1971, p. 115). Through a series of interactions, the transcendent function "progressively unites the opposites" (1955, p. 690). In describing the counter-position in the unconscious constantly interacting with consciousness, Jung refers to Goethe's analogy of the rhythmic beating of a heart: "Goethe's idea of a systole and diastole seems to have hit the mark intuitively. It may well be a question of a vital rhythm, of fluctuations of vital forces" (1921/1971, p. 253).

Other Jungian and post-Jungian theorists have also incorporated the idea of psychic rhythm into their writings. Fordham's deintegration-reintegration cycle, for example, is explicitly rhythmic in its operation. The process of the deintegration and reintegration is ongoing for the infant. "Fordham finds ego development [development of consciousness] to be a consequence of repeated deintegration of the self. This ego development . . . always reflects the dynamic operation of the self in its cycles of deintegrating and reintegrating"

(Naifeh, 1993, p. 9). Although he originally focused his thinking on the development of ego in the infant and child, Fordham later (1985) expanded his theory to hypothesize that the cycle is lifelong. An analogous notion of shifting consciousness is noted by Edinger (1972). In his discussion of the "ego-Self axis," a construct that he explicitly acknowledges (p. 38, fn. 3) was first named and explored by Neumann (1966), Edinger attempts to describe the pattern of consciousness that emerges from the "close structural and dynamic affinity" (p. 38) of the ego and the Self. He theorizes that we cycle between two states that he called "ego-Self separation" (an experience of separateness from the Self), similar to Fordham's deintegrative state, and "ego-Self union" (an experience of congruence between conscious and unconscious), similar to Fordham's reintegrative state (1972, p. 6). Edinger postulates that human consciousness is a lifetime process of shifting back and forth between the two states in a cycle or spiral:

> The process of alternation between ego-Self union and ego-Self separation seems to occur repeatedly throughout the life of the individual both in childhood and in maturity. Indeed, this cyclic (or better, spiral) formula seems to express the basic process of psychological development from birth to death (p. 5).

Others have expressed comparable ideas: "rhythmic back and forth movement" between I and the Other (Solomon, 1992, p. 132); movement "back and forth between layers of meaning" (Young-Eisendrath, 1992, p. 153); "active submission to deep and unknowable currents of change and recurrence, growth and decay, systole and diastole" (Joseph, 1997, p. 150); deintegration and reintegration cycle between people and between parts of people (Solomon, 1992, p. 132); and an oscillation "between experiences of plurality and unity" (Corbett, 1992, p. 398).

Support for the cyclic or spiraling shifts in consciousness can be found from a number of other disciplines and sources. In science, Corbett (1996) references Bohm's theories of a rhythmic interaction between the discrete, differentiated realm of physics that we know and a realm he calls the "implicate order" of undivided wholeness that is outside the bounds of time and space and is the common ground of both matter and consciousness (p. 137). Another physicist (Bentov, 1977) hypothesized that all creation can be divided into two alternating realms: the "absolute" that is fixed, eternal, and invisible and the "relative" that is the visible, manifest, and changing aspect (p. 89). Oscillating energy is a key part of chaos theory (Van Eenwyk, 1992, p. 276) as well as basic molecular physics. Alternating hemispheric activity has also been found to be an important part of brain chemistry (Ross, 1986, p. 238). In alchemy, moving toward the opus is seen as a cycle of steps between different stages and the *coniunctio*, the uniting of opposites is always followed by the *nigredo*, the state of disorganization and putrefication that breaks and transforms things (Schwartz-Salant, 1995, p. 12).

All these references converge to a single point: there is an attribute of energic matters that involves cycles, spirals, or oscillations back and forth. What Jung first theorized with the transcendent function is that psychological energy is no different; it will move in cycles or spirals. This point is summarized by Samuels:

> Parts of the psyche can move together and, conversely, apart. This rhythm of combining and uniting on the one hand, and on the other, separating, differentiating and discriminating, turns out to be an important theme in Jung and a vital one for the post-Jungians. (1985, pp. 8–9)

Though the different theories express the rhythm of consciousness in different terms, taken together they express the sense in which human existence is located in two experiences: (1) one part that feels localized within us, the personal, where we are each the subject of what happens, where we are differentiated and separated from others, and of which we are generally conscious; and (2) another part that feels like it may be located outside of us, the impersonal or transpersonal, where we are the object of things that happen to us promulgated by larger forces, where we are unified or merged with others in a kind of greater cosmic organism, and of which we are generally unconscious. What Jung may have first expressed is that these two parts of human experience are constantly held in a tension and/or interact in a sort of rhythm the exact nature of which we yearn to understand. The diagram below represents the rhythmic shifting of energy between these two realms.

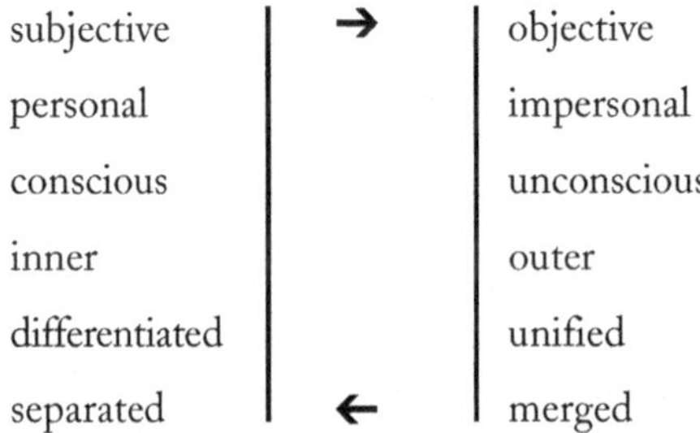

The cyclic movement of energy is a fact of both material and psychological life. It would occur with or without a transcendent function or any other liminal structure. The transcendent function is a label given to describe what we observe. It is an attempt to explain what appears to be an archetypal occurrence: the rhythm of consciousness.

THE TRANSCENDENT: CONNECTION WITH A GREATER CONSCIOUSNESS

The transcendent function clearly implicates matters of transcendence in a spiritual or divine sense. Though Jung took great pains to state explicitly in his writings that the transcendent function is not imbued with metaphysical or spiritual overtones (1921/1971, p. 480; 1928/1953, p. 224; 1957/1960, p. 68), saying it does not make it so. Dealing with matters deemed metaphysical or mystical to most, Jung had a real (and probably justified) sensitivity to being seen by his peers as unscientific. However, it is undeniable that his writing is replete with discussions of and references to religious and spiritual material. Jung attempted to deflect possible criticism "by constantly assuring us that all his theoretical statements . . . were not intended as metaphysical statements . . . and that he was, e.g., not speaking about God himself, but only about the God image in the psyche" (Giegerich, 1987, p. 110). This may be why some believe there is a clear reflection of the Divine in the transcendent function despite Jung's protestations to the contrary:

> This is what Jung means by the word transcendent—that third point of view which rises out of, unites, and thus transcends the warring opposites. He takes pains, almost protesting too much, to say he does not mean something metaphysical (Jung 1971, par. 828). I think Jung is avoiding the religious here and suggest that it is precisely through the workings of the transcendent function that we receive evidence of the Transcendent in the metaphysical sense operating within us, much like religious tradition describes the Spirit of God moving us to pray. What comes to us as a successful solution arising out of the transcendent function impresses us as a marvelous, novel, even grace-filled answer to our inner conflict, and convinces us of an abiding presence that knows us in our most intimate battles of our soul. (Ulanov, 1996, p. 194)

One author even asserts that Jung's relatively comprehensive explication of the more abstract aspects of the transcendent function, together with his failure to explore in detail its clinical applications, "raises the question of whether Jung ultimately became more of a theologian than a psychologist" (Horne, 1998, p. 26).

Whether Jung himself saw or acknowledged a connection between spirituality/divinity and the transcendent function is not the focus of this exploration. It is there; it is both unavoidable and important. Without advocating a particular religious orientation, there is something numinous and unexplainable about the transcendent function that implicates powers greater than ourselves. These "powers" may be psychological and not divine but in this context the distinction makes no difference. Indeed, in some sense, numinous, religious, and archetypal are synonymous qualities:

> Numinous experience is synonymous with religious experience. Translated into psychological parlance, this means the relatively direct experience of those deep intrapsychic structures known as archetypes. . . . In the religious literature, what the depth psychologist calls an archetype wold be referred to as spirit; operationally they are synonymous. (Corbett, 1996, p. 15)

The point is that the occurrence and engagement of the transcendent function moves us into a liminal place where we come into contact with the larger consciousness of which we are a part.

That the transcendent function arises from a broader and deeper divine landscape is evident from both Jung's writings and those of post-Jungian writers. In a letter written in 1954, just seven years before his death, Jung refers to the transcendent function as a natural phenomenon, part of the process of individuation, and says, "Psychology has no proof that this process does not unfold itself at the instigation of God's will" (1955, p. 690). In at least three other contexts, Jung connects the transcendent function to God, the voice of God, the grace of God, and the will of God (1939/1958, p. 488, 506; 1958/1964, p. 455). Post-Jungian writers also make frequent reference to the transcendent function as arising from the Transcendent. Ulanov (1992, 1996, 1997) makes extensive reference to the connection between the transcendent function and variously God, It, Isness, and the Transcendent. Her extensive work, *The Functioning Transcendent* (1996), explicitly refers to that connection and discusses the ways that the Transcendent and a conscious connection with it can be more fully incorporated into our everyday lives. Writers from other cultures have also drawn parallels with the operation of the transcendent function and the divine in their cultures. Joseph (1997), who coins the term "transcendent functioning" for the operation of the transcendent function, concludes that its foundation is the Transcendent:

> "God" is the Real, ineffable and vast beyond speaking or imagining, the ever-fresh source, known through world and wellspring. "God," the Real, is the true subject, the one who alone truly says "I." . . . And "transcendent functioning" is the name we give the *psychological* process of repairing and healing the Real and redeeming it from its exiles. (p. 155)

The Transcendent is elusive. Humanity is engaged in a perpetual effort to understand the Greater Consciousness. The world's religions have struggled to come to terms with it. The transcendent function, though couched in psychological terminology and encompassed by Jung's greater theory, is yet another effort to give voice to that connection. Maybe the musings about opposites, energy, symbol, and individuation are just our own frail, human way to explain something unexplainable; maybe psyche is really transformed and transcended by the grace of some Higher Power that we have attempted to understand since the dawn of humanity. The transcendent function clearly implicates a search for and contact with the Transcendent.

THE NEITHER/NOR AND AUTOCHTHONOUS URGES OF THE PSYCHE

The deeper roots of the transcendent function reflect a particular view of psyche that moves beyond divisions into dialogue and relationship. It is a vision of psyche that rejects either/or classifications and instead embraces a neither/nor stance. This perspective has been urged by Romanyshyn (1982, 1989, 1996, 2001, 2002) through his extensive writings and teachings on the harm done to psychological life through the either/or paradigm of modern science and technology and the need to reclaim key aspects of that life by, instead, adopting such a neither/nor posture. According to this way of thinking, when the psyche is confronted with mutually exclusive, logical opposites, it holds both and, in that holding, allows a new awareness to emerge; this is the neither/nor urge of the psyche. The dualistic thinking of human consciousness tends to block psychological growth and cause stagnation. Psyche, however, seeks to move beyond the "imagined" blockages into the terrain of neither/nor and it uses the transcendent function to do so. Put another way, psyche pushes us to seek the route between opposing positions to imagine what position (symbol or image) might hold pieces of them both without rejecting either; it demands that we find the neither/nor instead of choosing either/or. Introducing his concept of psyche or soul as the middle ground between idea (*esse in intellectu*) and thing (*esse in re*), and in so doing rejecting Kant's absolute formulation of *either* idea *or* thing, Jung (1921/1971) says:

> From the standpoint of logic, there is, as always, no *tertium* between the logical either-or. But between *intellectus* and *res* there is still *anima*, and this *esse in anima* makes the whole ontological argument [Kant's argument that there is a fundamental division between idea and thing] superfluous. . . . The *esse in anima*, then, is a psychological fact, and the only thing that needs ascertaining is whether it occurs but once, often, or universally in human psychology. (pp. 45–46)

Here Jung begins to articulate an idea that reaches full fruition in Hillman and archetypal psychology: that psyche is autonomous and does not "think" in logical ways. Psyche's primary activity is fantasy and image-making. It is neither required to follow, nor is it interested in being bound by, rational arguments. In its own time and in its own way, psyche seeks nonrational ways to find relationships between things that do not seem logically related. Jung describes that this process happens irrationally through the finding of an image that holds pieces of both and neither of the opposites:

> In practice, opposites can be united only in the form of a compromise, or *irrationally*, some new thing arising between them which, although different from both, yet has the power to take up their energies in equal measure as an *expression of both and of neither* [italics added]. (1921/1971, p. 105)

Psyche is not inside us; we are inside it. The either/or dualities we impose on the world around us are more for us to make sense of something we do not fully understand. Psyche pushes us toward the neither/nor reality where relationships rather than distinctions between things is the order of the day. By refusing to wall ourselves off with artificial dualities, we can move deeper into relationship with the world around us and with one another.

Thought of in this way, the transcendent function is simply psyche's way of reconnecting with the interiority of all things, of seeing the hidden dimensionality of itself and everything in reality. The transcendent function becomes a central subject in depth psychology because it helps us understand the constant urge of psyche to move deeper, to see more deeply into exactly what is transpiring. Hillman (1975) passionately exhorts us to avoid the more common psychological inquires of *why* and *how* and instead focus squarely on the deeper aspects of *what.*

> "What?" proceeds straight into an event. The search for "whatness" or quiddity, the interior identity of an event, its essence, takes one into depth. It is a question from the soul of the questioner that quests for the soul of the happening. "What" stays right with the matter, asking it to state itself again, to repeat itself in other terms, to re-present itself by means of other images. "What" implies that everything everywhere is matter for the psyche, matters to it—is significative, offers a spark, releases or feeds soul. (p. 138).

Elsewhere, Hillman (1979) has termed this urge of the psyche to constantly seek the deeper, invisible "whatness" of every event the "autochthonous" (from the Greek chthōn, meaning "earth" and *chthón(ios)* meaning "beneath the earth") urge of the psyche:

> The innate urge to go below appearances to the "invisible connection" and hidden constitution leads to the world interior to what is

> given. This autochthonous urge of the psyche, its native desire to understand psychologically, would seem to be akin to what Freud calls the *death drive* and what Plato presented as the desire for Hades. (p. 27)

In discussing the realm of Hades,[5] Hillman states emphatically that, "Hades is not an absence, but a hidden presence—even an invisible fullness" (p. 28). The underworld is a place of affirmative interiority, where the interior, deeper aspects of all things are present to be seen. Hillman moves even further, saying that the underworld should not be seen as a separate *place* that happens or is visited only at certain times but rather an everpresent perspective that views things in depth, in their darkness, in their invisibility at the same time that we see them in their light in the upper world:

> The brotherhood of Zeus and Hades says that the upper and lower worlds are the same; only the perspectives differ. There is only one and the same universe, coexistent and synchronous, but one brother's view sees it from above and through the light, the other below and into its darkness. Hades' realm is contiguous with life, touching it at all points, just below it, its shadow brother . . . giving life its depth and its psyche. (p. 32)

Thus, the underworld is a perspective more than a place, a perspective that is ever present, always available to us when we wish to see the darkness, hidden presence, invisible fullness of things—when we wish to see that which we do not allow in our conscious upper world.

The neither/nor and autochthonous urges of the psyche are at the root of the transcendent function. Psyche seeks to deepen events into experiences by moving beyond the paradigm of either/or dualities. It seeks to make connections and mediate relationships between things that might not otherwise be connected or related. In this vision of the radical nature of the psyche, its reason for seeking the interiority or invisible nature of all things is not based upon compensating for or balancing any conscious or ego position, but rather, in a manner of speaking, for its own pleasure, to see more deeply into itself. To put it another way, psyche uses the transcendent function to view the unseen because it wishes to understand its experiencess psychologically, to see itself more clearly.

This chapter has toured the deeper foundations of the transcendent function. Through an exploration of the universal themes of the opposites, the subject-object chasm, liminality and initiation, Hermes, the third, the rhythm of consciousness, and transcendence, we sought information about psyche's use of these psychological instrumentalities. The landmarks encountered throughout the trek all pointed in the same direction: toward finding connection and relationships where none seemed to exist, crossing boundaries not normally crossed, and transcending differences. Following the directions implicit in the material we arrived at the neither/nor and autochthonous urges of the psyche. With these deeper themes as our anchor, let us now turn to how the transcendent function may be used and applied in life outside the consulting room.

CHAPTER SEVEN

VIVIFYING THE TRANSCENDENT FUNCTION IN EVERYDAY LIFE

This final chapter focuses on synthesis and application. Having explored the transcendent function as a Jungian concept, as a root metaphor, and as an archetypal, mediatory phenomenon, we conclude by turning to more practical concerns. How can we better recognize and apply the transcendent function in our lives? How does the notion that Jung first described in 1916 manifest itself outside of the consulting room? Do we find it, for example, in relationships, in culture, and in our institutions? Are there ways in which we can increase its presence or at least increase our awareness of it? Is the expansive view of the transcendent function helpful in this regard? These questions require us to weave together the strands we teased out earlier.

Here we attempt to blend the concepts to bring the material to bear in a tangible way. Depth psychology serves only a limited purpose by remaining confined to the boundaries of the consulting room and the pages of scholarly works. Increasing awareness of and integration of the unconscious in individual psychotherapy is all well and good. But depth psychology needs to do more. The unconscious erupts into relationships, the culture, and the world in ways that require as much, if not more, attention by our field. Depth psychologists are conspicuously absent from the discussion of crucial issues of our time. Beneath each and every divisive split in our cultural, societal, and political lives lies unacknowledged material that needs to be identified, discussed, and brought to the surface. An expansive view and discussion of the transcendent function can assist us in addressing these issues. This chapter seeks to usher the transcendent function out of the relative quiet of the analytic situation and the academic world into the hustle and bustle of everyday life.

THE METAPHORICAL VIEW OF THE TRANSCENDENT FUNCTION

Notwithstanding Jung's effort to simply define and describe it in his 1916 paper, the transcendent function thwarts our efforts to give it clear outlines. Chapter 4 identified two distinct images of the transcendent function: the "narrow" transcendent function, a process within Jung's psychology pursuant to which opposites are united, and an "expansive" transcendent function, a much broader root metaphor for becoming psychological through an interaction with the unconscious, unknown, or other. Then in chapter 6, working explicitly with the transcendent function as a root metaphor, we explored the deeper archetypal patterns it implicates and enunciated the neither/nor and autochthonous urges of the psyche to find connections where none seemed possible and to move deeper.

Here we seek to further explore the expansive transcendent function as a metaphor for becoming psychological, a conversation between that which is known, conscious, or acknowledged and that which is unknown, unconscious, or hidden through which something new emerges. Though this metaphoric view of the transcendent function conjures up a core image that may best be described as "developing deeper awareness," it appears in various forms such as those discussed in chapter 6. Indeed, post-Jungian writers variously conceptualize the transcendent function in ways that are consistent with each of the archetypal patterns we discussed: the role of the transcendent function in overcoming the binary opposition inherent in consciousness;[1] its initiatory and transformative aspects;[2] its bridging or liminal qualities;[3] the rhythm of consciousness between differentiation and unity;[4] and the way it implicates divinity. Implicit in these references is the thrust of the second half of this book: beyond its delineated role in Jungian psychology (the "narrow" transcendent function), the transcendent function is a metaphor for psyche's yearning to create connections rather than separating, to savor the unknown rather than asserting knowledge as a way to order things. As one writer summarized it, "The transcendent function is realized synchronistically when there is a shift away from a desire to know and control toward a desire to relate and understand" (Beebe, 1992, p. 118).

The broader, metaphorical vision of the transcendent function is crucial to gaining greater insight into its appearance and use in interpersonal, cultural, and everyday contexts. Jung's description in his original essay, though helpful in understanding the abstract concepts implicated in a dialogue between consciousness and the unconscious, is not very useful in animating the transcendent function. His discussions in his other works are also interesting but they are devoid of how to bring the transcendent function more to life. In order to understand how the transcendent function affects us on a daily basis, the following discussion adopts the root metaphorical/expansive view of the transcendent function, the focus on the relationship between the known, conscious, or acknowledged and the unknown, unconscious, or hidden, through which something new emerges.

TILLING THE TRANSCENDENT FUNCTION WITH THE ALCHEMICAL METAPHOR

To further explore the metaphorical transcendent function and its impacts outside of the analytical situation, we turn to a curious analogy: alchemy, the ancient art of transmuting base metals into valuable ones. At the heart of the transcendent function is what some have called "alchemical thinking" or an "alchemical attitude" (see, e.g., Schwartz-Salant, 1998; Romanyshyn, 1996). Alchemy was concerned with creating qualitative changes in substances, specifically transforming base metals into gold or silver. Its importance to this work (indeed, to depth psychology generally) lies in its conviction that "outer" changes in the substances corresponded with "inner" changes in the alchemist's psyche; as the alchemical endeavor proceeds, transformation occurs in both the alchemist and the substance. Indeed, some would say that the transformation of the alchemist is the true focus of alchemy:

> Gold-making was not the major concern of alchemy but rather was part of the alchemical metaphor of personality transformation. . . . [A]lchemy was a system of transformation, and its genius lay in the assumption that change was part of an interaction between subject and object in which both were transformed. (Schwartz-Salant, 1998, p. 11)

Alchemy holds that subject and object, indeed all opposites, are joined in an unseen way by a universal process or substance, called the *lapis*, which imbues all creation, even the human mind and body. Alchemy also posited that "outer" and "inner" are merged in a space called the "subtle body" that mediates between spirit and matter. Instead of separating them, alchemy sees spirit/matter, inner/outer, and subject/object as related in some profound way.

Prevalent in Renaissance Europe during the fifteenth and sixteenth centuries, as reflected in historically important texts such as *Rosarium Philosophorum* (1550) and *Splendor Solis* (1582), alchemy experienced a precipitous fall from grace with the emergence of science, the tenets of which were in direct conflict with those of alchemy. Science trumpets objectivity, the ability and desirability of separating the observing subject from the observed object; alchemy believes in purposeful subjectivity, emphasizing the inherent role of the subject in changing the object. Science insists upon a strict separation of inner and outer whereas alchemy merges them in the subtle body:

> In contrast to modern scientific methods, the alchemical tradition is a testimony to the power of subjectivity. Rather than an "objective" attempt to carefully situate a difference between process in matter and the psychology of the experimenter, in alchemy the spiritual and physical transformation of the subject is an integral part of the work of transforming matter. . . . The merger of outer and inner occurs in a space that alchemists called the "subtle body," a strange area this neither material nor spiritual, but mediating between them. (Schwartz-Salant, 1998, p. 11)

Science seeks to find order in things and determine their cause; alchemy is more comfortable with disorder and is not concerned with causality. Rather than seeking the differences between things, alchemy searches for their connections. Relatedness, not causality, is alchemy's focus. Some have linked the emphasis on relationships in alchemy to its belief in the workings of soul, which lives in relationship:

> Alchemy's insistence on the linkage between subject and object followed its concern for the soul, the inner life that moves of its own accord, independent of cause. This quality of soul is the reason that causal concerns are of far less significance for the alchemical mind than for our own. Because the soul lives in relationship, the quality of relationship, characterized in alchemical science by a concern for the relation *per se*, and not the things related, defined alchemy. (p. 13)

The focus on the relationship between things (the relation per se) and the implications of that relationship rather than on what distinguishes and defines the things themselves is alchemy's fundamental difference with science.

One can see from this brief review that alchemy and the transcendent function have commonalities. Fundamental to each are the ideas of the relationship between opposites, the creation of a container in which the opposites are held, the mediating influence of a transcendent force, and the emergence of a transformation. The alchemical endeavor employs the transcendent function; the transcendent function is alchemical in its core.

THE NEITHER/NOR AND THE METAPHORICAL THIRD

Science and alchemy unfold in fundamentally different ways: scientific thinking is either/or in nature while alchemical thinking is metaphorical, and neither/nor in its focus. The workings of the transcendent function are alchemical and are psyche's way of overcoming the either/or. Hence we explore these parallel ideas further here.

This exploration is founded upon and is an extension of the teachings and writings of Romanyshyn (1982, 1989, 1996, 2001, 2002). In his work, he, among other things, mourns the loss in psychological life resulting from the advance of science and technology and its dualistic, either/or way of viewing reality. He espouses a renewed embrace of soul by using what he calls metaphoric sensibility and alchemical thinking through which apparent dualities are suspended opening psychological life to the emergence of new images, unseen connections, a relationship with the divine, and a truly living psyche.

The scientific attitude reflects the tendency in human consciousness to split and hold things in a dualistic, either/or way; we create mutually exclusive categories (such as mind/body, spirit/matter, fact/idea, subjective/objective, interior/exterior, self/other, etc.) and organize things by forcing them into one or the other. Though there are many theories about the genesis of this phenomenon, there is no doubt it profoundly affects how we view the world: we are immersed in the Cartesian assumption that all reality consists of an observing subject separated from the world outside.[5] This duality of the "observing self-subject" and the "outside world-object" then forms the foundation for seeing all reality in the very same either/or way. By consistently splitting reality into opposing camps, this approach weakens and even disclaims the connections between the very things it is categorizing; by portraying reality as sets of opposites, this way of knowing and being creates splits, rifts, gaps that jar and disorient. The interconnectedness between parts of the cosmos is so elemental that this dualizing consciousness feels foreign, like a built-in cognitive dissonance. The scientific way of knowing misses, even dismisses, the connections that form the basic fabric of cosmological existence.

Alchemical thinking, manifested in the transcendent function, rejects the either/or approach. Just as alchemy sought the ultimate substance that connects all things, alchemical thinking seeks the connection in seemingly unconnected things, indeed, in all things. It sees all dualities as neither one nor the other but rather as being related in some way. Alchemical thinking is based in the neither/nor of the alchemical metaphor that change in the physical world mirrors change in psyche. This metaphor, like all metaphors, does not say that the two things being compared are the same, but rather that there is some unseen relationship *between* them. Instead of splitting matters, alchemy invites them to combine. "The metaphorical basis of alchemy, like metaphor in general, combines different orders of reality, like matter and psyche. Science splits them and becomes the beholder of order, ordering the supposed disorder of matter" (Schwartz-Salant, 1998, p. 13). Just as a metaphor invokes an image that is separate from the subject of the metaphor and the thing to which it is compared, alchemical thinking invokes such a metaphorical, third presence. Unlike science which focuses on the things related, alchemy concerns itself with the relationship, space, or field between them:

> Thus, a different universe of experience is the object of the alchemical endeavor. It is an "in between" world of "relations," occurring in a space that is not-Cartesian, and instead is characterized by a paradoxical relationship in which "outer" and "inner" are alternatingly both distinct and the same. Within the paradoxical geometry of this space . . . an "intermediate" realm between matter and psyche, the alchemist believed that "relations *per se*" could be transformed. (p. 13)

Instead of seeing reality in "two's" (i.e., "observing subject" and "observed object"), the alchemical attitude emphasizes the "threeness" of every situation; between the observer and the object is the relationship between the two. The relationship, the intermediate space or field between the two, that is neither one thing nor the other, is the "metaphorical third." It is more a process than a thing, the process of being aware that every subject-object experience creates a neither/nor, metaphorical space where a relationship may be found between the two. The logos of psyche is not a linear, logical, causal tale to be tracked like the data of an experiment; it needs a different way of thinking. Alchemy, with its demands to engage in metaphor and constantly look for the relationship between, provides the model.

Thus, it comes as no surprise that Jung focused on alchemy. The metaphorical third provided him a necessary tool for the way he worked with psyche. Alchemical thinking, along with the metaphorical third that underlies it, is the foundation for understanding the transformation Jung himself went through and then posited in the form of the transcendent function. Speaking more broadly, alchemical thinking underlies all of the liminal phenomena examined in this book. The very role of all the transitional mechanisms is to form the connective tissue between disparate psychic states. The transcendent function is the tissue between consciousness and the unconscious; it is the expression of the space or field that mediates between the two. The other phenomena discussed are, in one way or the other, analogous. The transcendent function is the embodiment of the metaphorical third, a process or space in which opposites are held, where the choice between either one or the other is suspended so that the relationship between them becomes the focus.

THE GERMINATION OF THE ALCHEMICAL FOURTH

Alchemy also allows us to move a step deeper in understanding the archetypal patterns discussed in chapter 6. Jung and others make reference to an alchemical principle called "The Axiom of Maria," which hypothesizes that all transformation results from energy patterns involving the numbers one through four. It states "Out of the One comes the Two, out of the Two comes the Three, and from the Three comes the Four as the One" (Schwartz-Salant,

1998, p. 64). The One represents a state prior to order that is chaotic and confusing, "before opposites have separated" (p. 64). The Two is the "beginning of making 'sense' of the phenomenon, the emergence of a pair of opposites" (p. 64). This is the state where matters seem to emerge as pairs, the parts of which dynamically oppose one another. The Three "is the creation of the third thing, the field" (p. 64) from the Two. This is what was termed the "metaphorical third" in the discussion above. Here, the opposites are held so that they create a kind of vessel that is separate from but at the same time contains them. Jung described the "Three" flowing from the opposites:

> This vacillating between the opposites and being tossed back and forth means being contained *in* the opposites. They become a vessel in which what was previously now one thing and now another floats vibrating, so that the painful suspension between opposites gradually changes into the bilateral activity of the point in the centre. (1955–1956/1963, p. 223)

The field or vessel is paradoxical in that it is both distinct from and yet comprised of its elements. The Four is "the experience of the Third as it now links to a state of Oneness of existence" (Schwartz-Salant, 1998, p. 65). Through the experience of the Three (the vessel) something new emerges: the Four as One, a sense of Oneness.

> In the movement to the Fourth, the alchemical idea that all substances (such as sulphur, lead, and water) have two forms—one "ordinary" and the other "philosophical"—can be experienced. In essence, affects cease to be experienced as "ordinary," as "things," and instead become something more—states of wholeness. (p. 65)

The Axiom of Maria evokes imagery of movement from a primitive unity (the One), to separation of the opposites (the Two), into a vessel or field in which the opposites reside in tension (the Three), and to a place of transcendence or Oneness (the Four as the One).

The Axiom of Maria is extremely helpful in our work with the transcendent function. First, each of the archetypal patterns we discussed seems to fall within the numerical progression of the axiom. More importantly, however, the Axiom of Maria allows us to see that in the workings of the transcendent function there are actually four elements: the two opposites, the transcendent function process, and the transformed, new attitude, what we have been calling the third. The two opposites (psychic states) are mediated by the process or container of the transcendent function; thus, viewed through the lens of the Axiom of Maria, the process of the transcendent function is the movement from the Two to the Three. It is the metaphorical third, the field or the relationship between the two opposites. It is the metaphoric, neither/nor space where the opposites sit in tension, vacillate, oscillate, and allow a shift in consciousness. The new, third thing that emerges from the operation of the third is actually a fourth, what may be called the alchemical fourth. When it emerges, it is a totally new consciousness, not an amalgam of the two disparate elements but some part of the Oneness that connects them. Schematically, this view of transcendent function is represented by the following diagram:

new, third thing
(alchemical fourth)

▲

conscious position → transcendent function ← unconscious
(metaphorical third)

This discussion harkens back to and helps clarify the ambiguity in Jung's writings about whether the transcendent function is a function, process, or final result. The reader will recall that Jung variously refers to the transcendent function as the process by which that tension of the opposites is held and the final result that emerges. This is the difference between the metaphorical third and the alchemical fourth. The transcendent function is the field or vessel in which the opposites are cooked; the new thing that emerges is the alchemical fourth.

PLOWING THE TRANSCENDENT FUNCTION FIELD IN RELATIONSHIPS

Though we normally think of the transcendent function as a personal, intrapsychic phenomenon, it is much more. Since psyche is transpersonal, so are the presence and effects of the transcendent function. The unconscious is not something that is solely accessed and integrated within the confines of therapy. Every relationship, analytic or otherwise, is imbued with the unconscious and is a vessel in which the transcendent function is always at work. Depth psychology would do well to exit the relative quiet of the analytic situation and walk out into the bustling world where the unconscious raucously cascades over all of us.

It is not a new idea in depth psychology that the contents of the unconscious erupt in relationships. That notion is the very heart of the idea of projection. Freud and Jung both spent substantial time and effort exploring this idea and, though in slightly different ways, both saw the essence of projection as based on something unconscious being transmitted into a relationship. As one writer, commenting on Jung's conception of projection, states it, "Jung defined projection as an unconscious, that is unperceived and unintentional, transfer of subjective psychic elements onto an outer object" (von Franz, 1980b, p. 3). In essence, projection itself is a kind of imaginary relationship between a person and the image of unconscious material projected or transferred onto another person: "In these imaginary relationships the other person becomes an *image* or a *carrier of symbols*" (p. 6).

Though we often think of projection as something negative to be discouraged, the perspective offered here is that virtually all relationships, whether with people or with the world around us, are ontologically based in projection. Indeed, from a depth psychological perspective, the very purpose of relationships may be to provide us a mirror through which to view, experience, confront, know, and integrate unconscious parts of psyche. Succinctly stated, "As living forms of exchange, relationships mediate between a person and his or her unconscious psyche" (Schwartz-Salant, 1998, p. 218). Relationships are a vehicle (like drawing, sculpture, active imagination, journaling, therapy, meditation, prayer, etc.) through which unconscious material emerges; interactions with other people are ideal containers for viewing unconscious material that might otherwise remain hidden.

From the vantage point of this study, relationships are a vessel in which the transcendent function is constantly at work. Indeed, relationships reify the transcendent function. Just as in analysis, every relationship has both conscious and unconscious dyads constantly at work. Relationships create a field in which, in one way or another, we are always confronted with aspects of the unconscious. Schwartz-Salant (1998) calls this field a "third area" between the two participants, a space where distinctions between subject/object and inner/outer disappear, where the unconscious can be experienced and transformation achieved:

> We must move beyond the notion of life as consisting of outer and inner experiences and enter a kind of "intermediate realm" that our culture has long lost sight of and in which the major portion of transformation occurs. As we perceive such a shared reality with another person, and as we actually focus on it, allowing it to have its own life, like a "third thing" in the relationship, something new can occur. The space that we occupy seems to change, and rather than being the subjects, observing this "third thing," we begin to feel we are inside it and moved by it. We become the object, and the space itself and its emotional states are the subject. In such experiences, the old forms of relationship die and transform. It is as if we have become aware of a far larger presence in our relationship, indeed a sacred dimension. (pp. 5–6)

Though Schwartz-Salant never connects his notion of the "third thing" or "third area" to the transcendent function, it is functionally the same; his third area is the metaphoric third, the transcendent function, where conscious and unconscious come together to produce something new, the alchemical fourth.

The idea of the transcendent function as the field provides new perspective on relationships. An interaction between me and Mr. X involves, me, Mr. X, and the field (the metaphorical third) between us. It is important to remember that the field is not just the physical space but the emotional, mental, psychic, and spiritual presence around us. When a topic or feeling emerges, we can surrender the idea that one of us motivated it or even that it "belongs" to either of us. Instead, we can open to the possibility that this is the way psyche brings issues, emotions, and insights to us through a process we do not understand. Instead of focusing on our respective subjective experiences, using the transcendent function in this way requires us to let go of knowing whom the content of the interaction began with and assume that it relates to us both:

> To do this, one must be willing to sacrifice the power of knowing "whose content" one is dealing with and instead imagine that the content . . . exists in the field itself and does not necessarily belong to either person. The content can be imaginally thrust into the field . . . so that it becomes a "third thing." (Schwartz-Salant, 1995, p. 5)

Sacrificing the power of knowing is key to this process. By this way of being, psyche is a living, breathing presence bringing content to us for movement toward greater awareness. That is, nothing just happens; each person coparticipates in an autonomous, unconscious field generated by psyche, and there is something that each can gain by standing back and asking what the field offers. This view of personal interactions does not mean that we ignore what is occurring between the participants on an interpersonal level. Apologies or explanations may need to be made, communication styles may need to be talked about, ways of resolving similar issues may need to be discussed. This analysis holds, however, that there is generally something hidden or deeper going on and that the surface interaction is the doorway into that metaphoric field.

Envisioning the transcendent function as constantly at work in relationships has two notable impacts, both of which are critical to the depth psychological endeavor. First, rather than attempting to locate the source of the feeling in myself or the other person, I can fully experience it and search for the deeper meaning of its eruption. Instead of "I am angry at you" (which, of course, may be true), one would merely note that there is anger "in the field." Thus, in place of trying to resolve the anger, one might just ponder what growth experience it may be offering. By stepping back from the knowledge that the anger is "mine" or "yours," we can enter the field and seek a deeper meaning that transcends our respective positions. A second and even more important implication of this notion is that by entering the field instead of trying to locate and explain the feeling, the participants can actually open to the other issues that psyche is presenting. The anger may be a small passageway that opens into a larger psychic field where there is crucial learning for both people; by avoiding the trap of giving undue scrutiny to the doorway, we can enter the room where the real treasure lies. Viewing the transcendent function as the metaphoric field in every relationship interaction allows us to move beyond the issue that appears on the surface to the richer and more complex, psychic terrain beneath.

A personal illustration here may help. Soon after completing the first draft of this section, my wife and I were traveling in Italy. On an otherwise sunny morning in Venice, the storm clouds of marital strife gathered suddenly. Soon we were embroiled in a heated argument. I felt that my wife was being overly dependent on me and making me do things I did not want to do; she felt I was being nasty, selfish, and abusive. Since I had just the evening before been sharing my thinking about the transcendent function and the metaphoric third as expressed in the field, we decided to retreat from the battle and try a different approach. She pulled out a small notebook and drew a large circle, a representation of the field. Alternately, we wrote words in the circle describing the energy we were feeling. Without comment from either one of us we wrote the following words alternately in the location in the circle that "felt right" (we both believe that the locations are significant in that they probably express relationships or connections between the words, concepts, and/or energies):

Me	*My Wife*
Childishness	Oppression
Anger	Power
Boundaries	Control
Mother	Responsibility

At that point, we decided to pause and explore what we had written. We agreed that we would each talk about how any of the words struck us but not in relation to our fight or the other person but only in relation to our own lives generally. As we each spoke, the energy shifted to a deeper level almost immediately and we further agreed that either could add words to the field. The following were added: shame, frustration, incompetence, avoidance, locked-out, home, rage, escape. At one point, I was even drawn to connect Mother, control, and power with a triangle; my wife drew connections between Mother, responsibility, incompetence, oppression, and childishness. As we sat under a tree together doing this exercise, we were both profoundly struck by a psychic presence in the field that was separate from both of us. What had started out as an argument about relatively superficial things ended up as a mutual soul-searching exploration into what was being presented to both of us by psyche through the metaphoric field. Though the experience in the moment is not really susceptible to verbal description, we both felt the presence of Mother, control, boundary, and responsibility. Each spoke to us individually in a different way and in a way that moved us differently. When we got past trying to identify what each of us was "doing to the other," we were able to have an experience that felt sacred. What had begun as an adversarial, nasty dispute ended with us walking away, hand in hand, both feeling as though we had been touched by a numinous presence. Both of us attribute what happened to our decision in the heat of the moment to surrender the idea that we knew what was at work psychologically. We were willing to imagine that our emotions were openings into deeper, more powerful material in the field. What emerged was something entirely new, the Mother energy, the alchemical fourth; it transcended and joined the dependence and control I was feeling from my wife and the nastiness, abusiveness, and oppression my wife was feeling from me. As Schwartz-Salant (1995) describes, surrendering to a state of "unknowing" allows movement into a deeper place (the metaphorical third) and the emergence of a *coniunctio* (the alchemical fourth):

> I could, however, choose to forgo such knowledge [of the dynamics of myself or the other person] and to sacrifice it to the state of "unknowing," allowing the unknown to become the focus. I could then ask a silent question: What is the nature of the field between us, what is our unconscious dyad like? In this manner, we open to the field as to an object. . . . That is to say, giving up the power or knowledge *about* another person can leave one in the position of focusing on and being affected by the field itself. . . . A different kind of Three can then emerge in which the opposites are transcended. This can be a union state, the alchemical *coniunctio*. At this stage, one can often feel a current inherent in the field in which one feels alternately pulled toward, then separated from the other person. This is the rhythm of the *coniunctio* as a Three quality of the field becoming Four. (pp. 7–8)

This style of consciousness has two important effects. First, instead of projecting, blaming, and identifying events and people "outside of ourselves" as the source of reality, we must be responsible for cocreating that reality. In other words, there is no "outside of ourselves." Rather, we are always inside whatever metaphoric field we are cocreating. Further, within the metaphor, we have a responsibility to ascertain our role and ethical obligations. Living within a metaphorical consciousness is a continuing invitation to examine one's relationship to every experience and act in a responsible way. Living the transcendent function in this way demands nothing less than a radical shift in one's day-to-day approach to life.

But this attitude has an even more profound impact: creating the space for the alchemical fourth to emerge. Indeed, it offers each of us the ability to experience the numinous in the everyday experience. When I am able to free myself from the shackles of viewing an experience as something happening to me and see it as something that I cocreate, I free myself to see the sacred in the other person. I liberate myself to not only see the third thing (the relationship, the connection, the field) that links me and the other person but also to allow (or even invite) the emergence of the other, the telos, the numinosum, the alchemical fourth. The sense of sacrality that we feel when we realize that a particular moment is happening for a specific reason (even if we do not know what that reason is) would be available to us always. We are then open to the other in any interaction, that which is hidden or separate from me and the other person. We can see each interaction as the field calling to us for some response, an awareness of something bigger than the apparent interaction we are having.

The transcendent function in relationships means living perpetually in the attitude of seeing the mystery in what we used to take for granted; being a faithful witness without possessing; realizing the ordinary can be sacred; opening to whatever wants to be shared; living in a field of eros. The transcendent function is about the birth of soul in the moment; one can practice it every day by merely engaging the field that allows the epiphany of the other.

Surveying the Transcendent Function in Social and Cultural Issues

Bringing the awareness of the transcendent function to social and cultural problems requires the same search for the metaphorical third and an openness to the alchemical fourth. That is, with regard to each cultural issue, one must query: What is the metaphoric field within which we are located, and what is the presence, the new experience or insight, that is requesting voice? Applying Schwartz-Salant's language in relation to the analytic third, "the content [the larger spiritual or cultural issue] can be imaginally thrust into the field . . . so that it becomes a 'third thing'" (1995, p. 5). When the exploration can be focused on the metaphoric field, the issue can be moved to a deeper level of awareness with the opportunity for the emergence of a new, transcendent perspective, the alchemical fourth. If that deeper dialogue can then be followed by the added responsibility and ethical obligation to respond espoused by the alchemical attitude, even acute cultural problems can be transformed in significant ways and something new can emerge as a response or demand.

In the area of race relations, for example, we are witness to disputes about affirmative action, racism in the administration of justice, and discrimination in a variety of areas. Individuals and groups choose sides in the debate, and rarely do we see a truly open discussion of what is really underneath it all. Using the transcendent function as a metaphoric field, one might say the content or the field is the fear of differences, fear of the other, the human tendency to blame someone else for problems, selfishness and greed, or any combination of these. When racial incidents present themselves in the culture, the transcendent function requires us to see the fear, blame, and projection as the field that is presented to us all by psyche, the field which we cocreate together. Allowing ourselves to hold these things in tension without pointing the finger at the other side is the metaphoric third, the transcendent function at work out of which can flow the alchemical fourth, something new instead of the same old game of blame and recrimination.

The cultural application of the transcendent function raises two interesting issues. First, the nature of the container is more complex and problematic than in the intrapsychic or interpersonal context. Between any two people, the intrapsychic field can be accessed relatively easily, with Jung's active imagination and other techniques, as the Venice experience demonstrates. However, on a culture-wide basis, one must be much more imaginative in creating the instrumentalities for enunciating what is in the field. Let us not get confused here. The transcendent function is always present whether intrapsychically, in relationship, or in culture. My wife and I did not create the field in Venice; we merely concocted a way to consciously enter it. In the same way, the metaphoric field is always present in vexing cultural issues, but gaining access to it may be more difficult. Here, imagination and innovation are incredibly important. Those in positions of leadership in media, political, cultural, social, and religious institutions must find ways to bring the field to greater consciousness.

Second, and even more importantly, depth psychologists must leave the safety of the consulting room and become active participants in the discussion of such issues. In the last decade or so, James Hillman and others have begun to express this pointedly. It is time for depth psychology to stand up and be heard. We bemoan the fact that the culture is in denial about its shadow, about the field, but we do nothing outside the analytic situation to remedy that. Whether it is making these points in television discussions, writing articles for mainstream magazines and newspapers, or through community workshops, seminars, and the like, we must find a way to help move deeper in our cultural dialogue. This exhortation is not exclusive to depth psychologists. Why do we not have philosophers, teachers, clergy people, ethicists, and others who focus on values more involved in our public discourse? Bluntly put, it is not part of our culture to discuss things on this level. Only following an acknowledgment and discussion of the transcendent function and the metaphoric field at a cultural level can we take responsibility as a group for addressing the larger points being presented. Only then is there any possibility for the emergence of a paradigm-shifting event in consciousness.

The cultural application of the transcendent function can be profitably used particularly with social issues that manifest highly divisive positions since those positions probably evidence affect indicative of a deeper, denied field. One such issue is the persistent fight over abortion in this country. The very names "pro-choice" and "pro-life" exhibit the kind of antithetical, uncompromising positions that are the hallmark of the transcendent function analysis. What is the subject matter that constitutes the metaphoric field? What is really at work here? Sexuality, sexual freedom, and sexual responsibility are certainly implicated as well as family and family structure. Indeed, along with the intensification of the abortion debate has come the emergence of the religious right and the debate about family values. Viewed in this way, the abortion battle, and the antithetical positions of the opposing camps, may be metaphoric camouflage for the deeper division between the Puritan roots of our culture and the values inherent in the liberal tradition as it has grown during the twentieth century. This is not to say that the debate on abortion itself is not an important one, but rather an observation that it undoubtedly constitutes a doorway to a deeper set of issues. Any approach with the transcendent function at its core would seek to engage those in a cultural field so that an alchemical fourth, an entirely new and transcendent thing could emerge.

Gun control is another area that could benefit from the cultural application of the transcendent function. Gun owners, waving the Second Amendment, vehemently oppose any substantial form of gun control; those in favor of gun control decry the use of guns urging registration or even a full ban. But what is the field? What deeper set of issues is being denied and is surfacing in this ungainly way? Commentators might offer different ideas about the content of the field in this case. Certainly the revolutionary, anti-authoritarian roots (e.g., "I need my gun to protect against and resist the absolute power and force of the sovereign government that might oppress me") of the American culture are present. The preeminence of individualism over the good of the group, some might say, also plays a part. Others might point to the inherent lack of values and ideals in the capitalist system. Still others would undoubtedly comment on the breakdown of our social, religious, and family institutions. Or the content of the field might be all these things. Again, viewed from the perspective of the transcendent function, we need not decide which content is the right one. Merely by being open to what we imagine the underlying issue to be, we engage the transcendent function, the metaphoric third. It has an autonomy of its own and will, without guidance from us, move the psychic energy toward some new attitude or breakthrough.

One final contemporary cultural issue that could be seen through the lens of the transcendent function is the struggle between the genders. This century has certainly seen a massive shift in the roles of men and women in the workplace, in the home, and in our social and political institutions. Once again, gender equality has been and continues to be an incendiary issue, a clue that there is a deeper metaphoric field. What is really at work? What are the hidden issues? Here, we might be well served to look beneath the surface at traditionally male and female values and question whether it is really those values struggling for change. The male is generally associated with autonomy, power, intellect, rationality, individuality, and outward projection while the female with the body, emotions, intuition, nature, imagination, relating, and receiving. Is it possible that the struggle between men and women in culture is merely a surface manifestation of a deeper field, the reemergence of feminine archetypal values and the falling away of the dominance of the masculine? Some have posited this very theory (see, e.g., Tarnas, 1991, and Meador, 1994), and it has certainly surfaced within depth psychology, the feminist movement, and some New Age circles. However, it has not yet made its way into the mainstream debate of the culture. So long as we continue to divide into camps opposing one another instead of opening to the content of the field upon which the battle is being waged, we remain stuck. The transcendent function and its application to cultural issues provides a way around (or underneath) the barriers.

Turning to our institutions, we could particularly benefit from the transcendent function in our political and governmental discourse. Despite the avowed egalitarian and democratic foundations of our system, it is rife with inequality that creates fierce, disruptive competition for influence. Thus, political discussions are highly polemical and manipulative. In this case, the subject matter that the transcendent function seems to be working upon is competition for resources. The alchemical approach would be to at least be aware of that field, if not substitute it as the subject, in political discussions. The awareness of the metaphor would allow us to attempt an honest exchange on how resources and power can be shared and allocated in a way that reflects the underlying philosophy we espouse. If we truly accept responsibility for acting in an ethical and responsible way in sharing our resources, we open the possibility for the emergence of an alchemical fourth or a new insight as to how best to handle diminishing resources.

The transcendent function operates not only intrapsychically and in relationships but is also present in social issues. It offers us a way of envisioning cultural matters that avoids the either/or of opposing camps on important ideas. As it does with intrapsychic disparities, the transcendent function allows us to create a metaphoric field in which the antitheses of opposing camps can be held, creating the potential for the emergence of something new.

TRANSCENDENT FUNCTIONING IN THE GARDEN OF EVERYDAY LIFE

A metaphoric approach to the transcendent function is also instrumental in reclaiming it from the dusty shelves of academic depth psychology and ushering it into everyday life. Though the way Jung often spoke of the transcendent function may evoke for many only its application to clinical work, the present study has disinterred its far more expansive uses in the world. The transcendent function is a key participant in the constant process of psychological transformation that proceeds, whether inside or outside the consulting room, independent of one's conscious will. The unconscious is ever present; it is continually being integrated in varying doses into consciousness. The transcendent function is omnipresent as well, operating at various levels and at varying intensities throughout our daily activities.

The question is, how can we animate the transcendent function in our lives? This really amounts to several separate inquiries: How do we better recognize and increase the transcendent function? How can we be more in touch with the transcendent function when it is at work? How can we be more open to the transcendent function in situations where it would be helpful? Is there anything we can do to increase the incidence of the transcendent function? These questions can be addressed at several different levels, as the sections of this chapter illustrate.

First, at the most general level, animating the transcendent function is as much a perspective as it is an act. That is why alchemical thinking is so important to this discussion. In rejecting the splits between apparent opposites (e.g., mind/body, spirit/matter, and idea/fact), it acknowledges that consciousness and the world are always inextricably intertwined. By this way of thinking, the world exists only in relation to a participant observer. The relation between the observer and the world, the metaphorical third, creates the reality. The transcendent function allows us to see all the world as a way of embodying, relating to, and integrating the unconscious. The unconscious is not tucked away neatly so that we can periodically do some drawing or sculpting to allow it to emerge. It cascades forth constantly in our everyday reality.

At the interpersonal and cultural levels, the transcendent function requires a concerted effort to implement the ideas set forth in the previous two sections. Each relationship interaction provides an opportunity to engage the field, to see something we would not otherwise see or make conscious something that is unconscious. What is being presented to me and the other person with whom I am interacting? What is beneath the surface? What is the content of our interaction that might provide clues to unconscious material seeking to be made conscious? Is there any part of my shadow present here? This attitude is particularly effective in situations where there is conflict or dissonance in a relational interaction. Contentiousness is a good indicator that something unconscious is being activated. Using a vivified transcendent function, attempting to access the field in these situations, both defuses and deepens them. This approach does not mean that one hundred percent of every problematic situation is a message from the unconscious. There may well be concrete steps to be taken to address the dispute. An animated transcendent function would, however, engage an awareness that there is probably something else going on.

Having adopted this attitude while authoring the last part of this book, I can offer personal testimony as to its efficacy and profundity. I have experienced a huge increase in awareness and satisfaction. I have also noticed a significant decrease in my desire to blame others; it is not they with whom I have issue but something in the field that tugs at both of us, something unconscious demanding to be heard. It is as if I have hired this person to reveal something unconscious to me. Thought of in this way, the transcendent function has much in common with Martin Buber's concept of "the Word" in his seminal essay "Dialogue" (1948). There he speaks of "becoming aware," acknowledging words as calls to action that come from an autonomous place beyond the person speaking them:

> It is a different matter when . . . a man. . . . addresses something to me, speaks something to me that enters my own life. It can be something about this man, for instance that he needs me. But it can also be something about myself. The man himself in his relation to me has nothing to do with what is said . . . It is not he who says it to me, as that solitary man silently confessed his secret to his neighbour on the seat; but *it* says it.
>
> The effect of having this said to me is completely different from that of looking on and observing. . . . Perhaps I have to accomplish something about him; but perhaps I have only to learn something, and it is only a matter of my "accepting." It may be that I have to answer at once, to this very man before me; it may be that . . . I am to answer some other person at some other time and place, in who knows what kind of speech, and that it is now only a matter of taking the answering on myself. But in each instance a word demanding an answer has happened to me.
>
> We may term this way of perception *becoming aware.*
>
> It by no means needs to be a man of whom I become aware. It can be an animal, a plant, a stone. . . . Nothing can refuse to be the vessel for the Word. The limits of the possibility of dialogue are the limits of awareness. (p. 9)

A list of the ways in which the transcendent function can be brought into our everyday lives via relationships could go on forever. Suffice it to say that bringing this awareness into our daily interactions not only improves the relationships but deepens our psychological experience.

The last paragraph of Buber's quote opens a second key area for activating the transcendent function: the environment that we live in. This is the focus and message of the emerging field of ecopsychology, which asserts that ecology and psychology are inextricably intertwined because the planet and the individual are indivisible. Ecopsychology exhorts us to see the world around us as more than our physical container and acknowledge it as a living, breathing system that both contains us and with which we have an intimate relationship. As one writer phrases it, "[Ecopsychology's] goal is to bridge our culture's long-standing, historical gulf between the psychological and the ecological, to see the needs of the planet and the person as a continuum" (Roszak, 1992, p. 14).

The purpose here is not to comprehensively review the field of ecopsychology; others have done that elegantly. Rather, the aim is to discuss ecopsychology as a way to stimulate the transcendent function in our daily lives. Our interactions with the environment offer two such possibilities. First, we can apply the same alchemical sensibility to our relationship with the environment as that urged for human relationships. Just as another person can be seen as the other with whom I am creating a field to experience the transcendent function, so with the environment. We are constantly in a field with all that surrounds us, and it contains invaluable passageways into the unconscious. This perspective requires us, particularly when we are in some state of dissonance with our surroundings, to search deeper for the content that we need to hold in tension for the emergence of a new perspective. This can be done with large issues like global warming, pollution, or urban sprawl in much the same way that was set forth above for cultural issues. But it can also be done on a much more mundane, day-to-day level. Visualizing a field or presence between ourselves and an element of nature (e.g., a tree, a flowing river, a hummingbird, a rock) and inviting information from that field can generate surprisingly powerful perspectives. To the skeptic that sees such an endeavor as imagining or making believe, we would respond that fantasy, the metaphoric third, and the transcendent function are every bit as real to psyche as the concreteness of so-called reality. One way in which Jung forever changed depth psychology was by asserting that underneath each everyday experience were archetypal forces constantly at work. As he expressed in a 1936 seminar:

> That is the artificiality of our conscious world. It is like assuming that this room, in which there are doors and windows leading to the outer world, possesses no such doors and windows; or like turning our backs on them and imagining that this is the whole world. You see, that is the prejudice, the hubris of consciousness—the assumption that we are in a perfectly reasonable world where everything can be regulated by laws. We don't recognize the fact that just outside is a sea that can break in over our continent and drown our whole civilization. As long as we turn our eyes to the center of the room we are blissfully unaware of the fact that there is any archetypal situation whatever: we don't collide with the elemental world outside. As a matter of fact, the

> whole room is, as it were, suspended in an elementary world, as our consciousness is suspended in a world of monsters, but we simply won't see it; and when these monsters at times peep in or make a noise, we explain it by indigestion or something of the sort. . . . So it is as if we were building the most marvelous walls and dams, and then open the floodgates and let the water in, just that. For the soil of our consciousness dries up and becomes sterile if we don't let in the flood of the archetypes; if we don't expose the soil to the influence of the elements, nothing grows, nothing happens: we simply dry up. (1988a, pp. 973–74)

The openness to the transcendent function in the form of the metaphorical field allows us to experience the archetypal in our everyday contacts with the environment.

A second way that our surroundings can catalyze the transcendent function is by our accepting the more radical tenet of ecopsychology that the world around us is not other at all but is the subject of which we are a small part. This view holds that the individual human self is a fiction we concoct to make sense of things. According to this vision, drawing the line of demarcation between "me" and "not-me" at the boundary of our own skin is narcissistic; "me" is really the entire living ecosystem of which we are a part and "my psyche" is really the world psyche. Freud and Jung both posited parts of psyche that are explainable only by taking into account the entire physical world around us:

> If we listen to . . . Freud and Jung, the most profoundly collective and unconscious self is the natural material world. Since the cut between self and natural world is arbitrary, we can make it at the skin or we can take it as far out as you like—to the deep oceans and distant stars. (Hillman, 1995, p. xiv)

This conception of the world psyche makes the everyday use of the transcendent function with our environment seem, in a way, much more natural; my conscious attitude is like one component of the intrapsychic structure of the larger psyche, and I am merely seeking to make contact with the aspects of that psyche that are hidden to me. The use of the field or transcendent function would follow the same lines we have previously drawn.

Finally, there are numerous activities that, when incorporated into our normal lives, serve to increase or spark the transcendent function. Generally speaking, such activities are those which reduce the operation of our logical function and increase our awareness of an other or third between ourselves and our normal lives. Though there are countless examples of this kind of activity, the following are named by way of illustration only: meditation, artwork, music, yoga, poetry, reading, dance, theater, play, creative writing, and tai chi. These and other similar activities allow the mind to quiet down and thereby naturally come into closer contact with hidden, unknown, or unconscious material.

Viewed in this way, the transcendent function becomes a tool of daily living. Whether we acknowledge it or not, each situation we face is a kind of alchemical vessel in which consciousness and the imagos of the unconscious face each other. The transcendent function is the metaphorical field or relationship between them from which a new integration can occur: a new third, thing in Jungian terms, the alchemical fourth as we have called it in this chapter. Thus, the transcendent function is implicated in every situation, person, relationship, challenge, thought, and event we face each moment of each day. Though this may seem a huge responsibility, it carries with it untold magic. It potentiates transformation in each instant; in every interaction is the possibility of the emergence of something completely new, a new insight, a new image, an entity separate and apart from the participants and the field in which they sit. By holding each event, within and contained by the transcendent function, the metaphorical third, a new element is invited to emerge, the alchemical fourth, a *coniunctio*. Through this extension of Jung's ideas,[6] the alchemical attitude toward the transcendent function allows us to experience new insights, new dimensions and, indeed, the numinosum in our everyday experiences.

CONCLUDING REMARKS

Thus, we come to the end of our hermeneutic exploration of the transcendent function. Enunciated by Jung as an integral part of his psychology in 1916 immediately after his own unsettling confrontation with the unconscious, the transcendent function was seen by Jung as uniting the opposites, transforming psyche, and central to the individuation process. It also undoubtedly reflects his own personal experience in coming to terms with the unconscious. Jung portrayed the transcendent function as operating through symbol and fantasy and mediating between the opposites of consciousness and the unconscious to prompt the emergence of a new, third posture that transcends the two. In exploring the details of the transcendent function and its connection to other Jungian constructs, this work has unearthed significant changes, ambiguities, and inconsistencies in Jung's writings. Further, it has identified two separate images of the transcendent function: (1) the narrow transcendent function, the function or process within Jung's pantheon of psychic structures, generally seen as the uniting of the opposites of consciousness and the unconscious from which a new attitude emerges; and (2) the expansive transcendent function, the root metaphor for psyche or being psychological that subsumes Jung's pantheon and that apprehends the most fundamental psychic activity of interacting with the unknown or other. This book has also posited that the expansive transcendent function, as the root metaphor for exchanges between conscious and the unconscious, is the wellspring from whence flows other key Jungian structures such as the archetypes and the Self, and is the core of the individuation process.

The expansive transcendent function has been explored further by surveying other schools of psychology, with both depth and non-depth orientations, and evaluating the transcendent function alongside structures or processes in those other schools which play similar mediatory and/or transitional roles. The book has also identified and explored several archetypal patterns implicated by the transcendent function, including the binary opposition inherent in consciousness, the subject-object chasm, liminality and initiation, Hermes energy, the third, the rhythm of consciousness, and transcendence. Through that exploration, the transcendent function was traced in its archetypal core to the neither/nor, autochthonous yearnings of psyche to seek connection (even between seemingly unconnectable things) and to move deeper.

Finally, the book concluded with an examination of how the transcendent function can be accessed more in relationships, in culture and society, in our institutions, and in our daily lives. By looking at analogous concepts flowing from the ancient art of alchemy, we identified several techniques for applying the transcendent in these broader contexts and discussed how they might be used. Simply put, the transcendent function is realized whenever we open to the field, the metaphoric third, between us and other, whether the other is a person, a societal issue, the environment, or our daily routine. Through this process we can make space for the emergence of the alchemical fourth, a new attitude or situation, the core of psychological awareness and psychological transformation.

APPENDIX A

Textual Comparison of the 1916 Version to the 1958 Version of "The Transcendent Function"

TEXTUAL COMPARISON OF THE 1916 VERSION TO THE 1958 VERSION OF "THE TRANSCENDENT FUNCTION"

[Note: Text with line through it is text that was removed from the 1916 version when Jung revised it in 1958; text that is underlined is text that Jung added to the 1916 version when he revised it to create the 1958 version]

THE TRANSCENDENT FUNCTION

~~[(1916)]~~

There is nothing mysterious or metaphysical about the term " transcendent function." It means a psychological function comparable in its way to a mathematical function of the same name, which is a function of real and imaginary numbers. The psychological "transcendent function" arises from the union of *conscious* and *unconscious* contents.

Experience in analytical psychology <has> amply ~~[shows]~~ <shown> that the conscious and the unconscious ~~[have a curious tendency not to agree.]~~ <seldom agree as to their contents and their tendencies,> This lack of ~~[agreement]~~ <parallelism> is not just accidental or purposeless, but is ~~[because]~~ <due to the fact that> the unconscious behaves in a compensatory or complementary manner towards the conscious. We can also put it the other way <round> and say that the conscious behaves in a complementary manner towards the unconscious. The reasons for this <relationship> are:

1. ~~[The conscious]~~ <Consciousness> possesses a threshold intensity which its contents must ~~[attain]~~ <have attained>, so that all elements ~~[which]~~ <that> are too weak remain in the unconscious.

2. ~~[The conscious]~~ <Consciousness>, because of its directed functions, ~~[inhibits all incompatible material (also called]~~ <exercises an inhibition (which Freud calls> censorship) ~~[,whereby this]~~ <on all> incompatible material ~~[sinks into]~~ <, with the result that it sinks into> the unconscious.

3. ~~[The conscious forms]~~ <Consciousness constitutes> the momentary process of adaptation, ~~[while]~~ <whereas> the unconscious contains not only all the forgotten material of the individual's own past, but ~~[also]~~ all <the> inherited behaviour traces ~~[of the human spirit]~~ <constituting the structure of the mind>.

4. The unconscious contains all the fantasy combinations which have not yet attained the threshold intensity, but which in the course of time and under suitable conditions will enter the light of consciousness.

This <readily> explains the complementary attitude of the unconscious towards the conscious.

The definiteness and directedness of the conscious mind ~~[is a function which has]~~ <are qualities that have> been acquired relatively late in the history of the human race, and ~~[is]~~ <are> for instance largely lacking among primitives ~~[even]~~ today. ~~[This function is]~~ <These qualities are> often impaired in the neurotic patient, who differs ~~[to a greater or lesser extent]~~ from the normal person in that his threshold of consciousness gets shifted more easily ~~[, or]~~ <;> in other words ~~[this]~~ <,the> partition between ~~[the]~~ conscious and ~~[the]~~ unconscious is much more permeable. The psychotic <,> on the other hand <,> is ~~[completely]~~ under the direct influence of the unconscious.

The definiteness and directedness of the conscious mind ~~[is an]~~ <are> extremely important ~~[function,]~~ <acquisitions> which humanity has ~~[acquired]~~ <bought> at a very heavy sacrifice, and which in turn ~~[has]~~ <have> rendered humanity the highest service. Without ~~[it, neither science nor society could exist, for they both presuppose a]~~ <them science, technology, and civilization would be impossible, for they all presuppose the> reliable continuity <and directedness> of the ~~[psychic]~~ <conscious> process. For the ~~[professional man]~~ <statesman, doctor, and engineer> as well as <for> the simplest labourer ~~[this~~

~~function is indispensable. A man's worthlessness to society increases in proportion to the degree of impairment of this function}~~ <, these qualities are absolutely indispensable. We may say in general that social worthlessness increases to the degree that these qualities are impaired> by the unconscious. Great artists and others distinguished by creative gifts are <,> of course <,> exceptions to this rule. The very advantage ~~{of}~~ <that> such individuals ~~{lies}~~ <enjoy consists precisely> in the permeability of the partition separating the conscious and <the> unconscious. But<,> for <those> professions and ~~{trades}~~ <social activities> which ~~{demand}~~ <require> just this continuity and reliability ~~{of the function}~~ <,> these exceptional human beings are as a rule of little value.

It is therefore understandable <,> and even necessary <,> that in each individual ~~{this function}~~ <the psychic process> should be as ~~{steady}~~ <stable> and ~~{as}~~ definite as possible, since the exigencies of life demand it. But this involves a certain disadvantage: the quality of directedness makes for the inhibition or ~~{the}~~ exclusion of all those psychic elements which appear to be, or really are, incompatible ~~{, i. e.}~~ <with it, i.e.,> likely to ~~{change}~~ <bias> the ~~{preconceived}~~ <intended> direction to suit their ~~{purposes}~~ <purpose> and so lead to an undesired goal. ~~{How can it be recognized whether the collateral}~~ <But how do we know that the concurrent> psychic material is ~~{compatible or not? It can be recognized by an act of judgement which is based on the same attitude which determined the preconceived direction. This judgement is therefore}~~ <"incompatible"? We know it by an act of judgment which determines the direction of the path that is chosen and desired. This judgment is> partial and prejudiced, ~~{for it is based exclusively on what is considered to be compatible with the directed process at the time. This judgement arising from an opinion is always based in its turn on experience, i. e.}~~ <since it chooses one particular possibility at the cost of all the others. The judgment in its turn is always based on experience, i.e.,> on what is already known ~~{and acknowledged as true. It}~~ <. As a rule it> is never based on what is new, what is still unknown, and what under certain conditions might considerably enrich the directed process. It is evident that it cannot be, for the very reason that the unconscious ~~{is blocked}~~ <contents are excluded from consciousness>.

Through such acts of judgement the directed ~~{function}~~ <process necessarily> becomes ~~{of necessity }~~ one-sided, even though the rational ~~{judge-~~

~~ment]~~ <judgment> may appear many-sided and unprejudiced. The ~~[extremest prejudice may even lie in the rationality of the judgements]~~ <very rationality of the judgment may even be the worst prejudice>, since we call reasonable what appears ~~[to be]~~ reasonable to us. What appears to us unreasonable <is> therefore ~~[is]~~ doomed to be excluded because of its irrational character. It may really be irrational, but may equally well merely appear irrational without actually being so ~~[,]~~ when seen from another standpoint.

One-sidedness is an ~~[inevitable]~~ <unavoidable> and ~~[essential]~~ <necessary> characteristic of the directed process, for direction ~~[means]~~ <implies> one-sidedness. ~~[One-sidedness]~~ <It> is an advantage and a drawback at the same time. Even when ~~[there is no externally recognizable]~~ <no outwardly visible> drawback <seems to be present>, there is always an equally pronounced counter-position in the unconscious, unless it happens to be the ideal case where all the psychic components are ~~[moving]~~ <tending> in one and the same direction. This possibility cannot be disputed in theory, but in practice <it> very rarely happens. The counter-position in the unconscious is not dangerous so long as it does not possess any high energy <-> value. But if the ~~[energy value]~~ <tension> increases as ~~[the]~~ <a> result of too great ~~[a one-sidedness in consciousness, which affords the energy too little difference in potential, then the unconscious causes interference, disturbance in the form of symptoms, and interruption of the rational continuity, usually just in]~~ <one-sidedness, the counter-tendency breaks through into consciousness, usually just at> the moment when it is most ~~[vital to carry through]~~ <important to maintain> the conscious ~~[function]~~ <direction>. Thus the speaker makes a slip of the tongue just ~~[in the moment]~~ when he particularly wishes not to say anything stupid. This moment is critical because it possesses ~~[the highest]~~ <a high> energy tension ~~[, and]~~ <which,> when the unconscious is <already> charged ~~[it]~~ <,> may easily ~~[provoke the]~~ <"spark" and> release ~~[of]~~ the unconscious content.

~~[Life]~~ <Civilized life> today demands concentrated <,> directed <conscious> functioning and ~~[with it]~~ <this entails> the risk of <a> considerable dissociation from the unconscious. The further we are able to ~~[detach]~~ <remove> ourselves from the unconscious through directed functioning, the more readily ~~[can]~~ a powerful counter-position [be built] <can build> up in the unconscious, and when this breaks ~~[loose]~~ <out> it may have ~~[devastating]~~ <disagreeable> consequences.

~~[Through analytical psychology we have won deep]~~ <Analysis has given us a profound> insight into the ~~[significance]~~ <importance> of unconscious influences, and <we> have learnt so much from this for our ~~[conscious life, that we have found it unwise after termination of the analytical treatment to neglect the unconscious completely. Out of an obscure recognition of]~~ <practical life that we deem it unwise to expect an elimination or standstill of the unconscious after the so-called completion of the treatment. Many patients, obscurely recognizing> this state of affairs ~~[many patients are unable to decide]~~ <, have great difficulty in deciding> to give up the analysis, ~~[though they]~~ <although both they and the analyst> find the feeling of dependency irksome. ~~[Many]~~ <Often they> are ~~[even]~~ afraid to risk ~~[attempting to stand]~~ <standing> on their own feet, because they know from ~~[manifold]~~ experience that the unconscious ~~[in an]~~ <can intervene again and again in their lives in a disturbing and> apparently unpredictable ~~[way can break into and dangerously disturb their lives]~~ <manner>.

It was formerly assumed that patients were ready to cope with ~~[the problems of]~~ <normal> life as soon as they had ~~[themselves learnt so much of practical methods that they were in a position to analyse their dreams themselves. This idea was certainly good, as long as we knew nothing better. But greater experience has shown that even skilled analysts, who had completely mastered the method of dream analysis, were forced to]~~ <acquired enough practical self-knowledge to understand their own dreams. Experience has shown, however, that even professional analysts, who might be expected to have mastered the art of dream interpretation, often> capitulate before their own dreams ~~[not, to be sure, in regard to their analytic-reductive interpretation but their synthetic or constructive handling. It is of course much easier to tear down than to build up. If then]~~ <and have to call in the help of a colleague. If even one who purports to be> an expert in the method proves unable to ~~[deal adequately with]~~ <interpret> his own dreams <satisfactorily>, how much less can this be expected of the patient. <Freud's hope that the unconscious could be " exhausted" has not been fulfilled. Dream-life and intrusions from the unconscious continue—*mutatis mutandis*—unimpeded.

There is> ~~{I must interpolate here that there exists}~~ a widespread prejudice that ~~{the}~~ analysis is something like a "cure," to which one submits for a time ~~{,}~~ <and is> then ~~{to be}~~ discharged healed. That is a layman's error left over from the early days of ~~{analysis}~~ <psychoanalysis>. Analytical treatment ~~{is a new adjustment of the}~~ <could be described as a readjustment of > psychological attitude ~~{,}~~ achieved with the ~~{aid}~~ <help> of the ~~{physician}~~ <doctor>. Naturally this newly ~~{-}~~ won attitude, which is better suited to ~~{external}~~ <the inner> and ~~{internal}~~ <outer> conditions, can last a considerable time, but there are very few cases ~~{in which}~~ <where> a single "cure" ~~{has such success}~~ <is permanently successful>. It is true that medical optimism has ~~{at no time been sparing with blatant}~~ <never stinted itself of> publicity and has always been able to report ~~{miraculous cures of indisputable permanence}~~ <definitive cures>. We must, however, not let ourselves be deceived by the all-too-human attitude of the practitioner, but ~~{must always remember the warning that the good should not be the enemy of the better. We}~~ <should always remember that the life of the unconscious goes on and continually produces problematical situations. There is no need for pessimism; we> have seen too many ~~{good}~~ <excellent> results achieved ~~{by honest thorough work to be pessimistic with regard to analysis}~~ <with good luck and honest work for that>. But this need not prevent ~~{our}~~ <us from> recognizing that analysis is no once ~~{and for all cure but first of all an individual, basic, new adjustment. As far as individual attitudes are concerned, not a single one is valid unconditionally and}~~ <-and-for-all "cure"; it is no more, at first, than a more or less thorough readjustment. There is no change that is unconditionally valid> over a long period of time. ~~{There are, to be sure}~~ <Life has always to be tackled anew. There are, of course>, extremely durable collective attitudes which ~~{can be called collective morals or religion. But a}~~ <permit the solution of typical conflicts. A> collective attitude ~~{is not an individual one; its effect upon the individual is merely like that of}~~ <enables the individual to fit into society without friction, since it acts upon him like> any other condition of life. ~~{The individual must adjust to the latter, just as in one way or another he must adjust to the collective attitude. This is the reason why in practical analytical work we only have to deal with the individual attitude}~~ <But the patient's difficulty consists precisely in the fact that his individual

problem cannot be fitted without friction into a collective norm; it requires the solution of an individual conflict if the whole of his personality is to remain viable. No rational solution can do justice to this task, and there is absolutely no collective norm that could replace an individual solution without loss>.

The new attitude gained in the course of analysis tends sooner or later to become inadequate in one way or another, and necessarily so, because the constant flow of life again and again demands fresh adaptation. Adaptation is never achieved once and for all. One might ~~[of course]~~ <certainly> demand of analysis that it ~~[ought to]~~ <should> enable the ~~[individual]~~ <patient> to gain new orientations in later life, too, without ~~[difficulty. Experience shows this to be the case to a certain extent]~~ <undue difficulty. And experience shows that thesis true up to a point>. We often find that patients who have gone through a thorough analysis have considerably less difficulty with new adjustments later <on>. Nevertheless, these difficulties prove to be fairly frequent and may at times be really troublesome. ~~[This]~~ <That> is why even patients who have had a thorough analysis often <turn to their old analyst for help> at some later period ~~[turn again to their former physician for help. In comparison with]~~ <. In the light of> medical practice in general there is nothing very unusual about this, but it ~~[contradicts]~~ <does contradict> a certain misplaced enthusiasm on the part of the therapist <as well as the view that analysis constitutes a unique "cure." In the last resort it is highly improbable that there could ever be a therapy that got> ~~[, which not infrequently conceals a multitude of sins. We shall probably never be meant to possess a therapy which gets]~~ rid of all difficulties ~~[, otherwise normal people would be the most gratifying patients]~~. Man needs difficulties; they are necessary for health. What concerns us here is only an excessive amount of them.

<The basic question for the therapist is not how to get rid of the momentary difficulty, but how future difficulties may be successfully countered. The question is: what kind of mental and moral attitude is it necessary to have towards the disturbing influences of the unconscious, and how can it be conveyed to the patient?

The answer obviously consists in getting rid of the separation between conscious and unconscious. This cannot be done by condemning the contents of the unconscious in a one-sided way, but rather by recognizing their significance in compensating the one-sidedness of consciousness and by taking this significance into account. The tendencies of the conscious and the unconscious are the two factors that together make up> ~~[If, as pointed out, the synthetic or constructive treatment of the dream were a means which could be used subjectively, then the dream content together with the knowledge of the conscious mind would be an ideal combination of those two factors, of which]~~ the transcendent function ~~[is composed. The term]~~ <. It is called> "transcendent" ~~[designates the fact that this function mediates]~~ <because it makes> the transition from one attitude to another ~~[. The constructive method however presupposes some conscious knowledge, which the patient too can be made to realize in the course of treatment, since the physician is aware in principle of the potential existence of this knowledge. If the physician himself knows nothing about it, then in this respect]~~ <organically possible, without loss of the unconscious. The constructive or synthetic method of treatment presupposes insights which are at least potentially present in the patient and can therefore be made conscious. If the analyst knows nothing of these potentialities> he cannot help the patient <to develop them> either, unless ~~[physician]~~ <analyst> and patient together devote ~~[a]~~ proper scientific study to this problem, which as a rule is out of the question.

In actual practice, therefore, the suitably trained ~~[physician]~~ <analyst> mediates the transcendent function for the patient, ~~[i. e. he]~~ <i.e.,> helps him <to> bring ~~[together]~~ conscious and unconscious ~~[and, by compensating the onesidedness of the conscious mind, helps him make the transition to]~~ <together and so arrive at> a new attitude. In this function of the ~~[physician]~~ <analyst> lies one of the many important ~~[aspects]~~ <meanings> of the *transference.* ~~[By]~~ <The patient clings by> means of the transference ~~[the patient clings to the person who promises]~~ <to the person who seems to promise> him a renewal of ~~[adjustment]~~ <attitude>; through ~~[the transference]~~ <it> he seeks this change, which is vital to him, even though he may not be conscious of ~~[it]~~ <doing so>. For the patient, therefore, the ~~[physician frequently]~~ <analyst> has the character of ~~[something]~~ <an> indispensable ~~[, something]~~ <figure> absolutely necessary ~~[to]~~ <for> life. However infantile ~~[such]~~ <this> dependence may appear ~~[,]~~ <to be,> it [involves] <expresses> an extremely important demand which, if disappointed, [frequently] <often> turns to bitter [hate against] <hatred of> the [physician] <analyst>. It is therefore important to know what this demand concealed in the transference <is> really [is about] <aiming at>; there is a tendency to understand [this demand] <it> in [a] <the> reductive sense only, as [a projected] <an erotic> infantile fantasy. [That] <But that> would mean [however] taking this fantasy, which is usually concerned with the parents, literally <,> as though the patient<,> or rather [the] <his> unconscious [again, or] <,> still [,] had the expectations the child once had towards the parents. [In a certain sense] <Outwardly> it still is the same expectation of the child for the help and protection of the parents, but [now it should be taken only in a symbolic sense as an unconscious] <in the meantime the child has become an adult, and what was normal for a child is improper in an adult. It has become a> metaphorical expression of the [demand for help in achieving the new attitude. The unconscious metaphor for this demand often has a very definite sexual formulation, which of course should be reduced to repressed (infantile) sexual fantasies as long as the patient is not conscious of the fact of the repressed sexuality. It would, however, be a meaningless and useless schematization simply to continue in this reductive way, if] <not consciously realized need for help in a crisis. Historically it is correct to explain the erotic character of the transference in terms of the infantile eros. But in that way the meaning and purpose of the transference are not understood, and its interpretation as an infantile sexual fantasy leads away from the real problem. The understanding of the transference is to be sought not in its historical antecedents but in its purpose. The one-sided, reductive explanation becomes in the end nonsensical, especially when> absolutely nothing new [is gained] <comes out of it except the increased resistances of the patient>. The sense of boredom which then appears in the analysis is [nothing but the] <simply an> expression of the monotony and poverty of [ideas not] <ideas—not> of the unconscious, as is sometimes supposed, but of the analyst, who [forgets] <does not understand> that these fantasies [are] <should> not <be taken> merely [to be understood] in a concretistic-reductive sense, but [also] <rather> in a constructive one. When this is realized [the state of stagnation is then often relieved] <, the standstill is often overcome> at a single stroke.

~~[Through constructive]~~ <Constructive> treatment of the unconscious ~~[the foundation is laid for]~~ <, that is, the question of meaning and purpose, paves the way for the patient's insight into that process which I call> the transcendent function. ~~[However, at first, the transcendent function is artificial, in so far as the knowledge of the physician plays an essential part in it.~~

~~This is perhaps the point at which to say –]~~ <It may not be superfluous, at this point, to say > a few words about the frequently heard objection that the constructive method is <simply> "suggestion." The method is based <rather,> on ~~[the fact that]~~ <evaluating> the symbol ~~[(i. e. the]~~ <(i.e.,> dream ~~[picture]~~ <-image> or fantasy) ~~[, is no longer evaluated semeiotically]~~ <not *semiotically*>, as a sign for elementary instinctual processes, but [really] *symbolically* ~~[, whereby]~~ <in the true sense,> the word "symbol" ~~[is]~~ <being> taken to mean the best possible expression ~~[of]~~ <for> a complex fact not yet clearly ~~[grasped]~~ <apprehended> by consciousness. Through reductive analysis of this expression nothing is ~~[won but the elementary components, which could equally well be expressed by innumerable other analogies. Reductive analysis of the symbol in]~~ <gained but a clearer view of the elements originally composing it, and though I would not deny that increased insight into these elements may have its advantages, it nevertheless bypasses the question of purpose. Dissolution of the symbol at> this stage of analysis is therefore ~~[thoroughly reprehensible. The method of obtaining the complex meaning]~~ <a mistake. To begin with, however, the method for working out the complex meanings> suggested by the symbol is ~~[at first, it is true,]~~ the same as in reductive analysis. The ~~[free]~~ associations of the patient are obtained, and ~~[they are]~~ as a rule ~~[good]~~ <they are plentiful> enough to be used in the synthetic method. ~~[Again they are used, not in a semiotic, but in a symbolic sense. The formula runs: What is being looked for is comparable to the association A, B, C, etc., as well as the manifest dream content.]~~ <Here again they are evaluated not semiotically but symbolically. The question we must ask is: to what meaning do the individual associations A, B, C point, when taken in conjunction with the manifest dream-content?>

An unmarried woman patient dreamt ~~[,]~~ <that> someone ~~[gives]~~ <gave> her a wonderful, richly ornamented, ~~[ancient]~~ <antique> sword dug up out of a tumulus ~~[:]~~ <.>

Associations

Her father's dagger, which he once flashed in the sun in front of her. It made a great impression on her. Her father was in every respect an energetic, strong-willed man, with an impetuous temperament, and adventurous in love affairs. A *Celtic* bronze sword: Patient is proud of her Celtic ancestry. The Celts are full of temperament, impetuous, passionate. The ornamentation has a mysterious look about it, ancient tradition, runes, ~~[sign]~~ <signs> of ancient wisdom, ancient ~~[civilisations]~~ <civilizations>, heritage of mankind, brought to light again out of the grave.

Analytical Interpretation

Patient has a pronounced father complex and a rich tissue of sexual fantasies about her father, whom she lost early. She always put herself in her mother's place, although with strong resistances towards her father. She has never been able to accept a man like her father and has therefore chosen weakly, neurotic men against her will. Also in the analysis violent resistance towards the physician-father. The dream digs up her wish for her father's "weapon <.>" The rest is clear. <In theory, this would immediately point to a phallic fantasy.>

Constructive Interpretation

It is as if the patient needed such a weapon. Her father had the weapon. He was energetic, lived accordingly, and also took upon himself the difficulties inherent in his temperament. Therefore, though living a passionate, exciting life he was not neurotic. This weapon is a very ancient heritage of mankind, which lay buried in the patient and was brought to light through excavation (analysis). The weapon has to do with insight, with wisdom. It is a means of attack and defence. Her father's weapon was a passionate ~~[,]~~ unbending will, with which he made his way through life. Up till now the patient has been the opposite in every respect. She is just on the point of realizing that a person can also will something and need not merely be driven, as she had always believed. The will based on a knowledge of life and <on> insight is an ancient heritage of the human race, which also is in her, but till now lay buried, for ~~[she is]~~ in this respect, too, <she is> her father's daughter. But she had not appreciated this till now, because her character had been that of a perpetually whining, pampered, spoilt child. She was extremely passive and completely given to sexual fantasies.

In this case there was no [~~further~~] need of <any> supplementary analogies on the part of the [~~physician~~] <analyst> . The patient's associations [~~had~~] provided all that was necessary. [~~Against~~] <It might be objected that> this treatment of the dream [~~it is possible to make the objection that it~~] involves suggestion. But [~~then~~] this ignores the fact that [~~without inner readiness for it~~] a suggestion is never accepted [~~. Or,~~] <without an inner readiness for it, or> if after great insistence it is accepted, it is immediately lost again. A suggestion [~~which~~] <that> is accepted for any length of time [~~,~~] always presupposes a marked psychological readiness [~~,~~] which is merely brought [~~to the surface~~] <into play> by the so-called suggestion. This objection is therefore thoughtless [~~,~~] and [~~endows~~] <credits> suggestion with a magical power it in no way possesses, otherwise suggestion therapy would have an enormous effect and would render analytical procedures quite superfluous. But this is [~~by no means so~~] <far from being the case. Furthermore, the charge of suggestion does not take account of the fact that the patient's own associations point to the cultural significance of the sword>.

After this digression <,> let us return to the question of the transcendent function. We have seen that <during treatment> the transcendent function [~~during treatment~~] is <,> in a sense <, an> "artificial" [~~,~~] <product> because it is [~~substantially~~] <largely> supported by the [~~physician. If however~~] <analyst. But if> the patient is to stand on his own feet he must [~~make this function his own. I have already mentioned that the~~] <not depend permanently on outside help. The> interpretation of dreams would be an ideal [~~instance of cooperation between unconscious and conscious productions, but it comes to grief because~~] <method for synthesizing the conscious and unconscious data, but> in practice the difficulties of [~~mastering it~~] <analyzing one's own dreams> are too great.

We must now make clear what is required to [~~create~~] <produce> the transcendent function. First and foremost, we need [~~to procure~~] the unconscious material. The most readily accessible expression of unconscious processes is [~~represented by~~] <undoubtedly> dreams. The dream is <,> so to speak <,> a pure product of the unconscious. The ~~{changes}~~ <alterations> which the dream undergoes in the process of ~~{becoming conscious, although this happens in an as yet unknown degree}~~ <reaching consciousness, although undeniable>, can be considered irrelevant, since they ~~{also}~~ <too> derive from the unconscious and are not intentional distortions ~~{based on insight. The distortions which may possibly be present}~~ <. Possible modifications of the original dream-image> derive from a more superficial ~~{level}~~ <layer> of the unconscious and therefore contain ~~{useful unconscious}~~ <valuable> material ~~{.}~~ <too.> They are ~~{merely}~~ further ~~{fantasies}~~ <fantasy-products> following the ~~{line}~~ <general trend> of the dream. ~~{This also}~~ <The same> applies to the ~~{frequent}~~ subsequent <images and> ideas which <frequently> occur while dozing or ~~{arise as free associations immediately}~~ <rise up spontaneously> on waking. Since the dream ~~{is derived from}~~ <originates in> sleep, it bears all the characteristics of an "abaissement du niveau mental" (Janet) <,> or of low energy <-> tension: logical discontinuity, fragmentary character, ~~{poor formation of analogies, superficial speech, clang and visual associations, contaminations, meaningless}~~ <analogy formations, superficial associations of the verbal, clang, or visual type, condensations, irrational> expressions, confusion, etc. With an increase ~~{in}~~ <of> energy <-> tension ~~{in the unconscious}~~, the dreams acquire a more ordered character ~~{. They}~~ <; they> become dramatically composed ~~{,}~~ <and> reveal ~~{distinct meaningful}~~ <clear sense-> connections, and the ~~{feeling value}~~ <valency> of the associations increases. ~~{Stereotype dreams always signify particular tension in the unconscious.~~

~~Since the tension of the libido }~~ <Since the energy-tension> in sleep is usually very ~~{slight, the dreams are such}~~ <low, dreams, compared with conscious material, are > inferior expressions of unconscious contents ~~{, that they}~~ <and> are very difficult to understand from a constructive ~~{viewpoint}~~ <point of view>, but are usually easier to understand reductively. ~~{Dreams are therefore in general}~~ <In general, dreams are > unsuitable or difficult to make use of in developing the transcendent function ~~{because they are usually too difficult for the individual to understand}~~ <, because they make too great demands on the subject>.

We must therefore look to other sources ~~{in order to procure}~~ <for the> unconscious material <.> ~~{:}~~ There are, for instance, <the> unconscious interferences in the waking state, ~~[free associations, unconscious disturbances of action, etc. These phenomena are usually more valuable]~~ <ideas “out of the blue,” slips, deceptions and lapses of memory, symptomatic actions, etc. This material is generally more useful> for the reductive method than <for> the constructive one; ~~[they are]~~ <it is> too fragmentary and ~~[suffer from lack of]~~ <lacks> continuity, which is indispensable for a meaningful synthesis. ~~[Furthermore they occur so episodically and are so rare and fortuitous that they can hardly be used for our purpose.~~

~~Spontaneous]~~ <Another source is spontaneous> fantasies ~~[are another matter]~~. They usually have ~~[a]~~ more composed and coherent character and ~~[, if there is a greater tension in the unconscious, they]~~ <often> contain much that is <obviously> significant. ~~[The trouble, however, is that in the course of treatment they often disappear, so that finally just when they are required there are no more.]~~Some ~~[people]~~ <patients> are able <to produce fantasies> at any time ~~[to reproduce fantasies, which they allow]~~ <, allowing them> to rise up freely simply by eliminating critical attention. Such fantasies can be used, ~~[only]~~ <though> this particular talent is none too common. ~~[But with practice the]~~ <The> capacity to produce free fantasies can <, however,> be developed <with practice>. The training consists first of all in systematic ~~[practice to eliminate]~~ <exercises for eliminating> critical attention, ~~[whereby]~~ <thus producing> a vacuum ~~[is produced]~~in consciousness. This encourages the emergence of <any> fantasies ~~[which]~~ <that> are lying in readiness. A prerequisite <, of course,> is that fantasies with a high libido <-> charge are actually lying ready. This is ~~[, of course,]~~ <naturally> not always the case. Where this is not so, special measures are required.

Before ~~[I enter]~~ <entering> upon a discussion of these, I must yield to an ~~[urge]~~ <uncomfortable feeling> which tells me that the reader may be asking dubiously, what really is the point of all this? And why is it so absolutely necessary to bring ~~[out]~~ <up> the unconscious contents? Is it not sufficient if from time to time they ~~[just]~~ come up ~~[by themselves]~~ <of their own accord> and make themselves <unpleasantly> felt? Does one have to drag the unconscious ~~[onto]~~ <to> the surface by force? On the contrary, should it not ~~[rather]~~ be the job of analysis to empty the unconscious of fantasies and in this way ~~[to]~~ render it ~~[as]~~ ineffective ~~[as possible]~~?

It may be ~~[good]~~ <as well> to consider these misgivings in somewhat more detail, since the methods for ~~[making]~~ <bringing the> unconscious ~~[contents conscious]~~ <to consciousness> may ~~[appear to]~~ <strike> the reader ~~[new,]~~ <as novel,> unusual <,> and perhaps even rather weird. We must therefore first ~~[consider]~~ <discuss> these natural objections, so that they shall not hold us up when we begin demonstrating ~~[these]~~ <the> methods <in question>.

As we have seen, we need the unconscious contents to supplement the conscious attitude. If the conscious attitude were only to a slight degree "directed," ~~[then]~~ the unconscious could flow in quite of its own accord. This is ~~[the case with all those individuals in whom the conscious function is only to a slight extent directed, as for instance with the primitives. As far as the primitives are concerned of course]~~ <what does in fact happen with all those people who have a low level of conscious tension, as for instance primitives. Among primitives,> no special measures are required to bring ~~[out]~~ <up> the unconscious. Nowhere <,> really <,> are special measures required for this ~~[purpose, since the individual to whom his unconscious contents are of no concern at all is, without being aware of it, the most influenced by these contents. There is no means at all by which the unconscious can be excluded from participation in life. This]~~ <, because those people who are least aware of their unconscious side are the most influenced by it. But they are unconscious of what is happening. The> secret participation of the unconscious ~~[in life]~~ is everywhere present ~~[,]~~ without ~~[one]~~ <our> having to search for it ~~[. But it is so accidental that it can never be relied upon, either in a positive or negative sense. Since the contamination is unconscious to us, we never know what actually happens]~~<, but as it remains unconscious we never really know what is going on> or what to expect. ~~[It is not this participation which concerns us here; what]~~ <What> we are searching for is ~~[the means]~~ <a way> to make conscious those ~~[unconscious contents which are on the point of influencing our actions. By this means the secret contamination of conscious and unconscious is]~~ <contents which are about to influence our actions, so that the secret interference of the unconscious and its unpleasant consequences can be> avoided.

The ~~[question will of course be asked: Why cannot this contamination of the conscious with unconscious contents be left alone]~~ <reader will no

doubt ask: why cannot the unconscious be left to its own devices>? Those who have not already had ~~{very}~~ <a few> bad ~~{experience}~~ <experiences> in this respect will ~~{of course have}~~ <naturally see> no reason to control the unconscious. But anyone with ~~{sufficient}~~ <sufficiently> bad experience will eagerly welcome the ~~{mere}~~ <bare> possibility of ~~{controlling the unconscious.}~~ <doing so.> Directedness is ~~{an absolute necessity}~~ <absolutely necessary> for the conscious process, but as we have seen it ~~{inevitably }~~ entails ~~{a}~~ <an unavoidable> one-sidedness. Since the psyche is a self-regulating system, ~~{as much as the living body, the corresponding regulatory counter-action develops}~~ <just as the body is, the regulating counteraction will always develop> in the unconscious. ~~{If}~~ <Were it not for the directedness of> the conscious function ~~{were not directed, the regulating}~~ <, the counteracting> influences of the unconscious could set in unhindered. It is just this directedness ~~{however which}~~ <that> excludes them. This ~~{of course does not make for suppression of the counter-action in the unconscious, which takes place in spite of it. But the}~~ <, of course, does not inhibit the counteraction, which goes on in spite of everything. Its> regulating influence ~~{is suppressed as much as possible by all the might of}~~ <, however, is eliminated by > critical attention and the ~~{purposive will, in as far as by reason of the prejudice discussed above the regulating influence seems not to correspond}~~ <directed will, because the counteraction as such seems incompatible> with the conscious direction. To ~~{that}~~ <this> extent the ~~{human}~~ psyche ~~{, at least that}~~ of civilized man ~~{,}~~ is no <longer a> self-regulating system ~~{,}~~ but <could> rather ~~{could}~~ be compared to a machine ~~{,}~~ whose speed <-> regulation is so insensitive that it can continue to function to ~~{a}~~ <the> point of self-injury ~~{.}~~ <, while on the other hand it is subject to the arbitrary manipulations of a one-sided will.>

~~{It}~~ <Now it> is a peculiarity of psychic functioning that <when> the unconscious counteraction ~~{, once}~~ <is suppressed it loses> its regulating influence ~~{is eliminated, exchanges, as it were, its favourable character for an unfavourable one. If it cannot act in a regulating way, it}~~ <. It then> begins to have an accelerating <and intensifying effect on the conscious process. It is as though the counteraction had lost its regulating influence, and hence its energy, altogether, for a condition then arises in which not only no inhibiting

counteraction takes place, but in which its energy seems to add itself to that of the conscious direction. To begin with, this naturally facilitates the execution of the conscious intentions, but because they are unchecked, they may easily assert themselves at the cost of the whole. For instance, when someone makes a rather bold assertion and suppresses the counteraction, namely a well-placed doubt, he will insist on it all the more, to his own detriment> ~~{effect in the direction of the conscious process. It seems as if there exists an optimum for the regulating influence of the unconscious which must not be exceeded. If it is exceeded, then a condition arises which can best be described as a summation of conscious energy (libido) and of the energy of the unconscious counter-action. (This is of course only an attempt to formulate experience connected with this problem). It may be that the mere elimination of the regulating influence suffices as an explanation, in that, by the act of suppression, energy is withdrawn from the regulating influence and thus the regulating process is reversed. The result is an over-regulation in favour of the conscious process and unfavourable to the unconscious one. However that may be, suppression of the unconscious regulating influence in any case ends more or less in a catastrophe}~~.<

>The ease with which the ~~{unconscious regulating process is eliminated reflects an extensive atrophy of the instincts}~~ <counteraction can be eliminated is proportional to the degree of dissociability of the psyche and leads to loss of instinct>. This is characteristic of, as well as very necessary for, civilized man, since instincts in their original strength can render social adaptation almost impossible. ~~{After all, the atrophy of the instincts should not necessarily be considered as a degeneration, but merely as}~~ <It is not a real atrophy of instinct but, in most cases, only> a relatively lasting product of education, ~~{which}~~ <and> would never have ~~{prevailed to such a degree, if it did not serve important}~~ <struck such deep roots had it not served the> interests of the individual. ~~{Indeed, civilized man finds himself in a somewhat awkward dilemma between nature and civilization.~~

~~Many good examples can be found for}~~ <Apart from the everyday cases met with in practice, a good example of> the suppression of the unconscious regulating influence ~~{discussed here. In order not to speak of everyday cases met with in practice, I shall take as an illustration the classical case of~~

~~Nietzsche's in~~] <can be found in Nietzsche's > *Zarathustra.* The discovery of the "higher" man, [~~as ,well as~~] <and also> of the "ugliest" man, [~~reflects~~] <expresses> the regulating influence [~~of the unconscious~~], for the "higher" men want to drag Zarathustra down [~~into~~] <to> the collective sphere of average humanity [~~,~~] as it always has been [~~. The~~] <, while the> "ugliest" man [~~in particular is the symbol~~] <is actually personification> of the counteraction [~~of the unconscious~~]. But the roaring lion of Zarathustra's moral conviction forces all these influences, above all [~~,~~] the feeling of pity, back again into the cave of the unconscious. Thus the regulating influence is suppressed, but not the [~~hidden counter-action~~] <secret counteraction> of the unconscious, which from now on becomes clearly noticeable in Nietzsche's writings. First he seeks [~~the~~] <his> adversary in Wagner, whom he cannot forgive for [~~*Parsival.* Soon however~~] <*Parsifal,* but soon> his whole wrath turns against Christianity and in particular against St. Paul, who [~~had~~] <in some ways> suffered a [~~similar fate that Nietzsche was soon to suffer~~] <fate similar to Nietzsche's>. As is well known [~~the~~] <, Nietzsche's> psychosis first [~~of all~~] produced [~~in him~~] an identification with the "Crucified Christ" and <then> with the dismembered [~~Dionysos~~] <Dionysus>. With this catastrophe the [~~counter-action of the unconscious had reached~~] <counteraction at last broke through to> the surface.

[~~A very beautiful psychological~~] <Another> example is the [~~classical~~] <classic> case of [~~delusion of grandeur,~~] <megalomania> preserved for us in the [~~4th Chapter~~] <fourth chapter> of the Book of Daniel. Nebuchadnezzar at the height of his power had a dream which foretold disaster if he did not humble himself. Daniel interpreted the dream quite expertly, but without getting a hearing. Subsequent events [~~however~~] showed <that> his interpretation [~~to be~~] <was> correct, for Nebuchadnezzar, after suppressing the [~~regulating influences of the unconscious, succumbed to the psychosis which contained just that counter-action from which the king had wished to escape~~] <unconscious regulating influence, fell victim to a psychosis that contained the very counteraction he had sought to escape:> he, the lord of the earth, [~~became~~] <was degraded to> an animal.

[~~A distant~~] <An> acquaintance <of mine> once told me a dream in which *he stepped out into space from the* [~~*peak*~~] <*top*> *of a mountain.* I explained to him something of the influence of the unconscious and warned him against

~~[all too dangerous undertakings, which he was particularly fond of]~~ <dangerous mountaineering expeditions, for which he had a regular passion>. But he laughed at such ideas. ~~[Six]~~ <A few> months later while climbing a mountain he actually did step off into space and was ~~[dead]~~ <killed>.

Anyone who has seen these things happen ~~[time]~~ <over> and <over> again in ~~[all possible shades]~~ <every conceivable shade> of dramatic intensity is bound to ponder. ~~[One]~~ <He> becomes aware how easy it is to overlook the regulating ~~[influence and wants therefore to do it better. One has learnt the need for paying attention to the unconscious, in order not to overlook the regulating action,]~~ <influences, and that he should endeavour to pay attention to the unconscious regulation> which is so necessary for our mental and physical <health. Accordingly he will try to help himself by practising> ~~[well-being. It would therefore appear very important to be aware of the utterances of the unconscious early and interpret them correctly, in order to prevent catastrophic results. For all the reasons cited, it follows that mere]~~ self-observation and <self-criticism. But> mere <self-observation and intellectual> self-analysis are entirely inadequate as a means ~~[of getting]~~ <to establishing> contact with the unconscious. Although ~~[the]~~ <no> human being can ~~[never]~~ be spared ~~[evil experience, yet]~~ <bad experiences,> everyone ~~[certainly]~~ shrinks from risking ~~[it]~~ <them>, especially if he sees any ~~[chance at all of avoiding such experience]~~ <way by which they might be circumvented>. Knowledge of the regulating influences of the unconscious ~~[is]~~ <offers just> such a possibility ~~[, which]~~ <and> actually does render much bad experience unnecessary. We can avoid ~~[making]~~ <a great> many detours ~~[which]~~ <that> are distinguished ~~[not]~~ by ~~[any]~~ <no> particular attraction but <only> by tiresome conflicts. It is ~~[sufficient if we]~~ <bad enough to> make ~~[the]~~ detours and painful mistakes in unknown and unexplored territory, but to get lost in inhabited country on broad highways is merely exasperating. ~~[One can be spared this by working out the regulating processes of the unconscious. It should therefore be worth the trouble to speak of the ways and means as to how the unconscious material can be obtained.]~~ <What, then, are the means at our disposal of obtaining knowledge of the regulating factors?>

If ~~[therefore]~~ there is no capacity to produce fantasies freely, ~~[then]~~ we have to resort to artificial aid. The ~~[occasion]~~ <reason> for ~~[calling upon]~~

<invoking> such aid is generally a depressed <or disturbed> state of mind ~~[,]~~ for which no ~~[good]~~ <adequate> cause can be ~~[shown]~~ <found>. Naturally the patient ~~[has an abundance of rational causes; the]~~ <can give any number of rationalistic reasons—the> bad weather alone suffices as a ~~[cause]~~ <reason>. But none of them is <really> satisfying as an explanation, ~~[since]~~ <for> a causal explanation of these ~~[mental conditions]~~ <states> is usually satisfying only to ~~[the]~~ <an> outsider <, and then only up to a point>. The outsider is ~~[satisfied when his need for causality is appeased]~~ <content if his causal requirements are more or less satisfied>; it is sufficient for him to know ~~[from]~~ where the thing comes ~~[, for]~~ <from;> he does not feel the challenge which, for the patient, ~~[lies]~~ <lie> in the depression. The patient would like to know what it is all for and how to gain relief. *In the intensity of the ~~[affective phenomenon]~~ <emotional disturbance itself> lies the value, the energy ~~[,]~~ which ~~[the sufferer]~~ <he> should have at his disposal ~~[to enhance his feeling of vitality. This suggests the following possibility.]~~ <in order to remedy the state of reduced adaptation.* Nothing is achieved by repressing this state or devaluing it rationally.>

~~[One starts by taking the patients mental condition as the object to be worked out, and this is done as follows: He should occupy himself intensively with the mood in an uncritical frame of mind, becoming absorbed in it, and noting down on paper a description of the mood and all fantasies which emerge. In doing so the fantasies must be allowed widest free-play. Out of this occupation there emerges]~~ <In order, therefore, to gain possession of the energy that is in the wrong place, he must make the emotional state the basis or starting point of the procedure. He must make himself as conscious as possible of the mood he is in, sinking himself in it without reserve and noting down on paper all the fantasies and other associations that come up. Fantasy must be allowed the freest possible play, yet not in such a manner that it leaves the orbit of its object, namely the affect, by setting off a kind of "chain-reaction" association process. This "free association," as Freud called it, leads away from the object to all sorts of complexes, and one can never be sure that they relate to the affect and are not displacements which have appeared in its stead. Out of this preoccupation with the object there comes> a more or less complete expression of <the> mood, which reproduces the ~~[contents]~~ <content> of the depression ~~[as extensively and faithfully as possible]~~ <in some

way, either concretely or symbolically>. Since the depression was not {~~made by consciousness, but represents~~} <manufactured by the conscious mind but is> an unwelcome intrusion {~~on the part of the unconscious, then the expression of mood so produced is a picture of the~~ } <from the unconscious, the elaboration of the mood is, as it were, a picture of the contents and> tendencies of the unconscious {~~as a whole, which are contained~~} <that were massed together> in the depression. {~~By working on the mood, libido is transferred to the unconscious standpoint. The energy value of the unconscious is thus increased, enabling it to modify the conscious direction. This procedure by itself may have a very~~} <The whole procedure is a kind of enrichment and clarification of the affect, whereby the affect and its contents are brought nearer to consciousness, becoming at the same time more impressive and more understandable. This work by itself can have a> favourable and vitalizing influence{~~; this is understandable for the reasons described. At any rate, by working on the mood a material is created, which owes its existence in part to the unconscious and in part to conscious effort~~} <. At all events, it creates a new situation, since the previously unrelated affect has become a more or less clear and articulate idea, thanks to the assistance and cooperation of the conscious mind>. This is the beginning of the transcendent function {~~.~~} <, i.e., of the collaboration of conscious and unconscious data.>

{~~There is still another method, not so much of working out the mood directly, but at least of expressing it. Individuals who possess some sort of talent for painting or drawing~~} <The emotional disturbance can also be dealt with in another way, not by clarifying it intellectually but by giving it visible shape. Patients who possess some talent for drawing or painting> can give expression to their mood by means of a picture. It is not important for the picture to be technically or aesthetically satisfying, but merely for the fantasy to have free {~~-~~} play and for the whole thing to be done as well as possible. In principle this procedure agrees {~~in every respect with the one mentioned first. In this case, too, a part-conscious part-unconscious product is created, embodying the common function of the conscious and the unconscious.~~} <with the one first described. Here too a product is created which is influenced by both conscious and unconscious, embodying the striving of the unconscious for the light and the striving of the conscious for substance.>

~~[However, we often see]~~ <Often, however, we find> cases ~~[in which]~~ <where> there is no ~~[really]~~ tangible mood or depression <at all>, but just a general, dull discontent ~~[which is difficult to grasp]~~, a feeling of resistance to everything, a sort of boredom or ~~[something like disgust of a vague nature, a sort of torture which cannot be defined more closely]~~ <vague disgust, an indefinable but excruciating emptiness>. In these cases no definite starting point ~~[is at hand, it]~~ <exists—it> would first have to be created. Here <a> special introversion of ~~[the]~~ libido is ~~[required,]~~ <necessary, supported> perhaps ~~[even supported]~~ by favourable external conditions, such as complete rest, especially at night, when the libido ~~[anyhow]~~ has <in any case> a tendency ~~[towards]~~ <to> introversion. ~~[(Night it is]~~ <("'Tis night:> now <do> all fountains speak louder ~~[, and]~~ <. And> my soul ~~[, too,]~~ <also> is a <bubbling> fountain." ~~[(Nietzsche).]~~ <)> Critical attention must be ~~[excluded]~~ <eliminated>. ~~[]~~

Visual types should concentrate on the expectation that an inner image will be produced. As a rule such a fantasy <-> picture will actually ~~[arise, and should be noted down carefully. Auditory]~~ <appear—perhaps hypnagogically—and should be carefully observed and noted down in writing. Audio-verbal> types usually hear inner words, perhaps ~~[initially]~~ mere fragments of apparently meaningless sentences ~~[,]~~ <to begin with,> which however should ~~[also]~~ be carefully noted down ~~[.]~~ <too.> Others ~~[in]~~ <at> such ~~[moments]~~ <times> simply hear their "other" voice. There are <,> indeed <,> not a few <people> who are well aware that they possess a sort of inner critic or judge ~~[,]~~ who immediately comments on everything they say or do. ~~[The insane]~~ <Insane people> hear this voice directly as auditory hallucinations. But normal people <too>, if their inner life is ~~[reasonably]~~ <fairly well> developed, are ~~[also]~~ able to reproduce this ~~[annoying]~~ <inaudible> voice without difficulty ~~[. To be sure, since]~~ <, though as> it is notoriously irritating and ~~[obstinate, it is always repressed. In such persons, however, conditions are particularly favourable for]~~ <refractory it is almost always repressed. Such persons have little difficulty in procuring the unconscious material and thus> laying the foundation of the transcendent function.

~~[Again there]~~ <There> are others <, again,> who neither see nor hear anything inside themselves, but ~~[their hands are able to express]~~ <whose

hands have the knack of giving expression to> the contents of the unconscious. Such people <can profitably work with plastic materials. Those> {~~should work with clay, without anything definite in mind, just giving free rein to their fantasy. Those, finally,~~} who are able to express the {~~contents of the~~} unconscious by means of bodily {~~movement~~} <movements> are {~~fairly~~} <rather> rare. The {~~difficulty~~} <disadvantage> that movements cannot {~~be easily remembered~~} <easily be fixed in the mind> must be met by {~~concentrating on~~} <making careful drawings of> the movements afterwards {~~and practising them~~}, so that they shall not {~~escape~~} <be lost to> the memory. {} Still rarer, but equally valuable <,> is automatic writing, direct or with the planchette. This {~~procedure,~~} <,> too, yields {~~very~~} useful results.

We now come to the next question {~~,~~} <:> what is to be done with the material obtained in one of the manners described. To this question {~~, as to all other problems dealt with here,~~} there is <no> *a priori* {~~no single~~} answer <; it is only when the conscious mind confronts the products of the unconscious that a provisional reaction will ensue which determines the subsequent procedure>. Practical experience alone can give {~~the valid answer~~} <us a clue>. So far as my experience goes, there appear to be two {~~possibilities~~} <main tendencies>. One is the way of *creative formulation,* the other the way of *understanding.*

{~~In one class of cases~~} <Where> the principle of creative formulation predominates {~~:~~} <,> the material {~~obtained~~ }is continually <varied and> increased {~~, whereby~~} <until> a kind of condensation of motifs into more or less {~~stereotype symbols or symbolic expressions takes place. These symbols gain in importance through associations and become elaborated at the same time. They are very effective, often mainly~~} <stereotyped symbols takes place. These stimulate the creative fantasy and serve chiefly> as aesthetic motifs {~~, i. e. they become an~~} <. This tendency leads to the> aesthetic problem of artistic {~~expression. The libido therefore flows in the direction of artistic expression.~~} <formulation.>

{~~In another class of cases~~} <Where on the other hand,> the principle of understanding predominates {~~. The~~} <, the> aesthetic aspect {~~of the material obtained~~} is {~~there~~} of relatively little interest and may <occasionally> even {~~occasionally~~} be felt as a hindrance. {~~What takes place rather~~} <Instead,

there> is an intensive {, intellectual analysis, whereby the motifs} <struggle to understand the *meaning*> of the unconscious {material are more or less intensively abstracted into ideas} <product.

Whereas aesthetic formulation tends to concentrate on the formal aspect of the motif, an intuitive understanding often tries to catch the meaning from barely adequate hints in the material, without considering those elements which would come to light in a more careful formulation>.

Neither of these {possibilities is realized} <tendencies can be brought about> by an arbitrary effort of will {, but they result from the personality} <; they are far more the result of the peculiar> make-up of the individual <personality>. Both have their typical dangers {,} and may lead one astray. The danger of the aesthetic tendency is {over-valuation of the artistic worth of the expressions produced, whereby the libido is led away} <overvaluation of the formal or "artistic"worth of the fantasy-productions; the libido is diverted> from the real goal of the transcendent function and {directed along the false track of} <sidetracked into> purely aesthetic {, artistic} problems of <artistic> expression. The danger of wanting to understand {is over-valuation of the ideational, i. e. philosophical worth of the elaborated ideas, whereby the libido is enticed away onto the intellectual problem} <the meaning is overvaluation of the content, which is subjected to intellectual analysis and interpretation, so that the essentially symbolic character of the product is lost>. Up to a point these {false tracks must however be taken} <bypaths must be followed> in order to satisfy {the} aesthetic or intellectual {demand,} <requirements,> whichever {predominates} <predominate> in the individual case. But the danger of both {false paths} <these bypaths> is worth stressing, {since the expressions produced are as a rule greatly over-valued, because previously they have been grossly undervalued} <for, after a certain point of psychic development has been reached, the products of the unconscious are greatly overvalued precisely because they were boundlessly undervalued before>. This undervaluation is {typical and} one of the greatest {hindrances in giving expression to} <obstacles in formulating the> unconscious material. {This} <It> reveals the collective standards by which {something} <anything> individual is {measured: Nothing} <judged: nothing> is considered good or beautiful {, which} <that> does not fit into the collective schema [of good or beautiful.

~~Our whole over-valuation of technical perfection shows itself here. But what is usually missing is the just appreciation of the subjective value of a product over and beyond all collective standards. This deeply rooted}~~ <, though it is true that contemporary art is beginning to make compensatory efforts in this respect. What is lacking is not the collective recognition of the individual product but its subjective appreciation, the understanding of its meaning and value for the *subject*. This> feeling of inferiority for one's own product is of course not ~~{found}~~ <the rule> everywhere. Sometimes <we find> the <exact> opposite ~~{of this is seen, namely}~~ <:> a naive and uncritical ~~{over-valuation. But when the initial obstacle of the}~~ <overvaluation coupled with the demand for collective recognition once the initial> feeling of inferiority ~~{is overcome, it tends to turn into its opposite, namely into just as extreme an over-valuation of the product. Vice versa, an initial over-valuation is likely to change into a depreciatory scepsis. These erroneous judgements}~~ <has been overcome. Conversely, an initial overvaluation can easily turn into depreciatory scepticism. These erroneous judgments> are due to the individual's ~~{extreme lack of independence, since he is only able to measure}~~ <unconsciousness and lack of self-reliance: either he is able to judge only> by collective standards ~~{and cannot evaluate himself or his individual products correctly}~~ <, or else, owing to ego-inflation, he loses his capacity for judgment altogether>.

One tendency seems to be the regulating principle of the other; both are ~~{related}~~ <bound together> in a compensatory ~~{manner.}~~ <relationship.> Experience ~~{confirms}~~ <bears out> this formula. ~~{As}~~ <So> far as it is possible at this stage to draw <more> general conclusions, we could say that ~~{the tendency towards aesthetic expression seems to need the tendency towards understanding, and equally the tendency towards}~~ <aesthetic formulation needs understanding of the meaning, and> understanding needs ~~{that of}~~ aesthetic ~~{expression. Both}~~ <formulation. The two> supplement each other to form the transcendent function.

The first steps along both ~~{ways}~~ <paths> follow the same principle: consciousness ~~{lends}~~ <puts> its ~~{means}~~ <media> of expression ~~{to}~~ <at the disposal of> the unconscious ~~{contents, it}~~ <content. It> must not do more than ~~{that}~~ <this> at first, ~~{in order}~~ <so as> not to exert undue influence ~~{on the unconscious contents. Therefore it looks as if the unconscious were taking~~

~~the lead as regards form and content. This means a weakening of]~~ <. In giving the content form, the lead must be left as far as possible to the chance ideas and associations thrown up by the unconscious. This is naturally something of a setback for> the conscious standpoint ~~[, which the individual]~~ <and is> often ~~[experiences]~~ <felt> as painful. It is not difficult to understand this when we remember <how> the ~~[kind of contents in]~~ <contents of >the unconscious ~~[, all the]~~ <usually present themselves: as> things which ~~[either]~~ are too weak ~~[from the start]~~ <by nature> to cross the threshold ~~[of consciousness or which have been repressed from consciousness because they ran counter to the conscious direction. The contents coming up from the unconscious are either unwelcome or unexpected irrational things which had been banished from consciousness, partly unjustly, but to some extent quite rightly, if considered from the point of view of collective values. A small part appears to be of unusually great value, and another small part appears to be of absolutely no value at all, sheer dross adhering to the molten gold. But those contents which, considered from the collective standpoint, appear worthless can be of greatest value]~~ <, or as incompatible elements that were repressed for a variety of reasons. Mostly they are unwelcome, unexpected, irrational contents, disregard or repression of which seems altogether understandable. Only a small part of them has any unusual value, either from the collective or from the subjective standpoint. But contents that are collectively valueless may be exceedingly valuable when seen> from the standpoint of the individual ~~[, if they are strongly loaded with libido. To gain possession of the unconscious libido is one of our chief aims. This is, of course, primarily to the advantage of the individual and only benefits society in so far as the particular individual concerned is a useful member of society, and society is therefore interested in the continuance of his individual existence]~~ <. This fact expresses itself in their affective tone, no matter whether the subject feels it as negative or positive. Society, too, is divided in its acceptance of new and unknown ideas which obtrude their emotionality. The purpose of the initial procedure is to discover the feeling-toned contents, for in these cases we are always dealing with situations where the one-sidedness of consciousness meets with the resistance of the instinctual sphere>.

The two ways do not divide until the aesthetic problem becomes decisive for <the> one type of person and the intellectual <-moral> problem {~~decisive~~} for the other. The ideal case would {~~then~~} be if these two {~~possibilities~~} <aspects> could exist side by side or {~~succeed each other, that is understanding and expression alternating. The one can hardly exist without the other. In my experience at least, such one-sidedness in the long run had no stability. Experience has taught me that it is simply impossible by means of the intellect alone to bring about anything like an adequate understanding of the unconscious contents, the same applies to exclusively aesthetic expression. There are~~} <rhythmically succeed each other; that is, if there were an alternation of creation and understanding. It hardly seems possible for the one to exist without the other, though it sometimes does happen in practice: the creative urge seizes possession of the object at the cost of its meaning, or the urge to understand overrides the necessity of giving it form. The> unconscious contents {~~which cannot be made conscious in any way at all except by intellectual understanding; again others can only be experienced by means of aesthetic expression~~} <want first of all to be seen clearly, which can only be done by giving them shape, and to be judged only when everything they have to say is tangibly present. It was for this reason that Freud got the dream-contents, as it were, to express themselves in the form of "free associations" before he began interpreting them.

It does not suffice in all cases to elucidate only the conceptual context of a dream-content. Often it is necessary to clarify a vague content by giving it a visible form. This can be done by drawing, painting, or modelling>. Often the hands know how to solve a riddle {~~, which the mind tries to do in vain.~~} <with which the intellect has wrestled in vain. By shaping it, one goes on dreaming the dream in greater detail in the waking state, and the initially incomprehensible, isolated event is integrated into the sphere of the total personality, even though it remains at first unconscious to the subject. Aesthetic formulation leaves it at that and gives up any idea of discovering a meaning. This sometimes leads patients to fancy themselves artists—misunderstood ones, naturally. The desire to understand, if it dispenses with careful formulation, starts with the chance idea or association and therefore lacks an

adequate basis. It has better prospects of success if it begins only with the formulated product. The less the initial material is shaped and developed, the greater is the danger that understanding will be governed not by the empirical facts but by theoretical and moral considerations. The kind of understanding with which we are concerned at this stage consists in a reconstruction of the meaning that seems to be immanent in the original "chance" idea.>

~~[I am far from thinking that this account of how to obtain unconscious material is in any way conclusive. I am quite satisfied if I have succeeded to some extent in shedding some light on these extremely complicated matters.~~

~~In procuring the unconscious material we had to leave the lead entirely with the unconscious, in order to give it as adequate an opportunity as possible to unfold and take on shape. When this undertaking succeeds, then the second great problem arises: how this position of the unconscious is related to the ego. This brings us to the problem of how the unconscious and the ego]~~ <It is evident that such a procedure can legitimately take place only when there is a sufficient motive for it. Equally, the lead can be left to the unconscious only if it already contains the will to lead. This naturally happens only when the conscious mind finds itself in a critical situation. Once the unconscious content has been given form and the meaning of the formulation is understood, the question arises as to how the ego will relate to this position, and how the ego and the unconscious> are to come to terms. ~~[In the practical handling of this question]~~ <This is the second and more important stage of the procedure, the bringing together of opposites for the production of a third: the transcendent function. At this stage> it is no longer the unconscious ~~[which has the prerogative of leadership]~~ <that takes the lead>, but the ego.

~~[Here I must first say that when speaking of the ego in this connection I do not mean the persona but the individual ego, that smallest point in the indefinitely extensive, collective psyche, arising out of the analysis of the persona in the collective psyche. The ego, as a result of its identity with the individuals own body, has a unique and singular combination of qualities, in fact it consists just in that very uniqueness of the combination, while the elements making up the combination are qualities of a collective character.~~

~~This individually determined ego acts as a sort of counterpole to the collective psyche. Collective psyche and ego also have a compensatory relationship towards each other and in each case the one is the regulating principle of the other. Therefore the conscious ego representing the highest expression of the function of differentiation is of the same value as the collective psyche. The unconscious at this stage of psychological development is pure collective psyche and therefore has the tendency towards disintegration, which is contrary to that of the ego. The ego differentiates and builds up into a whole, while the collective psyche levels out and breaks up the whole into its parts]~~ <We shall not define the individual ego here, but shall leave it in its banal reality as that continuous centre of consciousness whose presence has made itself felt since the days of childhood. It is confronted with a psychic product that owes its existence mainly to an unconscious process and is therefore in some degree opposed to the ego and its tendencies>.

This standpoint is essential ~~[for any confrontation]~~ <in coming to terms> with the unconscious. The position of the ego must be maintained as being of equal ~~[importance as]~~ <value to> the counter-position of the unconscious ~~[. This is no mere empty phrase but]~~ <, and vice versa. This amounts to> a very necessary warning ~~[. For just as civilized man's psychology of consciousness has an enormously limiting]~~ <: for just as the conscious mind of civilized man has a restrictive> effect on the unconscious, <so> the ~~[re-discovered]~~ <rediscovered> unconscious <often> has a really dangerous ~~[and disintegrating effect on the conscious ego. The ego-synthesis can often be maintained only with the greatest effort in face of the action of the unconscious which is continually dissolving things into their elements. The danger is that the ego will disintegrate by being completely at sea in all the possibilities and chimaera of the unconscious. There would be no danger of this, or at least not much]~~ <effect on the ego. In the same way that the ego suppressed the unconscious before, a liberated unconscious can thrust the ego aside and overwhelm it. There is a danger of the ego losing its head, so to speak, that it will not be able to defend itself against the pressure of affective factors—a situation often encountered at the beginning of schizophrenia. This danger would not exist, or would not be so acute>, if the process of having it out with the unconscious ~~[were psychologically somehow limited, e. g. were merely intellectual]~~ <could somehow divest the affects of their dynamism. And this is what does in fact happen when the counter-position is aestheticized or intellectualized>. But the confrontation with the unconscious ~~[is, and]~~ must be ~~[,]~~ a many-sided ~~[process. For]~~ <one, for> the transcendent function is ~~[no psychological partial process, running an isolated course, but is rather a new regulation of the stream of life itself. Analytical treatment, too, rightly understood, is never an isolated process, a psychological bottle of medicine, or spa treatment, but a new adjustment to the conditions of life, and accordingly is thoroughly all-round, penetrating every sphere of life. The transcendent function must be of the same nature. It must be valid for every sphere of life and its results must be binding in action]~~ <not a partial process running a conditioned course; it is a total and integral event in which all aspects are, or should be, included. The affect must therefore be deployed in its full strength. Aestheticization and intellectualization are excellent weapons against dangerous affects, but they should be used only when there is a vital threat, and not for the purpose of avoiding a necessary task.

Thanks to the fundamental insight of Freud, we know that emotional factors must be given full consideration in the treatment of the neuroses. The personality *as a whole* must be taken seriously into account, and this applies to both parties, the patient as well as the analyst. How far the latter may hide behind the shield of theory remains a delicate question, to be left to his discretion. At all events, the treatment of neurosis is not a kind of psychological water-cure, but a renewal of the personality, working in every direction and penetrating every sphere of life>. Coming to terms with the ~~[unconscious viewpoint is accordingly an earnest matter,]~~ <counter-position is a serious matter> on which sometimes a <very> great deal depends. ~~[It]~~ <Taking the other side seriously> is an essential prerequisite of the ~~[transcendent function to take the unconscious seriously. By taking it seriously I acknowledge my readiness to accept the regulating effect of the unconscious and permit it to influence my actions. Taking the unconscious seriously does not mean taking it literally, but it does mean giving credit to the unconscious, thus allowing the unconscious a possibility of developing.]~~ <process, for only in that way can the regulating factors exert an influence on our actions. Taking it seriously

does not mean taking it literally, but it does mean giving the unconscious credit, so that it has a chance to cooperate with consciousness instead of automatically disturbing it.> ~~[In having it out]~~ <Thus, in coming to terms> with the unconscious, not only ~~[must]~~ <is> the standpoint of the ego ~~[be maintained]~~ <justified>, but the unconscious ~~[must be afforded]~~ <is granted> the same ~~[right]~~ <authority>. The ego takes the lead, but ~~[with due apprecia-tion of the standpoint of]~~ the unconscious <must be allowed to have its say too—*audiatur et altera pars*>.

The way this can be done is best shown by those cases in which the "other" voice is more or less distinctly heard. For such people it is technically very simple to note down the "other" voice in writing and to answer its statements from the standpoint of the ego. It is exactly as if a dialogue were taking place between two human beings with equal rights, each of whom gives the other credit for a valid argument and considers it worth while to modify the conflicting standpoints by means of thorough ~~[discussion, and in this way to strike a balance or at least make a compromise]~~ <comparison and discussion or else to distinguish them clearly from one another. Since the way to agreement seldom stands open, in most cases a long conflict will have to be borne, demanding sacrifices from both sides. Such a rapprochement could just as well take place between patient and analyst, the role of devil's advocate easily falling to the latter>.

The present day shows with appalling clarity how little able people are to let the other man's argument count ~~[. This]~~ <, although this> capacity ~~[however is an essential, basic]~~ <is a fundamental and indispensable> condition ~~[of]~~ <for> any human community. ~~[It is therefore of great educational interest for every-one to develop this faculty in himself as far as possible. And this is best done by having it out with the unconscious, which contains the other standpoint with all possible distinctness, since consciousness is largely one-sided.]~~ <Every-one who proposes to come to terms with himself must reckon with this basic problem. For, to the degree that he does not admit the validity of the other person, he denies the "other" within himself the right to exist—and vice versa. The capacity for inner dialogue is a touchstone for outer objectivity.>

~~[The confrontation with the unconscious appears simple in the situation discussed, but it is]~~ <Simple as the process of coming to terms may be in the

case of the inner dialogue, it is undoubtedly> more complicated in other cases ~~[, where only products are available which, though eloquent, are unsuitable for dialogue. It is however possible that the reaction on the part of the ego occasioned by these products leads in turn to a modification of later products, just as the products of the unconscious can modify the psychology of the ego. The modification process itself however remains pretty well in the dark. It is perhaps]~~ <where only visual products are available, speaking a language which is eloquent enough for one who understands it, but which seems like deaf-and-dumb language to one who does not. Faced with such products, the ego must seize the initiative and ask: "How am I affected by this sign?" This Faustian question can call forth an illuminating answer. The more direct and natural the answer is, the more valuable it will be, for directness and naturalness guarantee a more or less total reaction. It is> not absolutely necessary for the process of confrontation itself to become conscious in every detail. ~~[The main thing is that the union of conscious and unconscious, which we have called the transcendent function, should be achieved.]~~ <Very often a total reaction does not have at its disposal those theoretical assumptions, views, and concepts which would make clear apprehension possible. In such cases one must be content with the wordless but suggestive feelings which appear in their stead and are more valuable than clever talk.>

~~[The transcendent function lies between the conscious and the unconscious standpoint and is a living phenomenon, a way of life, which partly conforms with the unconscious as well as the conscious and partly does not. It is an individual-collective phenomenon which in principle agrees with the direction of life which anyone would follow, if he were to live in a completely unconscious, instinctive way. This explains why primitive man so often appears as the symbol for the transcendent function. Back to nature in Rousseau's sense is impossible and would only be a futile regression. One can however go forwards and through psychological development again reach nature, but this time consciously taking account of instinct]~~ <The shuttling to and fro of arguments and affects represents the transcendent function of opposites. The confrontation of the two positions generates a tension charged with energy and creates a living, third thing—not a logical stillbirth in accordance with the principle *tertium non datur* but a movement out of the suspension be-

tween opposites, a living birth that leads to a new level of being, a new situation. The transcendent function manifests itself as a quality of conjoined opposites. So long as these are kept apart—naturally for the purpose of avoiding conflict—they do not function and remain inert.

In whatever form the opposites appear in the individual, at bottom it is always a matter of a consciousness lost and obstinately stuck in one-sidedness, confronted with the image of instinctive wholeness and freedom. This presents a picture of the anthropoid and archaic man with, on the one hand, his supposedly uninhibited world of instinct and, on the other, his often misunderstood world of spiritual ideas, who, compensating and correcting our one-sidedness, emerges from the darkness and shows us how and where we have deviated from the basic pattern and crippled ourselves psychically>.

I must content myself here with a description of the ~~[external]~~ <outward> forms and possibilities of the transcendent function. Another ~~[equally important task would be to describe the contents of the transcendent function]~~ <task of greater importance would be the description of its contents>. There is already a mass of material on this subject ~~[. But]~~ <, but not> all the difficulties ~~[involved in a description of them have not]~~ <in the way of exposition have> yet been overcome. A number of preparatory studies are still ~~[necessary]~~ <needed> before the ~~[conceptional]~~ <conceptual> foundation is laid ~~[, upon which a comprehensive and unmistakable presentation]~~ <which would enable us to give a clear and intelligible account> of the contents of the transcendent function ~~[is possible]~~. I have unfortunately had the experience that the scientific public ~~[is]~~ <are> not everywhere in a position to follow <a> purely psychological ~~[considerations and descriptions, since either people]~~ <argument, since they either> take it too personally ~~[, or a sort of]~~ <or are bedevilled by> philosophical ~~[-]~~ <or> intellectual ~~[prejudice interferes]~~ <prejudices>. This renders any meaningful appreciation of the psychological ~~[relationships]~~ <factors> quite impossible. If people take it personally ~~[,]~~ their ~~[judgement]~~ <judgment> is always subjective, and they declare everything to be impossible which ~~[perhaps does]~~ <seems> not <to> apply in their case ~~[,]~~ or which they prefer not to acknowledge. They are quite incapable of realizing that <what is valid for them may not be valid at all> for another person with a different psychology ~~[things are just different. Philosophical prejudice~~

~~always wants to find out~~] <. We are still very far from possessing a general valid scheme of explanation in all cases.

One of the greatest obstacles to psychological understanding is the inquisitive desire to know> whether the psychological [~~relationship postulated is objectively real, and completely overlooks the fact that for the other person subjectively this condition actually exists, otherwise he could not have produced it at all. At the most the question might be raised, whether the condition is causal or creatively purposeful. As long as science identifies itself with the causal principle, only half of psychology will come within the realm of science. The other half however, which is orientated towards the goal, remains veiled by scientific prejudice~~] <factor adduced is "true" or "correct." If the description of it is not erroneous or false, then the factor is valid in itself and proves its validity by its very existence. One might just as well ask if the duck-billed platypus is a "true" or "correct" invention of the Creator's will. Equally childish is the prejudice against the role which mythological assumptions play in the life of the psyche. Since they are not "true," it is argued, they have no place in a scientific explanation. But mythologems *exist*, even though their statements do not coincide with our incommensurable idea of "truth."

As the process of coming to terms with the counter-position has a total character, nothing is excluded. Everything takes part in the discussion, even if only fragments become conscious. Consciousness is continually widened through the confrontation with previously unconscious contents, or—to be more accurate—could be widened if it took the trouble to integrate them. That is naturally not always the case. Even if there is sufficient intelligence to understand the procedure, there may yet be a lack of courage and self-confidence, or one is too lazy, mentally and morally, or too cowardly, to make an effort. But where the necessary premises exist, the transcendent function not only forms a valuable addition to psychotherapeutic treatment, but gives the patient the inestimable advantage of assisting the analyst on his own resources, and of breaking a dependence which is often felt as humiliating. It is a way of attaining liberation by one's own efforts and of finding the courage to be oneself>.

APPENDIX B

REFERENCES TO THE TRANSCENDENT FUNCTION IN JUNG'S WORKS, LETTERS, AND SEMINARS

REFERENCES TO THE TRANSCENDENT FUNCTION IN JUNG'S WORKS, LETTERS, AND SEMINARS

Listed below are the references to the transcendent function in Jung's written works, his published letters, and his published seminars. The first column gives the name and citation of the work (see the reference list for the full citation); the second column sets forth the pages of the work that the author believes will give the reader the relevant passages that lead up to and follow the specific reference to the transcendent function; the third column shows actual pages where the transcendent function is mentioned with multiple references on a given page indicated in parentheses.

Work/Citation	Excerpt/Pages	Reference(s)
Written Works		
Psychological Types (CW, Vol. 6)	Pages 105–115	Page 115
	Pages 125–126	Page 126
	Pages 251–252	Page 252
	Pages 478–481	Page 480
"Relations Between the Ego and the Unconscious" (CW, Vol. 7, pp. 123–241)	Pages 133–135	Page 134
	Pages 219–220	Pages 219(2), 220(2), 222, 223, 224
"Psychological Commentary on 'The Tibetan Book of Great Liberation'" (CW, Vol. 11, pp. 475–508)	Pages 488–492	Page 489(3), 491
	Pages 500–501	Pages 500, 501
	Pages 506–508	Pages 506, 508
"Conscious, Unconscious, and Individuation" (CW, Vol. 9I, pp. 275–289)	Pages 286–289	Page 289(2)
"On the psychology of the Unconscious" (CW, Vol. 7, pp. 3–119)	Pages 80–81	Page 80(3)
	Pages 97–99	Page 99
	Pages 109–116	Pages 109, 110, 116

WORK/CITATION	EXCERPT/PAGES	REFERENCE(S)
WRITTEN WORKS		
Symbols of Transformation (CW, Vol. 5)	Pages 430–434	Page 433
Mysterium Coniunctionis (CW, Vol. 14)	Pages 199–203	Pages 200(2), 203(2)
"A Psychological View of Conscience" (CW, Vol. 10, pp. 437–455)	Pages 453–455	Page 454
LETTERS		
Letter to A. Zarine, May 3, 1939 (Letters, Vol. I, 1906–1951)	Pages 269–271	Pages 267(3), 268(8), 269(2)
Letter to Père Lachat, March 27, 1954 (CW, Vol. 18)	Pages 675–691	Page 690(2)
Letter to Fr. V. White, April 10, 1954 (Letters, Vol. I, 1906–1951)	Pages 163–174	Page 168
Letter to E. Böhler, December 14, 1955 (Letters, Vol. II, 1951–1961)	Pages 282–284	Page 283
SEMINARS/LECTURES		
Lecture 2, March 30, 1925 (Seminar on Analytical Psychology)	Pages 9–14	Pages 10, 11
Lecture 4, April 13, 1925 (Seminar on Analytical Psychology)	Pages 26–34	Page 26(6), 34(2)
Summer, 1930 Lecture V, June 4, 1930 (Seminar on Dream Analysis)	Pages 637–653	Page 648(7)
Lecture V, June 3, 1936 (Seminar on Nietzsche's *Zarathustra*)	Pages 965–982	Page 975
Lecture II, May 11, 1938 (Seminar on Nietzsche's *Zarathustra*)	Pages 1230–1247	Page 1231

APPENDIX C

REVIEW OF LITERATURE RELATING TO "THE TRANSCENDENT FUNCTION"

REVIEW OF LITERATURE RELATING TO "THE TRANSCENDENT FUNCTION"

INTRODUCTION

This section reviews topics, references, and literature that is not emphasized in the body of the book so that the reader may have access to as much information on the transcendent function as possible. While reviewing the sources, the aim is not to achieve any final, objective interpretation of the literature but rather to set the stage for breaking new theoretical ground. This is not to imply that any of the writers reviewed are deficient in their analysis. Quite the contrary. The literature surveyed represents prodigious scholarship and profound thought. We honor the work by engaging it in a manner that will lead us to a new perspective and a fresh theoretical landscape upon which we can subsequently tread for further development.

The literature will be reviewed in several sections. Though categorization is helpful for systematic discourse, it must overtake neither the material's substance nor the way we engage it. This section does not attempt to include every possible source; further references are contained elsewhere in the book. The material will be covered in the following subsections: (1) Jung and Jung's writings; (2) basic reference materials relating to Jungian psychology and Jungian analysis; (3) others' comments on the transcendent function within Jung's metapsychology; (4) the origins of the transcendent function; (5) the role of the analyst in working with the transcendent function; (6) the manifestation of the transcendent function in depth clinical applications; (7) the transcendent function as it is reflected in cultural, political, and societal contexts; and (8) the relationship of the transcendent function to religious and spiritual matters.

JUNG AND JUNG'S WRITINGS

The heart of this book is Jung's paper "The Transcendent Function" (1957/1960). Though a detailed discussion of the paper is the subject of chapter 2, a brief list of the subjects Jung discusses include: (1) the definition of the transcendent function and the reason for its name (pp. 69, 73); (2) the definiteness and directedness of the conscious ego (pp. 69–73); (3) the way consciousness and the unconscious disagree with one another, thereby forming opposites (pp. 69, 73–75); (4) the synthetic or constructive method (pp. 73–75); (5) the role of transference and the analyst in mediating the transcendent function (p. 74); (6) the sources of unconscious material (pp. 76–78, 82–83); (7) the self-regulating influence and affect on the psyche of the unconscious (pp. 78–81); (8) the confrontation by the conscious ego of the unconscious material (pp. 84–88); and (9) the dialogue between the conscious and unconscious yielding the transcendent function (pp. 89–91).

Jung refers to or discusses the transcendent function in eight of his other works. In *Psychological Types* (1921/1971), for example, he connects the operation of the transcendent function to symbol and fantasy and shows how they are fundamental to it. In "Relations Between the Ego and the Unconscious" (1928/1953), Jung offers his view of how archetypal contents from the objective psyche guide the transcendent function in assimilating the unconscious to effect a change of personality. In "Conscious, Unconscious, and Individuation" (1939/1959), Jung makes the transcendent function fundamental to the teleological individuation process. Referring to how psyche consists of both conscious and unconscious, he describes "two incongruous halves which together should form a whole" (p. 287). Further, Jung gives interesting insights into his ideas about the transcendent function in four letters. All of these references, coincidentally, deal with subjects relating to religion. These and other references, discussed in chapter 3, raise the issue of the connection between the transcendent function and spiritual matters. Finally, Jung mentions or refers to the transcendent function in five public seminars. These references cover a wide range of topics: the appearance of the transcendent function in dreams (1984, p. 648); its appearance in Nietzsche's *Zarathustra* (1988a, p. 976; 1988b, p. 1231); the natural occurrence of the transcendent function in a patient's analysis (1989a, p. 11); and Jung's description of how the transcendent function worked to help him integrate his own inferior function (1989b, pp. 26, 34). These references are discussed in chapter 3.

BASIC REFERENCE MATERIALS

The transcendent function is, of course, also referred to and discussed in a variety of basic reference materials about Jungian psychology and psychotherapy. Though an exhaustive list of such reference materials would be impractical, a representative sampling is instructive both for context and for further reference by the reader. Samuels, Shorter, and Plaut (1986) place the transcendent function at the heart of Jung's psychology, saying that he "con-

the mechanisms of the transcendent function and chaos theory. He posits that when the tension of psychological opposites is held, seemingly chaotic symbols begin to form recognizable patterns through the transcendent function in ways that are analogous to the inherent ordering processes of nature. In his intriguing analysis of the workings of the transcendent function in Shakespeare's *A Midsummer Night's Dream*, Willeford (1992) posits that the opposites generate a symbol derived equally from the most highly differentiated and most primitive levels of psyche (p. 261). Other writers begin to explore the idea of opposites not only as between the conscious and unconscious, Jung's formulation of the classical transcendent function, but also the formulation of and tension between opposite positions that are both manifest in the conscious (Dehing, 1992, p. 28; Solomon, 1992, p. 128; Ulanov, 1992, p. 228).

At least two writers analyze how and why opposites function in human consciousness. Dehing (1992) states: "Any human being probably presents some degree of splitting. . . . [T]he very development of ego consciousness necessarily leads us to divide our subjective experience into poles: for example, good and bad, love and hate, life and death" (p. 27). Corbett (1996), states it somewhat differently: "Since consciousness requires discrimination, tension between its constituents is inevitable" (p. 138). Finally, and key to a debate within the Jungian community, is the issue of whether Jung's theory of opposites is accurate or whether it reflects a feature of Jung's personal psychology. Corbett (1992) offers a view, held by others (e.g., Samuels, 1985), that though there is a drive to unify and integrate, it does not flow from opposites but from a drive to recover psychological parts that are missing. This theme is explored in detail in chapter 3.

Symbol

Since Jung gave central importance to the symbol in bringing unconscious material to consciousness, there are several sources that discuss the importance of the symbol in the transcendent function. Corbett (1992) states: "Movement from unconscious into consciousness occurs in dreams or fantasies via the symbol" (p. 395). Van Eenwyk (1992) explains further:

> Symbolic images transcend not only categories, but themselves as well, challenging the perceptions and assumptions of those who encounter them. By expanding awareness beyond the immediately apparent, symbols and metaphors exert a compelling effect. . . .
>
> While all symbols transcend categories, a certain type of symbol integrates them into new amalgamations that, in a synergetic manner, become more than the sum of their parts. That is, each amalgamation incorporates greater realms of meaning than can any single conglomeration of the original images. Jung called the process by which such symbols are generated the "transcendent function." (p. 273)

Jung felt that symbols play a central role in bringing together conscious and unconscious material since the symbol itself is partly conscious and partly unconscious. As he stated in one of his early writings (1921/1971):

> The symbol is always a product of an extremely complex nature, since data from every psychic function have gone into its making. It is, therefore, neither *rational* nor *irrational* (qq.v.). It certainly has a side that accords with reason, but it has another side that does not; for it is composed not only of rational but also of irrational data supplied by pure inner and outer perception. . . .
>
> But precisely because the new symbol is born of man's highest spiritual aspirations and must at the same time spring from the deepest roots of his being, it cannot be a one-sided product of the most highly differentiated mental functions but must derive equally from the lowest and most primitive levels of the psyche. (p. 478)

Since symbols derive equally from humanity's highest and most primitive levels, the symbol has been considered key to bringing into consciousness matters we would otherwise avoid. Willeford (1992), for example, refers to the symbol as mediating the conflict between such extreme levels of consciousness (p. 261). Furthermore, symbols, containing both conscious and unconscious material, standing in the differentiated present and the primitive past, have incredible energy for transformation. As stated powerfully by von Franz:

> Differentiated and primitive, conscious and unconscious are united in the symbol [footnote omitted], as well as all other possible psychic opposites. . . . Jung called the unknown activity of the unconscious which produces real, life-giving symbols the *transcendent function* because this process facilitates a transition from one attitude to another. (1980, p. 83)

Thus, symbol is integral to the operation of the transcendent function.

Individuation

Jung postulated that the transcendent function is central to the individuation process. He assigned to it "a rather extraordinary task: the psyche consists of two incongruous halves which together should form a whole" (1939/1959, p. 287). Jung saw psychological health as requiring individuation and individuation as being impossible without the transcendent function. As stated somewhat differently by Corbett (1992), the transcendent function "describes the capacity of the psyche to change and grow toward individuation when consciousness and the unconscious join, revealing the essential person" (p.

395). Handel (1992) makes a connection between the transcendent function, synchronicity, and individuation. He posits that the transcendent function manifests through synchronicities that unite unconnected internal elements of the psyche and external elements of matter in seemingly coincidental but purposeful ways. He asserts that those synchronicities represent the union of spirit and matter and are integral to the individuation path:

> This union [of spirit and matter] is one of Jung's principal examples of an activation of the transcendent function.
>
> The most startling expression of the transcendent function is a synchronicity, defined as the acausal meaningful coincidence of two events, one of which is experienced internally to the psyche and the other externally. It rests upon an archetypal foundation.
>
> Jung attributed a central role to the transcendent function. It follows that the phenomena of synchronicity are of special significance for the individuation process. (p. 387)

A similar connection is made by Kiepenheuer (1992), who argues that psychosomatic symptoms are psychic matters made physical and, therefore, stand as examples of synchronicity offering the affected person a route to wholeness (pp. 281–82).

The Self

The Self is the central, guiding archetypal structure in Jung's psychology. The ego can be seen as the center of consciousness while the Self is the center of all of psyche, both conscious and unconscious (Edinger, 1972, p. 3). Communication between the ego and the Self, termed the "ego-self axis" (Edinger, 1972), is critical to the individuation process. Thus, one can see that the ego-Self conversation involves, at least in part, a conversation between consciousness and the unconscious, the transcendent function. In fact, Agnel (1992) described the transcendent function as the "initial experience of the Self" (p. 107). Samuels (1985) sees the transcendent function as a "facilitation of the processes of the self" (p. 59).

R. L. Moore (1992) argues that the "octahedral structure of the archetypal self" causes the transcendent function to manifest in order to activate and effectuate the "blueprint for individual development" (pp. 240–41). Nagy (1992) calls the transcendent function a "technique for developing a Self" (p. 293). Schellenbaum (1992) labels it the "spontaneous activity from the Self" (p. 414). Using a developmental Jungian approach giving equal emphasis to reductive and synthetic views, Corbett (1992) asserts that the transcendent function represents the unfolding of the demands of the Self into selfobject needs in analysis (p. 400).

Using Fordham's theory of development based upon the idea of an infant born with a "primary self" that contains all of that infant's possibilities (discussed further in chapter 5), Urban (1992) identifies the transcendent function as "an essential aspect of Michael Fordham's postulate of a primary self, the psychosomatic integrate that contains the potential of the organism" (p. 421). Williams (1983) makes a similar connection, arguing that the transcendent function is vitally linked to the deintegration of the Self as described by Fordham (p. 65). Finally, some (e.g., Hillman in the Editor's Preface of the 1916 version of "The Transcendent Function") have suggested that once Jung fully developed his concept of the Self, his need for the idea of and reference to the transcendent function were both diminished (Jung, 1957, p. 3). The linkage of the Self and the transcendent function is explored in chapter 3.

Typology

Part of Jung's thinking about the opposites and the transcendent function had to do with his work on personality typology. He felt that a person's inferior function was pushed into the unconscious and that the transcendent function is essential to locating it, conversing with it, and integrating it (see, e.g., Jung, 1989b, pp. 26, 33). Indeed, much of Jung's thinking on the transcendent function was formulated in his work with the fundamental opposites, introverts and extroverts, in *Psychological Types* (1921/1971). In a fascinating paper, Ross (1986) sought to locate the transcendent function and the Jungian typologies in the physical brain. She maps out the brain by identifying the left (or logical and sequential) and right (or analogical and intuitive) hemispheres and argues that the two principal states of consciousness, waking and sleeping, correspond roughly with the left and right hemispheres, respectively. She locates the transcendent function in the connection between the hemispheres and finds its existence in the hemispheric equilibrium existent in "hybrid states," states of consciousness between waking and sleeping, such as mystical states, hypnosis, meditation, and daydreaming. Finally, she gives a hypothesis for overlaying the physical structure of the brain with the four Jungian typologies.

Transformation and Change in Attitude

Key to all psychologies, particularly Jungian psychology, is transformation in attitude. That, in fact, is the core of the transcendent function. Indeed, Jung (1957/1960) says that it "is called 'transcendent' because it makes the transition from one attitude to another organically possible" (p. 73). In other writings, Jung refers again to the transcendent function as that which makes transition from one attitude to another possible (1921/1971, pp. 252, 480; 1939/1959, p. 289), and that which facilitates the transition from one psychic condition to another (1939/1958, p. 489); he even calls it the "transformation of personality" (1928/1953, p. 220).

Other writers also comment on the theme of psychic change. Corbett (1992), for example, calls it "the capacity of the psyche to change and grow toward individuation" (p. 395) and states that the "inexorable impulse for change familiar to all therapists marks the appearance of the transcendent function" (p. 397). Ulanov (1996) notes that the "transcendent function inaugurates transition to arrival of the new" (p. 126). Joseph (1997) calls the transcendent function the "process of bringing conscious and unconscious together for the sake of a renewal of attitude, a transformation of psychical organization" (p. 139) and says that it "involves at its core a letting go of fixed structures and identities" (p. 150). Ryce-Menuhin (1992) states it more dramatically by comparing the transcendent function to the experimental showing of the preference of a male grayling butterfly, which naturally is drawn to females of darker hue, to choose a female that is artificially stained a darker color than anything known in nature: "This inclination to reach after and beyond nature is comparable to the transcendent function as it brings forward the unconscious, unrealized yearnings of human beings" (p. 410). The ideas of psychic change and transformation are central to and inexorably tied to the transcendent function.

ORIGINS OF THE TRANSCENDENT FUNCTION

Because of the importance of the transcendent function in Jung's metapsychology, its origins have been the subject of speculation, investigation, and scholarship on the part of a number of writers. Though a full exploration of the origins of the transcendent function is beyond the scope of this book, here I will summarize the main contributions. At least a few authors have imagined that Jung's *VII Sermons Ad Mortuos (Seven Sermons to the Dead),* his anonymously authored work written in the same year as "The Transcendent Function," may contain "mythic prefigurations" of Jung's theory of the opposites and their reconciliation through the transcendent function (Beebe, 1992; Hubback, 1966; Sandner, 1992). Solomon (1992) points out the strong similarity between the transcendent function and Hegel's dialectic vision: the emergence of the third from the dialogue between the conscious and unconscious bears a striking resemblance to the emergence of the synthesis from the interplay of thesis and antithesis. Salman (1992), on the other hand, takes issue with Solomon, pointing out that though the transcendent function has a "dialectical motion," it is a much more psychological and transformative process; it "goes beyond dialectics into conscious dialogue by introducing creativity, suffering and ethical integrity into the interaction of opposites," creating an "alchemical *ferment* which transforms the dialectic process" (p. 143).

Beebe (1992) posits that the transcendent function was an inevitable development in Jung's personal psychology; once Jung accepted the reality and autonomy of the complexes, they "were sure to assert themselves as unruly guests" (p. 117) in Jung's own life. Beebe asserts that instead of finding a way to explain them, Jung sought a "relationship with the complexes themselves" (p. 118) that led him inescapably to dialogue with the unconscious and to finding a bridge across the "yawning ravine" between the ego and the unconscious (p. 118). Dehing (1992) follows a similar line arguing that the transcendent function was Jung's "attempt at self-healing" from his own "severe breakdown" (p. 21).

Others have noted the personal, family, and cultural forces at work in Jung's life. Nagy (1992) suggests that cultural and historical factors contributed to Jung's need to find a "higher level of moral authority" (p. 294) implicit in the concept of the transcendent function (i.e., the higher morality of the unconscious and the need to dialogue with it). She cites Jung's being out of step with others, his counter-cultural, heroic stance, and his inability to believe in the religion taught by his father (pp. 294–96). Samuels (1985) cites the views of two psychoanalysts who saw the transcendent function as "an expression of Jung's denial of the conflicts in life and his unconscious search for symbiotic reunion or merger with an idyllic object" (p. 60).

ROLE OF THE ANALYST

An important subset of literature addresses the role of the analyst in working with the transcendent function. In "The Transcendent Function" (1957/1960), Jung devotes a section to the relationship between the analyst and the analysand and talks about transference. He states that the analyst "mediates the transcendent function for the patient, i.e., helps him to bring conscious and unconscious together and so arrive at a new attitude" (p. 74). Joseph (1997) expresses it somewhat differently by noting that the transcendent function involves the analyst carrying "unrealized potentials for psychological transformation" (p. 153).

Agnel (1992) posits that the analyst must strive to maintain both "poles" of the transference relationship, the "familiar" and the "foreign," to facilitate the transcendent function (p. 109). Dehing (1992) and Sandner (1992) theorize that transference is a striking example of the transcendent function operating in the analytic relationship "in which the analyst takes one pole of the oppositorum and the analysand takes the other" (Sandner, 1992, p. 36). Ulanov (1997) offers fascinating connections between transference, the transcendent function, and transcendence. She argues that transference ushers in the transcendent function which in turn produces transcendence (pp. 125–26). In contrast, Byington (1992) states that through expressive techniques (he was writing about dramatic reenactment using marionettes) the analysand can experience "symbolic elaboration" directly, not through the analyst so as to "diminish the identification of the analyst with the transcendent function" (p. 405).

A valuable perspective is offered by Corbett (1992) who argues that the classical Jungian view of the transcendent function (i.e., intrapsychic change of attitude through the spontaneous emergence of symbol that unites the opposites in consciousness and the unconscious) is too narrow. Similar to the tone of Ulanov's work, Corbett states that the transcendent function operates as much through the analytic relationship as it does intrapsychically:

> Traditionally, the transcendent function was seen to manifest itself only as psyche's symbol-making capacity. The search for wholeness was assumed to proceed more intrapsychically than interpersonally. Hence in the classical Jungian literature the relationship between analyst and analysand was seen as of secondary importance to the elucidation of symbolic material. But completion is also sought within relationships, and in such cases is mediated no less by the transcendent function than is the symbol. (p. 399)

Corbett proceeds to cite the mirroring, idealizing, and twinship selfobject needs of the developing child postulated by Kohut and relates how those needs are reactivated and healed in the transference. In this way, the analytic relationship mediates the guidance of the Self and is used as a symbol to repair the selfobject deficits:

> The role of the analyst therefore is to mediate the demands of the Self as they unfold into selfobject needs, by allowing oneself to be used—in a symbolic sense—as a responsive and, when necessary, interpretive participant. Such unfolding represents the action of the transcendent function. (p. 400)

Essentially, Corbett offers the perspective that the analytic relationship, and the transference within it, become the symbol through which the transcendent function and change of attitude are effected. This is an important viewpoint because it offers us insight into the commonality between Jungian and psychoanalytic views.

S. Powell (1985) offers another fascinating dimension to the role of the analyst and the relationship between the analyst and analysand. She posits that the "work between the patient and analyst is a complex process of interpersonal and intrapsychic communication" (p. 30). She argues that it is the analyst's capacity to tolerate her own painful experiences, affects, and unconscious contents that contains and models the patient's ability to develop that capacity:

> Through the analyst's capacity to make sense of the "other," as she experiences it within herself, a bridge to understanding can be built and creative development can take place in the patient and, indeed, in the analyst. . . . [I]t is the *analyst's* transcendent function, her capacity to comprehend her own internal processes in relation to the patient, which allows her own unconscious to link with consciousness and so to make a bridge of understanding. (p. 30)

Corbett and Powell give us hints about the current thinking regarding the role of the analyst and the analytic relationship in fostering or containing the transcendent function.

CLINICAL ASPECTS AND APPLICATIONS

A variety of works address the manifestation or effective use of the transcendent function in clinical work. Some are focused on the use of various expressive techniques to access unconscious material. Barz (1992) and Strahan (1992), for example, write about the appearance of the transcendent function through the use of psychodrama. Byington (1992) shows how the transcendent function is at work bringing unconscious material to consciousness through the clinical use of marionettes with patients. Rosati (1992) makes the important connection between art in therapy and symbolism and, thus, between art and the transcendent function. Kiepenheuer (1992) writes about the use of sand play to evoke the transcendent function. Other writers have focused on the transcendent function in conjunction with the treatment of specific disorders. Affeld-Niemeyer (1992), for example, writes about the use of the transcendent function in treating victims of incest. Ledermann (1992) explores the transcendent function in the treatment of narcissistic disorders. Bovensiepen (1992) and Kiepenheuer (1992) both write about the use of the transcendent function to access somatized unconscious material.

Several writers have focused on the importance of the transcendent function in working with particular populations or modalities. Schellenbaum (1992) offers his thoughts about the particular application and use of the transcendent function in working with groups and couples. Ryce-Menuhin (1992) and Rosetti-Gsell (1992) both write about the significance of the transcendent function in play therapy with children, the former focusing on sand play and the latter on child analysis. Urban (1992) documents her experience with assisting a deaf girl to develop language skills through the use of the transcendent function. Ulanov (1992) gives a clinical presentation about how she used the transcendent function to help a patient break through his profound obsession with perversion. Roloff (1992) offers reflections about the significance of the transcendent function in the analysis of a child, a transsexual, and sexually regressed adult. N. Moore (1975) discusses the way the transcendent function operates in patients with egos that are not fully formed or that are impaired by some disorder and offers a developmental model of the transcendent function in various stages of ego formation.

Finally, Charlton (1986) offers a historical and clinical comparison between the transcendent function and free association. He argues that Jung's rejection of the Freudian technique was based on Jung's limited, personal, and negative experiences with it before it was fully developed as an analytic method. Further, he argues that free association is not a "totally reductive experience" (p. 166), as Jung alleged, but rather involves the "continual formation of new experience . . . looking at what is alive within the psyche at the present moment" (pp. 166–67). Moreover, Charlton argues, "when used correctly, free association is an avenue which leads towards the production of that 'tension of opposites' which Jung felt to be the central aspect of the transcendent function, of individuation, and of analysis" (p. 166).

CULTURAL, POLITICAL, AND SOCIETAL CONTEXTS

Several writers have explored the transcendent function as a phenomenon of culture, politics, and society. Stewart (1992), for example, draws parallels between democracy as a political system and the transcendent function. He posits that since the transcendent function and democracy are both based on a dialogue between coequal entities (the conscious and unconscious in the transcendent function, citizens in a democracy), democracy is a "sociopolitical . . . projection" (p. 65) of the transcendent function and the "psychic origins of democracy are to be found in the transcendent function" (p. 59). Zabriskie (1992) takes issue with Stewart, arguing that Jung's formulation was an intrapsychic phenomenon, not one that takes place between and among conscious egos as it does in the political world (p. 77). Samuels (1992), though not making specific reference to the transcendent function, talks of building a "bridge between depth psychology and politics" (p. 354) through the clinical setting; he suggests that just as the analyst explores personal, family, emotional, and moral development with a patient, "political development" is also an important subject for analytic investigation (p. 356). Similarly, Walcott (1992) sees the racial tensions embodied in the Rodney King riots as resulting from the splitting off by the Caucasian community of the enslaved, inferior, and alien and argues for the necessity of incorporating that unconscious material (pp. 365–66).

Several writers have also sought to provide a cross-cultural perspective to the transcendent function. Takeuchi (1992), for example, compares and contrasts the transcendent function as reflected in ego-oriented Western cultures and Self-oriented Eastern cultures. Similarly, Rhi (1992) compares the transcendent function to transcendence in Confucian teachings. A different cultural perspective is offered by Kujawski (1992), who finds the transcendent function reflected in the central African myth of Eshu-Elegba, the Yoruba trickster god who weaves webs of misrepresentations through which transformations and new syntheses take place. M. P. Johnson (1992) also offers an African perspective, positing that healers in the Zulu culture are called to their vocations in what she sees as analogous to the transcendent function.

Finally, two writers have commented on the way in which the transcendent function both fosters and is reflected in aesthetic experience. Real (1992) gives anecdotal examples of how artists and writers consider the product of their efforts not their own but a "voice" (p. 84) that emerges from dialogue with their work; he posits that aesthetic experience is an example of the transcendent function, saying that it is "the transformation of psychic energy from the undifferentiated biological form to the cultural-spiritual form of esthetic activity" (p. 83). Rosati (1992) emphasizes that "the symbolic function is the fundamental function of art" (p. 99) and connects it directly to the transcendent function.

RELIGIOUS AND SPIRITUAL MATTERS

Though Jung (1957/1960) denies any metaphysical dimensions to the transcendent function, its very name and nature seem to attract connections to religious and spiritual matters. Indeed, in the prefatory note of his central paper on the transcendent function, Jung himself responds to his own question of how to come to terms in practice with the unconscious: "Indirectly, it is the fundamental question of all religions and all philosophies. For the unconscious is not this thing or that; it is the Unknown as it immediately affects us" (1957/1960, p. 68). Thus, several authors have drawn connections between the transcendent function and matters pertaining to religion and spirituality.

Ulanov (1996), for example, believes that Jung was wrong to deny the spiritual implications of the transcendent function. She states flatly, "it is precisely through the workings of the transcendent function that we receive evidence of the Transcendent" (p. 194). Elsewhere, Ulanov compares what emerges from the transcendent function as "the voice of God" (1992, p. 215). Solomon (1992) also suggests that Jung may have been in denial about the spiritual implications of the transcendent function and that it may very well have represented a connection between "the self and an Other" (p. 128). Handel (1992), in his discussion about the connections between the transcendent function, synchronicity, and individuation, draws parallels between religious systems and psychological systems (p. 391). Finally, Young-Eisendrath (1992) urges a "new emphasis on the transcendent function in Jungian discourse about the Unknown" (p. 156).

NOTES

CHAPTER ONE. INTRODUCTION TO THE TRANSCENDENT FUNCTION

1. The book assumes a basic knowledge of psychology but will provide definitions where appropriate. "Ego" refers to the central core of conscious psychic activity.

2. This term, borrowed from the anthropologist Lévy-Brühl, is used to refer to a relationship in which the subject cannot distinguish himself from the thing. Here the term is used to describe the stage of development when humans considered themselves to be one with nature.

3. Self is capitalized herein throughout, as it is by many Jungian writers, whenever it refers to the Jungian, transpersonal Self as distinguished from other uses of the word.

4. Archetypes are a key concept and will be explored in greater depth later. For the present, archetypal phenomenon is used her to mean something that psyche does instinctually.

5. Hillman, archetypal psychology's chief architect, certainly agrees with many of Jung's core ideas, particularly about the autonomous and archetypal nature of the unconscious, but he believes, among other things, that the images of the unconscious are more numerous and varied and that they need not be analyzed but rather only experienced.

CHAPTER TWO. DETAILED ANALYSIS OF THE TRANSCENDENT FUNCTION ESSAY

1. The book will not delve deeply into this event. Suffice it to say that after years of being closely associated both personally and professionally, Jung and Freud had a falling out. Jung came to believe that parts of Freud's conception of psyche were incorrect, not the least of which were Freud's emphasis on the primacy of sexuality and erotic urges and his view that the unconscious was primarily a receptacle of repressed, unacceptable contents from the conscious. Jung broke with Freud in 1912 with his publication *Symbols of Transformation*. The break, though essential to Jung and the development of his psychology, left him isolated professionally and disoriented psychologically, leading in part to the turmoil described here.

2. Sandner (1992) refers to that as a period during which "a torrent of unconscious material came flooding in, temporarily overwhelming him" (p. 33). Dehing (1992) calls what Jung went through a "severe crisis" (p. 20). Agnel (1992) flatly labels what Jung experienced a "breakdown" (p. 103).

3. The 1916 version referred to "all behavior traces of the human spirit," whereas the 1958 version was revised to "all the behaviour traces constituting the structure of the human mind." This change is interesting given Jung's work during the period of his writing of the 1916 version around the development of the archetypes and the collective unconscious.

4. He explains how definiteness and directedness, acquired relatively late in human history (p. 69), have been instrumental in the development of science, technology, and civilization. Since these qualities have been crucial in adapting to the needs of the modern age, Jung reasons, "it is therefore understandable, and even necessary, that in each individual the psychic process should be as stable and definite as possible, since the exigencies of life demand it " (p. 70).

5. Each of the tendencies by itself has a danger according to Jung. The pitfall of creative formulation is overvaluing the artistic worth of unconscious material and missing its meaning; the danger of the way of understanding is overintellectualizing the material so that its "essentially symbolic character" (p. 85) is lost.

6. Some (e.g., Samuels, 1985, pp. 113–15; Corbett, 1992, p. 395) have suggested that Jung's concept of opposites is too restrictive, that it mischaracterizes the multiplicity of psychic life, and that it and "ignores the concurrent mutual support, complemantarity, incremental gradations of change and subtle transitions found within the psyche" (Corbett, 1992, p. 395).

7. This is the second mention of the idea of a rhythmic shifting of consciousness; the first was in Jung's discussion of the two ways to formulate the unconscious contents (i.e., the way of creative formulation and the way of understanding), when he indicated that the "ideal case would be if these two aspects could . . . rhythmically succeed each other" (1957/1960, p. 86).

CHAPTER THREE. TRACING THE TRANSCENDENT FUNCTION THROUGH JUNG'S WORKS

1. *Symbols of Transformation* (1952/1956); "Psychological Commentary on *The Tibetan Book of Great Liberation* (1939/1958); "Conscious, Unconscious, and Individuation" (1939/1959); *Mysterium Coniunctionis* (1955–1956/1963); "A Psychological View of Conscience" (1958/1964).

2. To M. Zarine in May, 1939 (1973a, pp. 267–69), to Père Lachat in March, 1954 (1955, pp. 679–91), to Father Victor White in April, 1954 (1973b, pp. 163–74) and to Professor E. Böhler in December, 1955 (1973c, pp. 282–84).

3. Two seminars on analytical psychology, one on March 30, 1925 (1989a, pp. 9–14) and a second on April 13, 1925 (1989b, pp. 26–34), a seminar on dream analysis

on June 4, 1930 (1984, pp. 637–53), and two seminars on Nietzsche's *Zarathustra*, one on June 3, 1936 (1988a, pp. 965–82) and a second on May 11, 1938 (1988b, pp. 1230–47).

4. Jung alludes to the idea that "the unconscious behaves in a compensatory or complementary manner towards the conscious" (1957, p. 5) and makes references to the "counter-position" in the unconscious (pp. 7, 8, 21) and the "counter-action" of the unconscious (pp. 14, 15, 16).

5. Hegel's dialectic is the idea that in every position (thesis) lies the seeds of its own destruction in the form of an internal contradiction (antithesis), and that the opposition of thesis and antithesis leads to a synthesis, a third position that combines the positive aspects of both. The synthesis of one stage of the dialectic can then serve as the thesis for a new dialectical movement. Hegel's philosophy has been the subject of extensive review and comment. See, for example, Honderich (1995), Norman (1976), and R. Singer (1983).

6. According to Jung realism, which places primacy on the abstract idea and posits that universal concepts (like beauty, goodness, animal, man, etc.) exist before any physical reality, goes back to Plato's universals (1921/1971, pp. 26, 38; 1943/1953, p. 54); nominalism, which asserts that universals are nothing but names and assigns primacy to nature and phenomena, was advanced by the Cynics and Megarians in opposition to Plato's ideas (1921/1971, pp. 26, 38; 1943/1953, p. 54).

7. For example, the shift in consciousness created by the discoveries of Copernicus that the Earth is not the fixed center of the universe planted the seeds for Cartesian duality (Tarnas, 1991, p. 416). Also, the development of linear perspective where the world is seen from the vantage point of a self that "becomes an observing *subject*, a *spectator*, as against a world that becomes a *spectacle*, an *object*, of vision" created the imaginal foundation for the Cartesian philosophical foundation of a subjective self separated from the objective world (Romanyshyn, 1989, p. 42).

8. As Hillman states: "Polytheistic mythical thinking seems quite nonchalant about binary oppositions" (1975, p. 171).

9. Jung has an extensive definition of "fantasy" (1921/1971, pp. 427–33). Generally, the term is used herein to mean a complex of ideas, images, or other sensory perceptions that "has no objective referent" (p. 427) and so cannot be objectively measured.

10. Jung also has an extensive definition of "symbol" (1921/1971, pp. 473–81). Here it is used to refer to an image that carries or implies a "description or formulation of a relatively unknown fact, which is none the less known to exist or is postulated as existing" (p. 474).

11. Schiller says: "The distance between matter and form, between passivity and activity, between sensation and thought, is infinite, and the two cannot conceivably be reconciled. The two conditions are opposed to each other and can never be made one" (Jung, 1921/1971, p. 103).

12. Note that though Jung did not capitalize the word *self,* it is a common Jungian convention, one used by this book, to capitalize it to differentiate Jung's

transpersonal Self from other uses of the word. When the book quotes Jung, however, it will do so without capitalizing.

13. See previous footnote.

14. In this interesting and profoundly useful piece, Jung for the first time gives an organized exposition of the concepts he had been working with for the first few decades of his work.

15. "A relation between two sets . . . as the expression $y=x^2$ . . . The kind of action or activity proper to a person, thing or institution, as in the *function* of the unconscious" (*Random House Webster's Collegiate Dictionary*, 1996, p. 539).

16. The archetypal psychologist might even call this a visitation by a person's daimon to effect change in line with one's destiny (see, e.g., Hillman, 1996).

17. Jungians hold that one cannot have a direct experience or contact with the archetype; it would be overwhelming. Here Jung refers to experience of the archetypal image.

18. Elsewhere, Jung questioned the strength/clarity of dream images: "As a rule dreams are too feeble and unintelligible to exercise a radical influence on consciousness" (1943/1953, p. 110)

19. See 1957/1960, p. 68; 1939/1958, p. 488, 491; 1952/1956, p. 433; 1973a, p. 268).

CHAPTER FOUR. THE TRANSCENDENT FUNCTION AS THE CORE OF JUNG'S WORK

1. This theme will be revisited in the last chapter in the section called "The Germination of the Alchemical Fourth."

CHAPTER FIVE. THE TRANSCENDENT FUNCTION AND THE THEORIES OF OTHERS

1. Here the word *self* is used in the non-Jungian sense and, therefore, not capitalized.

2. In his view, adult psychopathology flows from not "good enough" mothering that arrests the movement from absolute dependency to independence (Summer, 1994, p. 156). Winnicott felt that "all . . . adult creativity, as well as aesthetic experience, are transitional phenomena and that this intermediate area of experience must continue into adult life for creative and cultural living, which he identified as mental health" (p. 149).

3. The topographical model demarcated psychic life into spatially separated systems (conscious, preconscious, and unconscious). In contrast, the structural model held that inner conflicts were not simply between conscious/unconscious but between structural parts that had different goals.

4. The structural theory holds that, while the ego is largely associated with the conscious, perceptual realm of existence, it also has parts that reside in the preconscious and unconscious.

5. Corbett (1989) described it as the "a priori ordering, structure-giving principle within the psyche" (p. 24).

6. Corbett (1989) described the Kohutian self as "a permanent mental structure consisting of feelings, memories, and behaviors that are subjectively experienced as being continuous in time and as being 'me'" (p. 24).

7. "The 'selfobject experience' depends partly on the capacity for illusion and partly on the . . . object that is experienced as fulfilling selfobject functions. Neither alone constitutes a substantive basis for the development of a strong and vital self" (Bacal, 1989, p. 267).

8. See, e.g., Summers, 1994, pp. 73–136 for a fuller discussion.

9. He also sometimes uses the synonymous term, "original self." Note that Fordham, following Jung's practice, does not capitalize the "s" in Self. He is, however, referring to the Jungian, transpersonal Self.

10. Hillman (1983) calls his psychology "archetypal," in contrast to Jung's "analytical" psychology, to emphasize that "'archetypal' belongs to all culture, all forms of human activity, and not only to professional practitioners of modern therapeutics" (p. 9).

11. "'Soul' refers to the *deepening* of events into experiences . . . the imaginative possibility in our natures, the experiencing through reflective speculation, dream, image and *fantasy*–that mode which recognizes all realities as primarily symbolic and metaphorical" (Hillman, 1975, p. xvi).

12. "I find that when I am closest to my inner, intuitive self, when I am somehow in touch with the unknown in me, when perhaps I am in a slightly altered state of consciousness in the relationship, then whatever I do seems to be full of healing. Then simply my presence is releasing and helpful" (Rogers, 1986, p. 198).

CHAPTER SIX. THE DEEPER ROOTS OF THE TRANSCENDENT FUNCTION

1. Freud's ego mediates between the opposite demands of the drives and fantasies of the id, on the one hand, and the conventions of the superego and reality, on the other. Winnicott's transitional object mediates between inner/outer, me/not-me. Klein's depressive position represents a unification of good and bad. Kohut's selfobject is a transitional ground between self/other, fantasy/reality, inner/outer. Fordham's deintegration-reintegration cycle mediates between self and not-self, between unity and fragmentation. The analytic field is a transitional or mediatory space between the subjectivities and objectivities of the patient and analyst.

2. The brain has "two separate, hemispheric minds . . . with independent perceptual, learning and memory functions" (Ross, 1986, p. 234).

3. Freud's ego mediates between the subjective level of the ego/me and what is experienced as objective or foreign, the instinctual fantasies of the id. Winnicott's transitional object/transitional phenomena explain how subject and object are psychologically separated in the infant. Klein's depressive position shows what occurs psychically when the subject fully apprehends that the object (mother) is separate. Fordham's deintegration-reintegration cycle describes the interplay between subject (self) and object (other) in a cycle of merger and differentiation. Kohut's concept of selfobject is essentially an intrasubjective manifestation of the object. The analytic field is based in the idea of the merging of the psychic fields of the subject and object (analyst and analysand).

4. Though difficult to exactly define, postmodernism is a philosophy that "rejects epistemological assumptions, refutes methodological conventions, resists knowledge claims, obscures all versions of truth, and dismisses policy recommendations" (Rosenau, 1992, p. 3). Instead of trying to reduce, classify, or interpret information, postmodernists "register the impossibility of establishing any such underpinning for knowledge" (p. 6) and focus the totality of what is written and talked about on a particular topic to invite conversation or dialogue.

5. Hades denotes the god of the underworld and the underworld itself. Hillman (1979) describes Hades as "the God of depth, God of invisibles" (p. 27) and that which is in the realm of Hades as hidden, deep, interior.

CHAPTER SEVEN. VIVIFYING THE TRANSCENDENT FUNCTION IN EVERYDAY LIFE

1. Williams says its purpose is to induce a meeting between the "opposing but complementary realities" of the "reality of the known world" and the "images springing up from the archetypes of the collective unconscious" (1983, p. 65). Agnel identifies its role as assembling "within a more complex whole elements that are rational and irrational, imaginary and real" (1992, p. 105). Corbett says that the aim of the transcendent function is to "restore our sense of cohesiveness" from the "fragmented condition of everyday consciousness" (1992, p. 398).

2. Kujawski describes it as "the mysterious capacity of the human soul for change" (1992, p. 315); Corbett calls it "the capacity of the psyche to change and grow toward individuation" (1992, p. 395); and Ulanov says it is "the arrival of the new . . . a third point of view that includes and surpasses the former conflicting ones" (1997, p. 126).

3. Young-Eisendrath, for example, refers to the transcendent function as "a capacity to move back and forth between layers of meaning" and analogizes it to Winnicott's "potential space" (1992, p. 153). Savitz calls it "a bridge to help cross the abyss between affects, between affect and memory, between self and ego, between analyst and patient" (1990, p. 243).

4. Corbett says that the "movement from the unconscious into consciousness means a movement from undifferentiation into plurality" (1992, p. 398) and that the

purpose of the transcendent function is to "restore an original totality" (p. 398). Horne calls the transcendent function "the manifestation of the coherence and unity which is the ground of all matter" (1998, p. 31).

5. Whether his theories represent the beginning or a mere expression of an underlying dualistic way of thinking, Descartes' *cogito* clearly enunciated the theory that there was a subjective human self that was separate and apart from the objective world outside, that subject and object were split, that there was a fundamental rift between mind and matter. The so-called Cartesian split both underlies the scientific and technological revolution and creates serious limitations and drawbacks in the way humans think and experience.

6. I say extension of Jung's ideas here because, although the alchemical *coniunctio* was a central thesis in Jung's thinking, he focused on the union of opposites or of conscious/unconscious. In the framework I am offering here, the metaphorical field, as the alchemical vessel, can contain and allow the transformation of virtually any combination of forces in our world.

REFERENCES

Affeld-Niemeyer, A. (1992). "The transcendent function in therapy after incestuous violence." In M. A. Matoon (Ed.), *The transcendent function: Individual and collective aspects; Proceedings of the Twelfth International Congress for Analytical Psychology, August 23–28, 1992* (pp. 38–51). Einsiedeln, Switzerland: Daimon Verlag.

Agnel, A. (1992). "Another degree of complexity." In M. A. Matoon (Ed.), *The transcendent function: Individual and collective aspects; Proceedings of the Twelfth International Congress for Analytical Psychology, August 23–28, 1992* (pp. 101–15). Einsiedeln, Switzerland: Daimon Verlag.

Bacal, H. A. (1989). "Winnicott and self psychology: Remarkable reflections." In D. W. Detrick and S. P. Detrick (Eds.), *Self psychology: Comparisons and contrasts* (pp. 259–71). Hillsdale, N.J.: Analytic Press.

Barkin, L. (1978). "The concept of the transitional object." In S. A. Grolnick and L. Barkin (Eds.), *Between reality and fantasy: Transitional objects and phenomena* (pp. 513–36). Northvale, N.J.: Jason Aronson.

Barz, H. (1992). "The transcendent function and psychodrama." In M. A. Matoon (Ed.), *The transcendent function: Individual and collective aspects; Proceedings of the Twelfth International Congress for Analytical Psychology, August 23–28, 1992* (pp. 173–88). Einsiedeln, Switzerland: Daimon Verlag.

Beck, A. T., and Weishaar, M. E. (1989). "Cognitive therapy." In R. J. Corsini and D. Wedding (Eds.), *Current Psychotherapies* (4th ed., pp. 285–320). Itasca: F. E. Peacock.

Beebe, J. (1992). "Response to A. Agnel: Another degree of complexity." In M. A. Matoon (Ed.), *The transcendent function: Individual and collective aspects; Proceedings of the Twelfth International Congress for Analytical Psychology, August 23–28, 1992* (pp. 116–22). Einsiedeln, Switzerland: Daimon Verlag.

Bentov, I. (1977). *Stalking the wild pendulum.* Rochester, Ver.: Destiny.

Berry, T. (1988). *The dream of the earth.* San Francisco: Sierra Club.

Biedermann, H. (1989). *Dictionary of symbolism: Cultural icons and the meanings behind them.* New York: Meridian.

Bovensiepen, G. (1992). "The body as container for the transcendent function: Thoughts on its genesis." In M. A. Matoon (Ed.), *The transcendent function: Individual and collective aspects; Proceedings of the Twelfth International Congress for Analytical Psychology, August 23–28, 1992* (pp. 242–49). Einsiedeln, Switzerland: Daimon Verlag.

Bradway, K. (1982). "Gender identity and gender roles: Their place in analytical practice." In M. Stein (Ed.), *Jungian Analysis* (pp. 275–93). LaSalle: Open Court.

Buber, M. (1948). "Dialogue." In *Between Man and Man* (pp. 1–39). New York: Macmillan.

Byington, C. A. B. (1992). "The marionettes of the Self: The transcendent function at work." In M. A. Matoon (Ed.), *The transcendent function: Individual and collective aspects; Proceedings of the Twelfth International Congress for Analytical Psychology, August 23–28, 1992* (pp. 402–08). Einsiedeln, Switzerland: Daimon Verlag.

Charlton, R. S. (1986). Free association and Jungian analytic technique. *Journal of Analytical Psychology* 31 (2), 153–71.

Chodorow, J. (Ed.). (1997). *Jung on active imagination.* Princeton: Princeton University Press.

Corbett, L. (1989). "Kohut and Jung: A comparison of theory and therapy." In D. W. Detrick and S. P. Detrick (Eds.), *Self psychology: Comparisons and contrasts* (pp. 23–47). Hillsdale, N.J.: Analytic Press.

Corbett, L. (1992). "Therapist mediation of the transcendent function." In M. A. Matoon (Ed.), *The transcendent function: Individual and collective aspects; Proceedings of the Twelfth International Congress for Analytical Psychology, August 23–28, 1992* (pp. 395–401). Einsiedeln, Switzerland: Daimon Verlag.

Corbett, L. (1996). *The religious function of the psyche.* New York: Rutledge.

Cwik, A. J. (1991). "Active imagination as imaginal play-space." In N. Schwartz-Salant and M. Stein (Eds.), *Liminality and transitional phenomena* (pp. 99–114). Wilmette: Chiron.

Dallett, J. (1982). "Active imagination in practice." In M. Stein (Ed.), *Jungian analysis* (pp. 173–91). La Salle: Open Court.

Dehing, J. (1992). "The transcendent function: A critical re-evaluation." In M. A. Matoon (Ed.), *The transcendent function: Individual and collective aspects; Proceedings of the Twelfth International Congress for Analytical Psychology, August 23–28, 1992* (pp.15–30). Einsiedeln, Switzerland: Daimon Verlag.

Douglas, C. (1997). "The historical context of analytical psychology." In P. Young-Eisendrath and T. Dawson (Eds.), *The Cambridge companion to Jung* (pp. 17–34). Cambridge: Cambridge University Press.

Downing, C. (1993). *Gods in our midst.* New York: Crossroad.

Edinger, E. F. (1972). *Ego and archetype.* Boston: Shambhala.

Eigen, M. (1991). "Winnicott's area of freedom: The uncompromisable." In N. Schwartz-Salant and M. Stein (Eds.), *Liminality and transitional phenomena* (pp. 67–[illegible]). Wilmette: Chiron.

Fordham, M. (1969). *Children as individuals*. New York: G. P. Putnam's. (Originally published as *The life of childhood*, 1944)

Fordham, M. (1985). *Explorations into the self*. London: H. Karnac Books.

Frattaroli, E. J. (1997). "The historical context of analytical psychology." In P. Young-Eisendrath and T. Dawson (Eds.), *The Cambridge companion to Jung* (pp. 164–84). Cambridge: Cambridge University Press.

Freud, S. (1949). *An outline of psycho-analysis* (J. Strachey, Trans. and Ed.). New York: W. W. Norton. (Original work published 1940)

Gadamer, H.-G. (1989). *Truth and method* (Second Rev. ed., J. Weinsheimer and D. G. Marshall Trans. of Rev. ed.). New York: Continuum. (Original work published 1960)

Giegerich, W. (1987). "The rescue of the world: Jung, Hegel, and the subjective universe." *Spring 1987*, 107–14.

Greene, A. (1975). "The analyst, symbolization and absence in the analytic setting." *International Journal of Psycho-Analysis 56*, 1–21.

Hall, C. S., and V. J. Nordby. (1973). *A primer of Jungian psychology*. New York: Penguin.

Hall, J. A. (1991). "The watcher at the gates of dawn: The transformation of self in liminality and by the transcendent function." In N. Schwartz-Salant and M. Stein (Eds.), *Liminality and transitional phenomena* (pp. 33–51). Wilmette: Chiron.

Handel, S. (1992). "Mirabile dictu." In M. A. Matoon (Ed.), *The transcendent function: Individual and collective aspects; Proceedings of the Twelfth International Congress for Analytical Psychology, August 23–28, 1992* (pp. 387–94). Einsiedeln, Switzerland: Daimon Verlag.

Hannah, B. (1953). "Some remarks on active imagination." *Spring 1987*, 38–58.

Henderson, J. L. (1967). *Thresholds of initiation*. Middletown: Wesleyan University Press.

Hillman, J. (1975). *Re-visioning psychology*. New York: HarperCollins.

Hillman, J. (1979). *The dream and the underworld*. New York: Harper and Row.

Hillman, J. (1983). *Archetypal psychology: A brief account*. Woodstock, Conn.: Spring.

Hillman, J. (1995). "A psyche the size of the earth: A psychological foreword." In T. Roszak, M. E. Gomes, and A. D. Kramer (Eds.), *Ecospychology: Restoring the earth, healing the mind* (pp. xvii–xxiii). San Francisco: Sierra Club.

Hillman, J. (1996). *The soul's code: In search of character and calling*. New York: Random House.

Homans, P. (1995). *Jung in context*. Chicago: University of Chicago Press.

Honderich, T. (1995). *The Oxford companion to philosophy*. New York: Oxford University Press.

Hopke, R. H. (1989). *A guide to the collected works of C. G. Jung*. Boston: Shambhala.

Horne, M. (1998). "How does the transcendent function?" *The San Francisco Jung Institute Library Journal 17* (2), 21–42.

Hubback, J. (1966). *"VII Sermones ad Mortuos." Journal of Analytical Psychology 11* (2), 95–111.

Humbert, E. G. (1988). *C. G. Jung: The fundamentals of theory and practice.* (R. G. Jalbert, Trans.). Wilmette: Chiron.

Jaynes, J. (1976). *The origins of consciousness in the breakdown of the bicameral mind.* Boston: Houghton-Mifflin.

Johnson, M. P. (1992). "African healers: Called to be Isangoma or prophet." In M. A. Matoon (Ed.), *The transcendent function: Individual and collective aspects; Proceedings of the Twelfth International Congress for Analytical Psychology, August 23–28, 1992* (pp. 343–50). Einsiedeln, Switzerland: Daimon Verlag.

Johnson, R. A. (1986). *Inner work: Using dreams and active imagination for personal growth.* San Francisco: Harper and Row.

Joseph, S. M. (1997). "Presence and absence through the mirror of transference: A model of the transcendent function." *Journal of Analytical Psychology 42* (1), 139–56.

Jung, C. G. (1953). "The structure of the unconscious." In R. F. C. Hull (Trans.), *The Collected Works of C. G. Jung* (Vol. 7). Princeton: Princeton University Press. (Original work published in 1916)

Jung, C. G. (1953). "Relations between the ego and the unconscious." In R. F. C. Hull (Trans.), *The Collected Works of C. G. Jung* (Vol. 7). Princeton: Princeton University Press. (Original work published in 1928)

Jung, C. G. (1953). "On the psychology of the unconscious." In R. F. C. Hull (Trans.), *The Collected Works of C. G. Jung* (Vol. 7). Princeton: Princeton University Press. (Original work published in 1943)

Jung, C. G. (1953). "Introduction to the religious and psychological problems of alchemy." In R. F. C. Hull (Trans.), *The Collected Works of C. G. Jung* (Vol. 12). Princeton: Princeton University Press. (Original work published in 1944)

Jung, C. G. (1954). "Psychology of the transference." In R. F. C. Hull (Trans.), *The Collected Works of C. G. Jung* (Vol. 16). Princeton: Princeton University Press. (Original work published in 1946)

Jung, C. G. (1955). Letter to Père Lachat, March 27, 1954. In R. F. C. Hull (Trans.), *The Collected Works of C. G. Jung* (Vol. 18). Princeton: Princeton University Press.

Jung, C. G. (1956). "Symbols of transformation." In R. F. C. Hull (Trans.), *The Collected Works of C. G. Jung* (Vol. 5). Princeton: Princeton University Press. (Original work published in 1952)

Jung, C. G. (1957). *The transcendent function* (A. R. Pope, Trans.). [Pamphlet]. Zurich: Students Association, C. G. Jung Institute.

Jung, C. G. (1958). "Psychology and religion." In R. F. C. Hull (Trans.), *The Collected Works of C. G. Jung* (Vol. 11). Princeton: Princeton University Press. (Original work published in 1937)

Jung, C. G. (1958). "Psychological commentary on *The Tibetan Book of Great Liberation.*" In R. F. C. Hull (Trans.), *The Collected Works of C. G. Jung* (Vol. 11). Princeton: Princeton University Press. (Original work published in 1939)

Jung, C. G. (1958). "A psychological approach to the Trinity." In R. F. C. Hull (Trans.), *The Collected Works of C. G. Jung* (Vol. 11). Princeton: Princeton University Press. (Original work published in 1948)

Jung, C. G. (1958). "Answer to Job." In R. F. C. Hull (Trans.), *The Collected Works of C. G. Jung* (Vol. 11). Princeton: Princeton University Press. (Original work published in 1954)

Jung, C. G. (1959). "The archetypes of the collective unconscious." In R. F. C. Hull (Trans.), *The Collected Works of C. G. Jung* (Vol. 9, Part I). Princeton: Princeton University Press. (Original work published in 1934)

Jung, C. G. (1959). "Conscious, unconscious, and individuation." In R. F. C. Hull (Trans.), *The Collected Works of C. G. Jung* (Vol. 9, Part I). Princeton: Princeton University Press. (Original work published in 1939)

Jung, C. G. (1959). "The psychology of the child archetype." In R. F. C. Hull (Trans.), *The Collected Works of C. G. Jung* (Vol. 9, Part I). Princeton: Princeton University Press. (Original work published in 1941)

Jung, C. G. (1959). "Aion." In R. F. C. Hull (Trans.), *The Collected Works of C. G. Jung* (Vol. 9, Part II). Princeton: Princeton University Press. (Original work published in 1951)

Jung, C. G. (1960). "On psychic energy." In R. F. C. Hull (Trans.), *The Collected Works of C. G. Jung* (Vol. 8). Princeton: Princeton University Press. (Original work published in 1928)

Jung, C. G. (1960). "On the nature of psyche." In R. F. C. Hull (Trans.), *The Collected Works of C. G. Jung* (Vol. 8). Princeton: Princeton University Press. (Original work published in 1947)

Jung, C. G. (1960). "The transcendent function." In R. F. C. Hull (Trans.), *The Collected Works of C. G. Jung* (Vol. 8). Princeton: Princeton University Press. (Original work published in 1957)

Jung, C. G. (1963). *Mysterium Coniunctionis.* In R. F. C. Hull (Trans.), *The Collected Works of C. G. Jung* (Vol. 14). Princeton: Princeton University Press. (Original work published in 1955–1956)

Jung, C. G. (1964). "A psychological view of conscience." In R. F. C. Hull (Trans.), *The Collected Works of C. G. Jung* (Vol. 10). Princeton: Princeton University Press. (Original work published in 1958)

Jung, C. G. (1967). *VII sermones and mortuos* (H. G. Baynes, Trans.). London: Stuart & Watkins. (Original work published in 1925)

Jung, C. G. (1967). "Commentary on 'The secret of the golden flower.' " In R. F. C. Hull (Trans.), *The Collected Works of C. G. Jung* (Vol. 13). Princeton: Princeton University Press. (Original work published in 1929)

Jung, C. G. (1971). *Psychological Types.* In R. F. C. Hull (Trans.), *The Collected Works of C. G. Jung* (Vol. 6). Princeton: Princeton University Press. (Original work published in 1921)

Jung, C. G. (1973a), Letter to A. Zarine, May 3, 1939. In G. Adler (Ed.) and R. F. C. Hull (Trans.), *C. G. Jung Letters,* Vol. I, 1906–1951. pp. 267–69. Princeton: Princeton University Press.

Jung, C. G. (1973b). Letter to Fr. V. White, April 10, 1954. In G. Adler (Ed.) and R. F. C. Hull (Trans.), *C. G. Jung Letters,* Vol. II, 1951–1961, pp. 163–74. Princeton: Princeton University Press.

Jung, C. G. (1973c). Letter to E. Böhler, December 14, 1955. In G. Adler (Ed.) and R. F. C. Hull (Trans.), *C. G. Jung Letters,* Vol. II, 1951–1961, pp. 282–84. Princeton: Princeton University Press.

Jung, C. G. (1973d). Letter to Herr N., December 14, 1955. In G. Adler (Ed.) and R. F. C. Hull (Trans.), *C. G. Jung Letters,* Vol. II, 1951–1961, pp. 423–24. Princeton: Princeton University Press.

Jung, C. G. (1984). *Dream analysis: Notes of the seminar given in 1928–1930.* W. McGuire (Ed.). Lecture V, June 4, 1930, pp. 637–53. Princeton: Princeton University Press.

Jung, C. G. (1988a). *Nietzsche's Zarathustra: Notes of the seminar given in 1934–1939.* J. L. Barret (Ed.). Lecture V, June 3, 1936, pp. 965–82. Princeton: Princeton University Press.

Jung, C. G. (1988b). *Nietzsche's Zarathustra: Notes of the seminar given in 1934–1939.* J. L. Barret (Ed.). Lecture II, May 11, 1938, pp. 1230–47. Princeton: Princeton University Press.

Jung, C. G. (1989a). *Analytical psychology: Notes of the seminar given in 1925.* W. McGuire (Ed.). Lecture 2, March 30, 1925, pp. 9–14. Princeton: Princeton University Press.

Jung, C. G. (1989b). *Analytical psychology: Notes of the seminar given in 1925.* W. McGuire (Ed.). Lecture 4, April 13, 1925, pp. 26–34. Princeton: Princeton University Press.

Jung, C. G. (1989c). *Memories, dreams, reflections.* New York: Vintage.

Kerényi, K. (1976). *Hermes: Guide of souls.* M. Stein (Trans.). Woodstock, Conn.: Spring. (Original work published in 1944)

Kiepenheuer, K. (1992). "Illness as oracle: Symptoms as synchronistic occurrences." In M. A. Matoon (Ed.), *The transcendent function: Individual and collective aspects; Proceedings of the Twelfth International Congress for Analytical Psychology, August 23–28, 1992* (pp. 201–[illegible]). Einsiedeln, Switzerland: Daimon Verlag.

Kohut, H. (1977). *The restoration of the self.* New York: International Universities Press.

Kujawski, P. (1992). "Eshu-Elegba, master of paradox: An African experience of the transcendent function." In M. A. Matoon (Ed.), *The transcendent function: Individual and collective aspects; Proceedings of the Twelfth International Congress for Analytical Psychology, August 23–28, 1992* (pp. 315–25). Einsiedeln, Switzerland: Daimon Verlag.

Lederman, R. (1992). "Narcissistic disorder and the transcendent function." In M. A. Matoon (Ed.), *The transcendent function: Individual and collective aspects; Proceedings of the Twelfth International Congress for Analytical Psychology, August 23–28, 1992* (pp. 265–72). Einsiedeln, Switzerland: Daimon Verlag.

Lee, P. (1988). "Hermeneutics and vitalism." *ReVision* 10 (3), 3–13.

López-Pedraza, R. (1989). *Hermes and his children.* Einseideln, Switzerland: Daimon Verlag.

Mattoon, M. A. (Ed.). (1993). *The transcendent function: Individual and collective aspects (Proceedings of the Twelfth International Congress for Analytical Psychology, August 23–28, 1992).* Einsiedeln, Switzerland: Daiomon Verlag.

Meador, B. (1994). *Uncursing the dark.* Wilmette: Chiron.

Moore, N. (1975). "The transcendent function and the forming ego." *Journal of Analytical Psychology* 20, 164–82.

Moore, R. L. (1992). "Decoding the diamond body: The structure of the self and the transcendent function." In M. A. Matoon (Ed.), *The transcendent function: Individual and collective aspects; Proceedings of the Twelfth International Congress for Analytical Psychology, August 23–28, 1992* (pp. 233–41). Einsiedeln, Switzerland: Daimon Verlag.

Mueller-Vollmer, K. (Ed.). (1997). *The hermeneutics reader: Texts of the German tradition from the Enlightenment to the present.* New York: Continuum.

Nagy, M. (1992). "Reflections on self as internalized value: Ancient and modern techniques." In M. A. Matoon (Ed.), *The transcendent function: Individual and collective aspects; Proceedings of the Twelfth International Congress for Analytical Psychology, August 23–28, 1992* (pp. 293–301). Einsiedeln, Switzerland: Daimon Verlag.

Naifeh, S. (1993). "Experiencing the Self." *The San Francisco Jung Institute Library Journal* 12 (1), 5–27.

Neumann, E. (1966). "Narcissism, normal self-formation, and the primary relation to the mother." *Spring 1966,* 81–106.

Norman, R. (1976). *Hegel's phenomenology: A philosophical Introduction.* London: Brighton Press.

Ogden, T. (1994). *Subjects of Analysis.* Northvale, N.J.: Jason Aronson.

Olson, E. E. (1990). The transcendent function in organizational change. *Journal of Applied Behavioral Science* 26 (1), 69–81.

Palmer, R. E. (1969). *Hermeneutics: Interpretation theory in Schleiermacher, Dilthey, Heidegger, and Gadamer.* Evanston: Northwestern University Press.

Paris, G. (1990). *Pagan grace.* Woodstock, Conn.: Spring Publications, Inc.

Pinker, S. (1997). *How the mind works.* New York: W. W. Norton.

Powell, R. (1989). *Why does God allow suffering?* Berkeley: AHP.

Powell, S. (1985). A bridge to understanding: The transcendent function in the analyst. *Journal of Analytical Psychology* 30, 29–45.

Random House Webster's college dictionary. (1996). New York: Random House.

Raskin, N. J., and C. R. Rogers. (1989). "Person-centered therapy." In R. J. Corsini and D. Wedding (Eds.), *Current Psychotherapies* (pp. 155–94). Itasca: F. E. Peacock.

Real, B. (1992). "Esthetic experience and the transcendent function." In M. A. Matoon (Ed.), *The transcendent function: Individual and collective aspects; Proceedings of the Twelfth International Congress for Analytical Psychology, August 23–28, 1992* (pp.79–93). Einsiedeln, Switzerland: Daimon Verlag.

Rhi, B. (1992). "Heaven's decree: Confucian contributions to individuation." In M. A. Matoon (Ed.), *The transcendent function: Individual and collective aspects; Proceedings of the Twelfth International Congress for Analytical Psychology, August 23–28, 1992* (pp. 302–09). Einsiedeln, Switzerland: Daimon Verlag.

Rogers, C. R. (1986). "Client-centered therapy." In I. L. Kutash and A. Wolf (Eds.), *Psychotherapist's casebook: Therapy and technique in practice* (pp. 197–208). San Francisco: Jossey-Bass.

Roloff, L. (1992). "Living, ignoring, and regressing: Transcendent moments in the lives of a child, a transsexual, and a sexually regressed adult." In M. A. Matoon (Ed.), *The transcendent function: Individual and collective aspects; Proceedings of the Twelfth International Congress for Analytical Psychology, August 23–28, 1992* (pp. 195–211). Einsiedeln, Switzerland: Daimon Verlag.

Romanyshyn, R. D. (1982). *Psychological life: From science to metaphor.* Austin: University of Texas Press.

Romanyshyn, R. D. (1989). *Technology as symptom and dream.* New York: Routledge.

Romanyshyn, R. D. (1996, November). "The alchemical way of knowing and being." Unpublished lecture, Pacifica Graduate Institute, Carpinteria, Cal.

Romanyshyn, R. D. (2001). *Mirror and metaphor: Images and stories of psychological life.* Pittsburgh: Trivium Publications.

Romanyshyn, R. D. (2002). *Ways of the heart: Essays toward an imaginal psychology.* Pittsburgh: Trivium Publications.

Rosati, M. P. (1992). "Response to B. Real: Esthetic experience and the transcendent function." In M. A. Matoon (Ed.), *The transcendent function: Individual and colle tive aspects; Proceedings of the Twelfth International Congress for Analytical Psychology, August 23–28, 1992* (pp. 94–100). Einsiedeln, Switzerland: Daimon Verlag.

Rosenau, P. M. (1992). *Post-modernism and the social sciences.* Princeton: Princeton University Press.

Rossetti-Gsell, V. (1992). "Play and the transcendent function in child-analysis." In M. A. Matoon (Ed.), *The transcendent function: Individual and collective aspects; Proceedings of the Twelfth International Congress for Analytical Psychology, August 23–28, 1992* (pp. 436–42). Einsiedeln, Switzerland: Daimon Verlag.

Ross, V. (1986). "The transcendent function of the bilateral brain." *Zygon Journal of Religion and Science* 21 (2), 233–47.

Roszak, T. (1992). *The voice of the earth: An exploration of ecopsychology.* New York: Touchstone.

Roszak, T., M. E. Gomes, and A. D. Kramer. (Eds.). (1995). *Ecospychology: Restoring the earth, healing the mind.* San Francisco: Sierra Club.

Ryce-Menuhin, J. (1992). "The interface of developmental and archetypal images in sandplay: The ground of the transcendent function." In M. A. Matoon (Ed.), *The transcendent function: Individual and collective aspects; Proceedings of the Twelfth International Congress for Analytical Psychology, August 23–28, 1992* (pp. 409–13). Einsiedeln, Switzerland: Daimon Verlag.

Salman, S. (1992). "Response to H. M Solomon: Hegel's dialectical vision and the transcendent function." In M. A. Matoon (Ed.), *The transcendent function: Individual and collective aspects; Proceedings of the Twelfth International Congress for Analytical Psychology, August 23–28, 1992* (pp. 143–50). Einsiedeln, Switzerland: Daimon Verlag.

Samuels, A. (1985). *Jung and the post-Jungians.* New York: Routledge.

Samuels, A. (1992). "Analytical psychology and politics; the political development of the person." In M. A. Matoon (Ed.), *The transcendent function: Individual and collective aspects; Proceedings of the Twelfth International Congress for Analytical Psychology, August 23–28, 1992* (pp. 353–60). Einsiedeln, Switzerland: Daimon Verlag.

Samuels, A., B. Shorter, and F. Plaut. (1986). *A critical dictionary of Jungian analysis.* New York: Routledge.

Sandner, D. F. (1992). "Response to Jef Dehing." In M. A. Matoon (Ed.), *The transcendent function: Individual and collective aspects; Proceedings of the Twelfth International Congress for Analytical Psychology, August 23–28, 1992* (pp. 31–37). Einsiedeln, Switzerland: Daimon Verlag.

Savitz, C. (1990). "The double death." *Journal of Analytical Psychology* 35, 241–60.

Schellenbaum, P. (1992). "Animation of the transcendent function in couples and groups." In M. A. Matoon (Ed.), *The transcendent function: Individual and collective aspects; Proceedings of the Twelfth International Congress for Analytical Psychology, August 23–28, 1992* (pp. 414–20). Einsiedeln, Switzerland: Daimon Verlag.

Schimmel, A. (1993). *The mystery of numbers*. New York: Oxford Press.

Schwartz-Salant, N. (1995). "On the interactive field as the analytic object." In M. Stein (Ed.), *The interactive field in analysis* (pp. 1 –36). Wilmette: Chiron.

Schwartz-Salant, N. (1998). *The mystery of human relationship: Alchemy and the transformation of self*. New York: Routledge.

Sidoli, M. (1993). "When the meaning gets lost in the body: Psychosomatic disturbances as a failure of the transcendent function." *Journal of Analytical Psychology* 38 (2), 175–89.

Singer, J. (1972). *Boundaries of the soul*. New York: Anchor Books/Doubleday.

Singer, R. (1983). *Hegel*. New York: Oxford University Press.

Slater, G. A. (1996). *Surrendering to psyche: Depth psychology, sacrifice and culture*. Unpublished doctoral dissertation, Pacifica Graduate Institute, Carpinteria, Cal.

Solomon, H. M. (1992). "Hegel's dialectical vision and the transcendent function." In M. A. Matoon (Ed.), *The transcendent function: Individual and collective aspects; Proceedings of the Twelfth International Congress for Analytical Psychology, August 23–28, 1992* (pp. 123–42). Einsiedeln, Switzerland: Daimon Verlag.

Steelman, E. Y. (1991). "Playing with the opposites: Symbolization and transitional space." In N. Schwartz-Salant and M. Stein (Eds.), *Liminality and transitional phenomena* (pp. 151–68). Wilmette: Chiron.

Stein, M. (1991). The muddle in analysis. In N. Schwartz-Salant and M. Stein (Eds.), *Liminality and transitional phenomena* (pp. 1–12). Wilmette: Chiron.

Stewart, L. H. (1992). "The world cycle of change: Political leadership and the transcendent function." In M. A. Matoon (Ed.), *The transcendent function: Individual and collective aspects; Proceedings of the Twelfth International Congress for Analytical Psychology, August 23–28, 1992* (pp. 59–74). Einsiedeln, Switzerland: Daimon Verlag.

Storr, A. (1983). *The essential Jung*. Princeton: Princeton University Press.

Strahan, E. (1992). "Response to H. Barz: The transcendent function and psychodrama." In M. A. Matoon (Ed.), *The transcendent function: Individual and collective aspects; Proceedings of the Twelfth International Congress for Analytical Psychology, August 23–28, 1992* (pp. 189–94). Einsiedeln, Switzerland: Daimon Verlag.

Summers, F. (1994). *Object relations theories and psychopathology*. Hillsdale, N.J.: Analytic Press.

Takeuchi, M. (1992). "Culture and the transcendent function." In M. A. Matoon (Ed.), *The transcendent function: Individual and collective aspects; Proceedings of the Twelfth International Congress for Analytical Psychology, August 23–28, 1992* (pp. 310–14). Einsiedeln, Switzerland: Daimon Verlag.

Tarnas, R. (1991). *The passion of the western mind*. New York: Ballantine.

Turner, V. (1974). *Dramas, fields and metaphors: Symbolic action in human society*. Ithaca: Cornell University Press.

Turner, V. (1987). "Betwixt and between: The liminal period in rites of passage." In L. C. Mahdi, S. Foster, and M. Little (Eds.), *Betwixt and between: Patterns of masculine and feminine initiation* (pp. 3–19). La Salle, Ill.: Open Court.

Ulanov, A. B. (1992). "The perverse and the transcendent." In M. A. Matoon (Ed.), *The transcendent function: Individual and collective aspects; Proceedings of the Twelfth International Congress for Analytical Psychology, August 23–28, 1992* (pp. 212–29). Einsiedeln, Switzerland: Daimon Verlag.

Ulanov, A. B. (1996). *The functioning transcendent*. Wilmette: Chiron.

Ulanov, A. B. (1997). Transference, the transcendent function, and transcendence. *Journal of Analytical Psychology* 42 (1), 119–38.

Urban, E. (1992). "Out of the mouths of babes: The transcendent function and the development of language." In M. A. Matoon (Ed.), *The transcendent function: Individual and collective aspects; Proceedings of the Twelfth International Congress for Analytical Psychology, August 23–28, 1992* (pp. 421–27). Einsiedeln, Switzerland: Daimon Verlag.

Van Eenwyk, J. R. (1992). "The chaotic dynamics of the transcendent function." In M. A. Matoon (Ed.), *The transcendent function: Individual and collective aspects; Proceedings of the Twelfth International Congress for Analytical Psychology, August 23–28, 1992* (pp. 273–80). Einsiedeln, Switzerland: Daimon Verlag.

van Gennep, A. (1960). *Rites of Passage*. Chicago: University of Chicago Press.

von Franz, M.-L. (1980). "The journey to the beyond." In *Inward journey: Art as therapy* (pp.125–33). London: Open Court.

von Franz, M.-L. (1980). *Projection and re-collection in Jungian psychology: Reflections of the soul*. Peru, Ill.: Open Court.

Walcott, W. O. (1992). "Armageddon next time: The Los Angeles riots." In M. A. Matoon (Ed.), *The transcendent function: Individual and collective aspects; Proceedings of the Twelfth International Congress for Analytical Psychology, August 23–28, 1992* (pp. 361–67). Einsiedeln, Switzerland: Daimon Verlag.

Willeford, W. (1992). "The transcendent function in *A Midsummer Night's Dream*." In M. A. Matoon (Ed.), *The transcendent function: Individual and collective aspects; Proceedings of the Twelfth International Congress for Analytical Psychology, August 23–28, 1992* (pp. 257–64). Einsiedeln, Switzerland: Daimon Verlag.

Williams, M. (1983). "Deintegration and the transcendent function." *Journal of Analytical Psychology* 28 (1), 65–66.

Winnicott, D. W. (1953). "Transitional object and transitional phenomena." *International Journal of Psycho-Analysis* 34, 89–97.

Winnicott, D. W. (1971). *Playing and reality*. New York: Basic.

Young-Eisendrath, P. (1992). "Locating the transcendent: Inference, rupture, irony." In M. A. Matoon (Ed.), *The transcendent function: Individual and collective aspects; Proceedings of the Twelfth International Congress for Analytical Psychology, August 23–28, 1992* (pp. 151–65). Einsiedeln, Switzerland: Daimon Verlag.

Zabriskie, B. (1992). "Response to L. H. Stewart: The world cycle of change: Political leadership and the transcendent function." In M. A. Matoon (Ed.), *The transcendent function: Individual and collective aspects; Proceedings of the Twelfth International Congress for Analytical Psychology, August 23–28, 1992* (pp. 75–78). Einsiedeln, Switzerland: Daimon Verlag.

INDEX

Made in United States
North Haven, CT
02 September 2022

23574891R00137